Heidegger and the Measure of Truth

Denis McManus presents a new interpretation of Martin Heidegger's early vision of our subjectivity and of the world we inhabit. Heidegger's 'fundamental ontology' allows us to understand the creature that thinks as also one which acts, moves, even touches the world around it, a creature at home in the same ordinary world in which we too live our lives when outside of the philosophical closet; it also promises to free us from seemingly intractable philosophical problems, such as scepticism about the external world and other minds. But many of the concepts central to that vision are elusive; and some of the most widely accepted interpretations of Heidegger's vision harbour within themselves deep and important unclarities, while others foist upon us hopeless species of idealism. Drawing on an examination of Heidegger's work throughout the 1920s, *Heidegger and the Measure of Truth* offers a new way of understanding that vision. Central is the proposal that propositional thought presupposes what might be called a 'measure', a mastery of which only a recognizably 'worldly' subject can possess. McManus shows how these ideas emerge through Heidegger's engagement with the history of philosophy and theology, and sets out a novel reading of key elements in the fundamental ontology, including Heidegger's concept of 'Being-in-the-world', his critique of scepticism, his claim to disavow both realism and idealism, and his difficult reflections on the nature of truth, science, authenticity, and philosophy itself. According to this reading, Heidegger's central claims identify genuine demands that we must meet if we are to achieve the feat of thinking determinate thoughts about the world around us.

Heidegger and the Measure of Truth

Themes from his Early Philosophy

Denis McManus

OXFORD
UNIVERSITY PRESS

OXFORD
UNIVERSITY PRESS

Great Clarendon Street, Oxford, OX2 6DP,
United Kingdom

Oxford University Press is a department of the University of Oxford.
It furthers the University's objective of excellence in research, scholarship,
and education by publishing worldwide. Oxford is a registered trade mark of
Oxford University Press in the UK and in certain other countries

© Denis McManus 2012

The moral rights of the author have been asserted

First published 2012
First published in paperback 2016

All rights reserved. No part of this publication may be reproduced, stored in
a retrieval system, or transmitted, in any form or by any means, without the
prior permission in writing of Oxford University Press, or as expressly permitted
by law, by licence or under terms agreed with the appropriate reprographics
rights organization. Enquiries concerning reproduction outside the scope of the
above should be sent to the Rights Department, Oxford University Press, at the
address above

You must not circulate this work in any other form
and you must impose this same condition on any acquirer

Published in the United States of America by Oxford University Press
198 Madison Avenue, New York, NY 10016, United States of America

British Library Cataloguing in Publication Data

Data available

Library of Congress Cataloging in Publication Data

Data available

ISBN 978–0–19–969487–7 (Hbk.)
ISBN 978–0–19–874812–0 (Pbk.)

Links to third party websites are provided by Oxford in good faith and
for information only. Oxford disclaims any responsibility for the materials
contained in any third party website referenced in this work.

For Joanna

Preface

As an undergraduate student, I encountered Heidegger's name once: on a poster advertising a series of lectures in the Faculty of Modern Languages, entitled 'The Irrationalists'. That gives some sense of the estimation of Heidegger at the end of the 1980s in British universities. Though much has changed since then, the Anglophone philosophical world still very largely sees his work as arcane, as using a peculiar, and perhaps wilfully contrary, idiom to convey esoteric knowledge—or possibly nothing much at all, who can tell? There are many reasons behind this view, many tied to the issue of that idiom.

The way in which Heidegger writes, of course, is contrary, though not merely so. Heidegger believes that philosophers have become estranged from the understanding that they display in their everyday lives of what we are and of what the world in which we live is like; instead they have become captivated by what are, in fact, pseudo-problems, framed in questionable terms. To distance oneself from those problems is to distance oneself from those terms; and to do that is to distance oneself from the terms in which philosophy has come to express itself, the language in which we who study philosophy have learned to think, and in which we have learned to think philosophical claims are expressed and ought to be defended. Heidegger's effort to distance himself from that language is problematic in all sorts of ways; but it is not merely contrary.

There are other reasons why his idiom is difficult. One is that the philosophical context in which Heidegger worked is itself now unfamiliar. Contemporary philosophers are largely no longer aware of the movements that shaped the ideas of thinkers only two or three generations ago, such as the brands of idealism from which Russell and Moore strove to extract themselves and the psychologistic philosophies of logic against which Frege and Husserl reacted. So too in reading Heidegger, we read someone whose thought juxtaposes itself to brands of neo-Kantianism and *Lebensphilosophie*, as well as early species of phenomenology, that have since vanished beneath the waves. But what perhaps makes the context in which Heidegger thought most remote for us now is its breadth; the ambition to engage not only with one's contemporaries but also with Aristotle, Plato, St Paul, St Augustine, Duns Scotus, Luther, Kant, Kierkegaard, Nietzsche, Dilthey, and Husserl is itself remote for the specialists which—for all sorts of questionable reasons—we academic philosophers have now very largely had to become.

Many philosophers also, of course, see Heidegger as belonging to an alien 'tradition'. Philosophy is divided now in a way in which it was not when he wrote, though it is a division for which some hold him principally responsible. I refer here to the cluster of linguistic, geographical, historical, sociological and (perhaps even) philosophical issues that go by the name of 'the Analytic/Continental divide'. It's extremely hard to say in any general way what this 'divide' is and there is an increasing number of philosophers who happily cross it in their work; but it remains the case that philosophy is so divided, a fact expressed in differences in whom one might read, one's sense of what 'the issues' are, and even one's manners.

In as much as I was 'trained', it was as an analytic philosopher and, unsurprisingly, I believe that some of the most interesting recent work that has been done on Heidegger has been written by those who share such a background but who similarly wilfully decided to take a walk on the wild side. Some who were 'raised Continental' see that work as sacrificing Heidegger's most profound thoughts for the sake of a clarity of questionable value and status; they may see my own work in that way too. But there is not much I can do about that; like everyone else, I have to start from where I find myself and the basic impetus behind this book is an attempt to make sense of Heidegger's thinking in terms I feel I understand. However, I hope that one or two others might benefit from my having made this effort.

Recent attempts to undo the historical remoteness of Heidegger's work can also help analytically-minded readers keep 'the real Heidegger' in focus. Through the continuing publication of Heidegger's lecture courses and other works from the 1920s, and—over the last couple of decades in particular—the labour of some admirable scholars, we have acquired a much clearer picture of the process by which Heidegger emerged as an independent thinker. What we see now is no longer the isolated monolith, *Being and Time*, but instead a continuous body of work beginning in the 1910s that runs up to and through that undeniably central book. The work on Heidegger that I have found most useful of all combines an appreciation of that history with a recognizable concern for clarity; and it is the example that that work provides that I have attempted to follow here.

I have benefited from discussing the ideas presented in this book with many friends, colleagues and students. For helpful comments on material on which this book is based, and for other kinds of help besides, I would like to thank Maria Alvarez, Mike Beaney, Adam Beck, Taylor Carman, Gordon Claridge, John Collins, Jim Conant, Steven Galt Crowell, Daniel Dahlstrom, Peter Dews, John Divers, Hubert Dreyfus, Matthias Fritsch, Adrian Furnham, Sebastian Gardner, Neil Gascoigne, Paul Gilbert, Simon Glendinning, Charles Guignon, Uli Haase, Adrian Haddock, Beatrice Han-Pile, Cressida Heyes, Joanna Hodge, John Hyman, Dylan Jaggard, Nicholas Joll, Vasso Kindi, Oskari Kuusela, Peter McLeod, Joanna McManus, David McNeill, Penelope Mackie, Rudolph Makkreel, Wayne Martin, Alex Miller, Ray Monk, Adrian Moore, Dermot Moran, Lenny Moss, Alex Neill, Felix O Murchadha, Matthew Ostrow, David Owen, George Pattison, Dawn Phillips, John Preston, Aaron Ridley, Michael Roubach, Genia Schönbaumsfeld, Mark Sinclair, David Smith, Graham Stevens, Jim Tully, Dan Watts, Mark Wrathall, and, in particular, Ed Minar, Stephen Mulhall, and Daniel Whiting. Apologies to anyone I may have forgotten.

My work has also benefited from the comments of members of audiences at research seminars at the Universities of Amsterdam, Bristol, Cambridge, Chicago, Copenhagen, Durham, East Anglia, Essex, Leeds, Manchester Metropolitan, Middlesex, Reading, the Sorbonne, Southampton, and University College Dublin, as well as at the conference, 'Art. Truth and Imagination', held in memory of Barrie Falk at the University of Birmingham, the 2009 'Wittgenstein' conference at the University of Athens, and the first of the series of workshops entitled 'Selfhood, Authenticity and Method in Heidegger's *Being and Time*' that I co-organised with George Pattison and Beatrice Han-Pile. The series was funded by the British Academy and provided me with a marvellous opportunity to discuss Heideggerian matters during the twelve months in which this book was completed, in some cases with people whose work I have been reading for years but whom I'd never actually met. That has been a real pleasure.

Several generations of undergraduate and postgraduate students here at Southampton have had to listen to the ideas presented here; their forbearance and their many thought-provoking questions are much appreciated. I would also like to thank the University of Southampton and the Arts and Humanities Research Council for periods of research leave during which the book was written, and Eleanor Collins, Bob Marriott, Joy Mellor,

Subramaniam Vengatakrishnan, and Peter Momtchiloff of Oxford University Press for their help in getting this book into print.

My regular readers will be sad to hear that the Fleming Park Monday Night Football boys have now disbanded, due to advancing age and increasing idleness; though those I continue to see socially (Bateman, Foster, Gardner) retain some lingering doubts, I trust this book will help convince them of the essential work we philosophers do for UK plc. Others who I know will be mortified if they are not given some kind of acknowledgement here include Chenine Bathena, Scott Curtis, Tim Grayson, Leila Jancovitch, Jonny Pallas, Danny Sullivan, Julian Timm, and Richard Hindley, who actually bought a copy of my previous book. Well done, Rich! I would also like to thank the proprietors and patrons of the Volunteer public house in Ventnor, Isle of Wight.

The book is dedicated to my wife, Joanna, who maintains that what I really ought to be studying is *Being on Time*; she puts up with an awful lot but remains remarkably supportive of me and my work. I am a very lucky chap. Another wonder is my son Jamie, who has been very keen to be involved in the writing of 'Daddy's story book' and is a top lad.

In what follows, references to Heidegger's work use abbreviations given in the bibliography, followed by page numbers. In the case of BT, the German pagination is also given in brackets. I am grateful to Adam Beck for access to his translation of the *Einleitung in die Philosophie* (GA 27) lectures and to Tom Sheehan for access to an earlier version of his now-published translation of the *Logik: Die Frage nach der Wahrheit* (GA 21) lectures. When quoting BT, I will generally use Macquarrie and Robinson's translation; it is often criticised but it strikes me as as good a starting point as any, not least because of the useful explanations that they provide for the decisions that they make and the fact that some of their questionable decisions are now reasonably widely recognized as such. Nevertheless, when necessary, I will diverge from their translation and from the translations of Heidegger's other works upon which I draw: for example, where translators' differing choices of terms might suggest a variation in terminology that is not to be found in Heidegger's original texts. In a similar spirit, I will capitalise the noun, 'Being [*Sein*]', throughout.

Contents

Introduction	1

Part I

1	The Concept of 'Constitution'	11
	1.1 'Constitution' and a phenomenological project	11
	1.2 The project illustrated: The objecthood of God and the 'how' of Christian faith	17
	1.3 Further 'original havings'	20
2	'Constitution' and the Categories	28
	2.1 Con-formity and the 'application' of the categories	28
	2.2 Constitution and idealism	35
	2.3 'Living in the categories'	37
	2.4 Intimations of 'Being-in-the-world' and the vanishing of talk of 'constitution'	41
	2.5 The 'subject-correlates' of science and philosophy	45

Part II

3	*Vorhandenheit*	51
	3.1 Themes in the discussion of *Vorhandenheit*	53
	3.2 *Vorhandenheit* and assertion	59
	3.3 *Vorhandenheit* and science	62
	3.4 *Vorhandenheit* and *Zuhandenheit*	68
4	Dreyfus's Concept of the 'Background'	76
	4.1 What is the 'background' meant to do for us?	77
	4.2 A first 'regress of rules'	80
	4.2.1 Rules for applying rules	80
	4.2.2 A problem to be solved or dissolved? The 'master thesis' and 'depicturization'	81
	4.3 A second 'regress of rules'	89
	4.3.1 The impossibility of 'spelling out' '*ceteris paribus* rules'	89
	4.3.2 A problem to be solved or dissolved? 'Closure' and the 'view from sideways on'	92

Part III

5 The Measure of Truth	103
5.1 Constitution and measure	105
5.2 'Empty intending' and truth as 'fulfilment'	107
5.3 'Living in the *Hinblick*'	111
5.4 A skeleton for some themes of the fundamental ontology	115
5.4.1 An abstract case for our 'Being-in-the-world'	118
5.4.2 Heidegger's critique of scepticism	123
5.4.3 Truth I: The puzzles of BT sec. 44	125
5.4.4 Truth II: Measures and methods of comparison	130
6 The 'Founding' of Measurement in Understanding without Fit	135
6.1 Understanding without fit: Manipulating the *Zuhanden*	138
6.2 The 'founding' of measurement	141
6.3 Objections and clarifications	144
6.3.1 'Impure beholding' and the manipulating/seeing distinction	144
6.3.2 Improvement in methods of measurement	146
6.3.3 'Impure facts' I: Projection, falsification, parochialism, and perspectives	148
6.4 'Appropriating' or 'being lived by' one's measures	154
6.4.1 'Impure facts' II: Artefacts and emptiness	154
6.4.2 A sketch of an example: Methodological fetishism in psychology	156
6.4.3 Emptiness and inauthenticity	159

Part IV

7 Being-in-the-World and Truth Revisited	165
7.1 The 'soul/external world gulf'	165
7.2 Finite knowing, 'presupposing truth', 'living in the truth' and 'in untruth'	166
7.3 'Empty intending', 'logical space', and the 'most obvious objection'	174
7.4 On the 'real/ideal gulf'	176
7.5 Truth's dependency on *Dasein*	181
8 *Vorhandenheit* and *Zuhandenheit* Revisited	190
8.1 *Zuhandenheit* revisited	190
8.2 *Vorhandenheit* and the Theoretical Attitude revisited	193
8.3 *Seinsvergessenheit* and '*Vorhandenheit* in the broadest sense'	195
8.4 *Vorhandenheit* and assertion revisited	198
8.5 Inauthenticity and the 'double meaning' of the 'Theoretical Attitude'	202

9 Metaphilosophical Issues and Further Questions 208
   9.1 'Original havings' and the 'Being and Time' project 210
   9.2 Recalling the measure 215
   9.3 Philosophy's 'subject-correlate' revisited 222

Appendix: Heidegger's Critique of Husserl 226
Abbreviations 229
Bibliography 232
Index 243

Introduction

Heidegger believed that philosophy has characteristically focused its attention on modes of thought that are not, in fact, fundamental, and, as a result, has arrived at a distorted picture of our subjectivity and of the world around us. In his early work in particular, he argued that we must recognize instead that these modes—roughly, the theoretical and the propositional—are 'founded' in what he called our 'Being-in-the-world'. The alternative vision that those early works offer is one to which many are drawn. It can appear to be simply truer to life, allowing us to understand the creature that thinks as also one which acts, moves, even touches the world around it—a creature at home in the same ordinary world in which we too live our lives when outside of the philosophical closet. Moreover, this vision promises to free us from seemingly intractable philosophical problems, such as scepticism about the external world and other minds. But its key notions—not least those of 'founding' and 'Being-in-the-world'—are elusive; indeed some of the most widely accepted interpretations of Heidegger's claim that theoretical and propositional thoughts are 'derivative', 'non-primordial', or 'founded' harbour within themselves deep and important unclarities, while others would seem to foist upon us hopeless species of idealism. It is the purpose of this book to offer a new way of understanding this claim and, with it, the challenge that Heidegger's early philosophy poses for us.

At the heart of the reading I will offer are two proposals: firstly, that making assertions and entertaining propositions, theoretical and otherwise, presuppose—are 'founded' in—a mastery of what might be called a 'measure', and, secondly, that mastery of such a 'measure' requires a recognizably 'worldly' subject. Grasping a proposition and considering whether it corresponds to the facts presuppose a mode of understanding—the grasp of a 'measure'—that cannot itself be understood as the grasp of a correspondence between the 'inner' 'mental' life and a world 'outside'; and I will argue that this realization underpins central elements of Heidegger's 'fundamental ontology', including his critique of scepticism, his controversial view of truth, his identification of a myopic 'Theoretical Attitude', and his vision of our mode of existence as necessarily a Being-in-the-world. According to this interpretation, many of Heidegger's central claims also appear to be true, providing insights into demands that we must meet if we are to achieve the feat of thinking determinate thoughts about the world around us.

To come to appreciate the alternative perspective that this reading offers, and the particular senses that it ascribes to 'measure' and 'worldliness', we must explore the broader, and less well known, context in which the better known of Heidegger's early works emerged, and I will devote a significant amount of attention here to some rarely discussed lecture courses, including, in particular, the 1925–26 *Logik* lectures and the series from 1920–21 collected in *The Phenomenology of Religious Life*. Part I begins this process. Chapter 1 examines the appropriation of Husserl's concept of 'constitution' that we find in Heidegger's very early work (which, following convention, I will refer to as that of 'the young Heidegger'). Roughly speaking, this concept directs us to reflect on how the subject must be in order for it to be intentionally related to different kinds of object; the young Heidegger's appropriation of this notion allows him to articulate his sense of the diversity of forms of subjectivity and of the corresponding forms taken by the entities to which that subjectivity is intentionally related. Importantly for what follows, a notion emerges here of an 'original having', a distinctive mode of intentionality that cannot be assimilated to any other and whose 'objects' are revealed only through that particular mode. I illustrate the young Heidegger's 'constitutive' reflections by presenting a preliminary sketch of several such 'havings', concentrating in particular on his early discussion of religious experience; this illustration gives a preliminary indication of what Heidegger, at the beginning of his emergence as an independent thinker, understood by 'the Theoretical Attitude', an expression I will capitalize in an effort to indicate that what this Attitude is is itself a significant issue.

Chapter 2 explains how the above interests tap into more traditional philosophical interests in the 'categories', and explores a crucial issue that the 'categories' raise: namely, how there can be 'categories' that characterize both forms of subjectivity and the objects towards which a subject may be intentionally related. This exploration will sharpen our sense of how use of the notion of 'constitution' may seem to commit one to a problematic idealism. That a doctrine of such a form can be found in the early Heidegger is a charge with a long history; one of the fates that Ryle predicted for Heidegger's phenomenology was its leading into a 'self-ruinous Subjectivism' (Ryle 1928: 222); but authors of more recent and far more comprehensive studies than Ryle's have come to similar conclusions.[1] Heidegger himself claimed to reject both realism and idealism; but giving a concrete sense to such a claim is a difficult task. We will take a first step towards doing so when we explore how 'constitutive' considerations point the way towards Heidegger's notion of Being-in-the-world; but the same considerations also ultimately raise doubts about the concepts used in articulating the very notion of 'constitution', as well as raising significant questions about the form of understanding that philosophy itself involves.

In the course of his 'constitutive' reflections, Heidegger came to characterize previous philosophers, including Husserl, as assimilating diverse forms of subjectivity to the Theoretical Attitude; this provides one sense for why the Theoretical Attitude might be thought to be 'non-primordial'. Part Two examines two others: its being 'founded' in other forms of understanding, and its revealing only a specific kind of entity—the *Vorhanden*, or 'present-at-hand'. Neither of these proposals, though familiar to readers of Heidegger and commentary upon his work, is easy to pin down. One factor which complicates matters is that both identify features that the Theoretical Attitude shares with a broader set of phenomena in which Heidegger includes assertions, propositions, and propositional attitudes—though why these phenomena should be so grouped together is less than clear. A further complication is the question of whether 'the Theoretical Attitude' denotes the form of subjectivity we must adopt if we are to entertain theoretical propositions, or whether instead it denotes a philosophical misapprehension of what that form of subjectivity involves and reveals.

Part II explores these and other problems that these proposals raise. Chapter 3 examines the multiplicity of different notions seemingly wrapped up in the claims in question: in, for example, Heidegger's discussion of the *Vorhanden*, the *Zuhanden* (the 'ready-to-hand'), and the supposed 'priority' of 'the practical'—in some sense of that expression—over 'the theoretical'. It argues that some of the central distinctions invoked in commentary on these notions are unstable, and threaten to lead us into forms of pragmatism or idealism which are implausible as well as incompatible with the early

[1] Cf., e.g., Blattner 1999 and Lafont 2000.

Heidegger's own broader, considered views, including his understanding of science. Perhaps the most influential interpretation of the 'founded' character of the theoretical and the propositional is that embodied in Hubert Dreyfus's reading of Heidegger and his notion of the 'background'; Chapter 4 explores and criticizes that interpretation in some depth.

Finding solutions to the problems with which Part II leaves us is crucial, I believe, if we are to stand by the claim that Heidegger's conception of subjectivity, understanding, and truth merits our philosophical attention, and Part III draws on the ideas that Part I sets out to present an alternative reading of Part II's problematic themes. Chapter 5 begins by showing how Heidegger's early understanding of 'constitution' is interwoven with a concern with the need for an 'always already pre-existent' understanding of the entities with which we deal—a concern further shaped by Heidegger's appropriation of another important notion of Husserl's, that of truth as the 'fulfilment' of an 'empty' 'intending'. What emerges is a focus on what could be called an 'anticipatory', 'constituting' 'measure' to which entities may or may not match up—a form of understanding of those entities which can be said to 'found' our entertaining propositional attitudes about those entities but which cannot itself be seen as the appreciation of a correspondence or fit between thought and world. By exploring how this notion is expressed in Heidegger's 1925–26 *Logik* lectures, I show how it provides a skeleton upon which we can hang crucial themes from his early philosophy, including his idiosyncratic and much-discussed remarks on the 'superficiality' (PS 10) of the correspondence conception of truth. But our guiding notion also raises significant idealist concerns, as indeed, in related ways, do all of the notions that I shall arrange on that 'skeleton'.

If we are to address such concerns, we need a more concrete sense of what Heidegger's vision proposes. Despite BT's initial focus on the circumstances of our 'everyday [*alltäglich*]' life, Heidegger provides us with very few illustrations of what the structure of our Being-in-the-world might, so to speak, look like. Some of his examples have become very well known—in particular, his now-famous hammer. But his discussions of such examples are few and far between, and do not help us resolve the difficulties that Part II identifies, nor to allay the suspicion of idealism. Chapter 6 attempts to address this problem, taking the abstract account set out in Chapter 5 and demonstrating how that account might be true.

Taking Chapter 5's 'measure' motif literally, and following up clues from some of Heidegger's remarks about the sciences, Chapter 6 offers what could be called a 'phenomenological' examination of some very basic measurement practices; in doing so, it shows that the forms of judgement that such practices involve are 'founded' in a form of understanding which is recognizably 'worldly' and—subject to appropriate interpretation—'practical', and which cannot itself be seen as the appreciation of a correspondence between thought and world. But it also argues that the need for this 'founding' understanding leads to brands of neither idealism nor pragmatism; nor does it otherwise undermine what seem to be Heidegger's own considered views of the forms of judgement in question.

Part IV goes on to clarify how the vision that emerges here gives content to the skeletal 'fundamental ontology' that Chapter 5 sets out, and provides answers to most of the questions that our earlier discussion raises. To mention only four of the difficult topics that these chapters address, I explain how that vision finds expression in Heidegger's remarks on truth and how his critique of scepticism is compatible with what one might call the 'finitude' of human knowing, present an alternative vision of what is at stake in Heidegger's problematic remarks on the *Vorhanden*, the *Zuhanden*, and the Theoretical Attitude, and identify a sense in which Heidegger might indeed be seen as rejecting both realism and idealism.

The latter involves drawing on two important ideas from Chapter 6: its questioning of the intelligibility of a certain kind of evaluation of our most basic descriptive practices and their depiction instead as 'original havings', as modes of understanding whose 'objects' cannot be understood as the 'object' of any other, 'rival' understanding. Chapter 6 closes, however, by sketching another mode of evaluation to which such practices might be subjected—one which draws on some aspects of Heidegger's discussion of authenticity. This form of criticism charges the descriptive practices in question with yielding descriptions that are not false but instead empty, this failing perhaps best seen as reflecting a certain lack of self-knowledge—a kind of 'self-forgetting'—on the part of those who engage in those practices, rather than those practices failing to 'correspond' to the world which they supposedly describe. This is one of a number of occasions here on which we will consider the possible philosophical significance of Heidegger's often derided notion of authenticity.

That notion will also play a role when in Chapter 9 we return to the question of philosophy's own form—the manner in which philosophical insight is 'had'. Heidegger's depiction of propositional truth as 'superficial' and 'secondary' has prompted some commentators to suspect that his insights might themselves resist capture in propositional form. This is a perplexing claim, which might seem to suggest that the other fate that Ryle predicted for Heidegger's work—a descent into 'windy mysticism' (Ryle 1928: 222)—is indeed what awaits it.[2] But I will sketch what I believe to be a non-mysterious construal of that claim—one which builds on Chapter 8's reinterpretation of the supposed 'superficiality' of assertions. A notion central to this construal is that of our 'forgetting', and needing to be 'reminded' of, the 'measures' through which our assertions are articulated—a notion that figures in Chapter 6's discussion of authenticity and in the broader analysis of philosophical problems that this book presents. The metaphilosophical vision that emerges stands in what might seem rather stark contrast with that which BT itself suggests; but I argue that the vision I present has textual support, and that any such tension must be considered in the broader context of the early Heidegger's thought. The continuing emergence of Heidegger's lecture courses and unpublished work from the 1920s shows that he placed a number of different 'frames' around his evolving work during that period, and that the frame one finds presented in BT is quite distinctive, emerges shortly before the book is written, and equally rapidly loses its shaping influence on Heidegger's ideas. Though I offer some suggestions about how that particular frame came to emerge, the philosophical and metaphilosophical notions that I argue most profoundly shaped Heidegger's thought originated significantly earlier than, find expression in, but also survive the demise of, the project that Heidegger conceived for BT.

Any interpretation of a significant philosopher's work will inevitably stress certain themes at the expense of others; but Heidegger's early work in particular perhaps demands a multiplicity of readings: his early thought is hungrily synthetic, with many sources of inspiration all exerting an influence. The writings that emerge are, unsurprisingly, not obviously always coherent and, as mentioned, Heidegger himself struggled to give an adequate setting to all of the ideas that pressed themselves upon him. For these

---

[2] For readings to this effect, cf., e.g., Okrent 1988: 292 and Philipse 1998: 302.

reasons, although the reading that I offer here will, I hope, shed light on Heidegger's early philosophy, it can only do so from a certain angle; it offers one arrangement of his complex, and complicatedly related, concerns. There is much that it leaves unexamined, and much that it runs the risk of distorting; but I hope that it may provide some readers with new reference points by which to consider what Heidegger has to teach us.

PART I

1

The Concept of 'Constitution'

1.1 'Constitution' and a phenomenological project

In analytic philosophical circles, the term 'phenomenology' is typically taken to refer to the way in which our engagement with some domain of objects 'feels', to what such an engagement is 'like', or how those objects 'first strike us' or 'initially seem to us to be'. Except when the objects in question are themselves 'ways that something feels' or 'seems'—such as when reflecting on qualia and the so-called 'hard problem' of consciousness—a reflection on such phenomenology is seen as having a necessarily preliminary or provisional character and the idea of a philosophy that gives some kind of *authority* to such seemings appears an oddly naïve, uncritical, or even simply unphilosophical one by virtue of its leaving no room for the following kind of question: 'That may well be what it feels like to engage with x or how x seems to us to be, but how is x *really?*'[1] For related reasons, phenomenology is often criticized for presenting no more than a psychology—as Heidegger saw Husserl as doing in his early *The Philosophy of Arithmetic*[2]—or an anthropology—as Husserl saw Heidegger as doing in BT.[3]

In this section I will sketch an interest in 'seemings' that has philosophical bite, a need for a 'turn to the subject', in light of which phenomenological 'psychologies' or 'anthropologies' could, in principle, be philosophically significant.[4] The guiding thought is that a certain kind of naivety or crudity in our thinking about the ontological character of the entities with which we deal might be exposed as such by reflecting on what it is to know or

---

[1] For example, John Searle asks of Dreyfus' phenomenological descriptions of intentional action ('all these puzzling remarks about how it seems to Larry Bird, etc.') 'so what? . . . [W]hy should we care how it seems to the agent?' (2000: 85, 91). Cf. also Blattner 1999: 9–12.
[2] Cf. L 31–2. As is well-known, Frege made the same charge in his 1894.
[3] Cf. Moran 2000b: 191.
[4] Quite how distinctive this form of reflection is to phenomenology is a question that Section 1.3 will examine.

otherwise engage with these entities. A revival of our sense of the diverse forms that that engagement takes may then revive a sense of the diverse forms that the entities we engage with take. In this way, a reflection on 'seemings', in the sense of the characteristic ways in which the subject is in its engagement with different kinds of entity, may have consequences not only for the ontology of subjectivity but for ontology in general. I suggest that Heidegger saw this kind of reflection as present, but underdeveloped, in the work of his principal mentor, Husserl.

'Constitution' is a central term in Husserl's phenomenology; in its use there, it is also surely one of the most misleading expressions in philosophy, and just about every commentator—Heidegger included[5]—feels the need to pause to say, 'No, he does not mean that!' The following passage from a recent book illustrates this, and also presents the basic outline of the concept I want to examine:

[E]very object in the world is 'constituted' through its correlation with a system of meanings that present the object in various possible ways in actual or possible acts of consciousness... This is not to say that the object is brought into being by consciousness or dependent in its being on actual or possible consciousness of it. Questions of dependence are a further issue of ontology. (D. W. Smith 2007: 76)

Opinions differ about just what or how much this kind of qualification ought to take back if Husserl's broader philosophy is to be presented correctly, and the thought that there is a substantial brand of idealism in Husserl is common enough.[6] However, I will not address those questions, and want instead to show how the above notion of 'constitution', for which I would also wish to suggest '[q]uestions of dependence are a further issue', can help us read the early Heidegger.

I will begin by looking at a very basic example and the interpretation of what it shows, which can be found in Heidegger's discussion of 'constitution' in lectures from 1925 (HCT sec. 6). In the *Logical Investigations*, Husserl proposes that, on the basis of 'straightforward acts of perception' which function as 'foundational acts', 'new acts of conjunction, of disjunction', etc.

---

[5] Cf., e.g., HCT 71.
[6] Cf., e.g. the works cited by Hall 1982: 169; Hall also provides a useful sample of passages that encourage idealist as well as opposed realist readings of Husserl (pp. 175–6 and 182).

set up new objects, acts in which something *appears as actual and self-given*, which was not given, and could not have been given, as what it appears to be, in these foundational acts alone. (2001, vol. 2: 282)[7]

After we have dispensed with the interpretation that the ubiquitous 'No, he did not mean that!' says he did not mean, the next that is likely to strike us is an eliminativist or phenomenalist interpretation, according to which these 'new objects'—in the above case, conjunctions and disjunctions—are 'subjective additions', 'made' or 'thought into [the real] by the subject' (HCT 68, 70, 58), the stress falling now on their '*appear[ing]* as actual and self-given'.[8] But a further possibility is to hear such a passage as expressing a view about how the subject must be in order for it to be capable of experiencing certain objects—objects which are not under suspicion of 'being in the least bit less objective than what is given as real' (HCT 66) and calling for, for example, some kind of reductive elimination.[9] Rather

'*Constituting*' does not mean producing in the sense of making and fabricating; it means *letting the entity be seen in its objectivity*. (HCT 71)

So, for example, it is the subject who is capable of 'acts of conjunction [and] disjunction' who can experience conjunctions and disjunctions: a wider region of what there is reveals itself to such creatures than reveals itself to those capable only of 'straightforward acts of perception'.[10] 'Objectivity in its broadest sense is much richer than the reality of a thing', that 'reality correlative to simple sense perception', which we must now come to recognize as a very particular concept of 'real' (HCT 66, 61).

Husserl's account of our experience of material objects offers another example.[11] It takes as its starting point the fact that when we encounter such an object we always perceive it from one particular side or other, leaving its other sides hidden. Husserl proposes that each perception of such an object sits within a 'horizon' or 'manifold' of other such perceptions in which we would experience the different 'profiles' of that object were we to move around it. Now, such ideas could inform a phenomenalist or eliminative

---

[7] Heidegger discusses this example in HCT 57–60.
[8] For objections to a reading of Husserl in such terms, cf., e.g., Pietersma 1989: 233.
[9] Cf. also Moran 2000a: 47. On the relationship between such reductionism and 'phenomenological reduction', cf. Hall 1982: 177.
[10] Cf. HCT 64, 65.
[11] Cf. HCT 43, 49, and 60–2 for a brief discussion.

account of 'material object talk', according to which such talk *is really just* summarizing talk of perceptions of 'profiles'. But these ideas could also inform an account of what kind of *subject* it is that can experience material objects: namely, a subject whose perceptions of 'sides of material things' are accompanied by a surrounding manifold of further, related expectations of what we will experience when . . . a 'changing but always co-posited horizon' (Husserl 1982: 107) of further possible acts of perception that correspond to other 'profiles'; to use a formulation of Moran's, each such act 'already looks beyond itself to those other profiles, assumes them in grasping the object' (2000a: 43), and to be capable of grasping that object is to be capable of such acts.

Such an account aims to explore not just the 'merely psychological' question of how humans, for example, encounter a particular kind of entity, but rather, what it *is* to encounter that particular kind of entity: 'something such as a physical thing in space is only intuitable by means of appearances in which it is and must be given in multiple but determined changing "perspective" modes' (Husserl 1982: 362). One way to understand Husserl's famous *epoché*—which 'brackets' the question of whether the entities that we supposedly encounter actually exist—is as the adoption of an attitude which focuses our attention directly upon the structure of such 'intuitings', making vivid the '*ideal* system of possible cognitive processes by virtue of which [an entity] and the truths about it would be given to *any* cognitive subject' (Husserl 1917: 11, both emphases added): a 'physical thing in space' is the kind of thing that is 'given' in 'multiple but determined changing "perspective" modes' 'not just for human beings but also for God' (1982: 362).

I suggest that we can usefully consider Heidegger's early thought as shaped by something like this notion of 'constitution', which floats free of reductive and sceptical concerns and instead takes as its focus the question of how a subject must be in order to experience different kinds of thing. But why ought philosophers to be interested in such a notion? Reductive/sceptical notions of 'constitution' have a clear and familiar philosophical pay-off if the projects they inform actually can be carried out. So what would be the philosophical pay-off of the notion I am presenting? My suggestion is that, for Heidegger at least, turning our attention to the question of the form that subjectivity takes breaks up certain prejudices not only about subjectivity but also about objectivity, about the 'objects' of our intentionality, about what one might call the 'Question of Being'. In adapting another Husserlian idiom, Heidegger proposes that a reflection on the 'how' of our experience will make clearer to us how diverse the 'what' of our experience really is. '[I]n the ... course of life, I do not become aware of the different *hows* of my reactions to' the 'quite different things' with which I 'deal'; an awareness of this '*indifference [Indifferenz]* with regard to the manner of experiencing [*die Weise des Erfahrens*]' (PRL 9) might make us aware of corresponding forms of indifference with regard to the Being of the experienc*ed*. In doing so, we would undermine two symbiotically related confusions: a *Verstehensvergessenheit*, along with what Heidegger called '*Seinsvergessenheit*'.

There would be something misleading in suggesting that intentionality is offered here as a 'channel' through which we can come to recognize Being—a possibility that might seem to be suggested by Heidegger's presentation of his 'analytic of *Dasein*'—his label for the entity that 'understands Being' (BT 32 (12))—as 'preparatory' to addressing 'the Question of Being' (BT 38 (17)); that would give a misleading impression of both a 'distance' between us—we *Dasein*—and Being, and of a 'proximity' between us and our understanding. Firstly, it suggests that Being is something to be identified 'out there', whereas for Heidegger, 'Being is never alien but always familiar, "ours"' (MFL 147), though we can, in some sense, 'forget' it.[12] Secondly, it suggests that our own intentionality is somehow unproblematically available to our reflection, when our view of its diverse modes can be obscured too.[13]

Rather, Heidegger's thought seems to be something like the following. In turning our philosophical attention away from the 'objects' of our intentional states and towards how they are 'constituted'—how the subject who intends such objects must be—we turn away from ground over which the philosophical tradition has already marked out deeply rutted tracks, into which our thinking naturally falls, Heidegger's intention being ultimately to return to that ground with a new freshness. Given that modes of intentionality are modes of

---

[12] We will return to the nature of this 'forgetting' in Chapter 9.

[13] This has a bearing on the apparent 'dogmatism' (Blattner 1999: 3) of a passage early in BT in which Heidegger gives what seems to be a definition of Being: 'In the question which we are to work out, *what is asked about* is Being—that which determines entities as entities, that on the basis of which entities are already understood, however we may discuss them in detail' (BT 25–6 (6)). A reason why these remarks stand at the *beginning*, not the end, of Heidegger's road is that it will turn out that there are diverse 'structures' that 'determine entities as entities' and diverse forms in which 'entities are already understood', neither diversity ordinarily being recognized in philosophy which misunderstands our understanding as well as its objects.

understanding of Being, one should make ontological progress and phenomenological progress at the same time: the latter aids the former, and the former, in principle, could aid the latter. I say 'in principle' because pursuing the former directly is a more difficult project, because it attempts to cross that deeply rutted field.[14] But when we come to reflect deliberately on 'constitutive' questions, we engage in a mode of reflection that is *less familiar, less 'calcified'* (WDR 164); this may lead us to identify unacknowledged prejudices about intentionality which sustain our ontological prejudices.

Thus, by exposing diversity in what Heidegger calls 'subject-correlates [*Subjektkorrelate*]'[15]—in the forms that 'subjects' must take in order to encounter the diversity of 'objects' they encounter—phenomenological reflection also promises to undermine corresponding crudities in our thinking about the character of those 'objects'.[16] In this way we may 'broaden the idea of objectivity'—this objectivity being 'exhibited in its content in the investigation of the corresponding intuition' (HCT 72), though Heidegger went on to abandon talk of 'diverse forms of intuition', 'consciousness', or indeed 'experience' precisely because it too directs attention away from the diversity of forms that 'subject-correlates' take. As Dahlstrom notes, Heidegger turns to

locutions such as 'having' (*haben*), 'comporting' (*verhalten*), or 'understanding' (*verstehen*) in order to emphasise that [our] original, unthematic 'having' or 'comporting' is for the most part not some sort of deliberate, meditative act of knowing something. (Dahlstrom 1994: 781)[17]

We might even come to think that conceiving of the 'experienced' as different *kinds* of 'thing' or 'object' is a distortion—a turning away from possibly profound differences between the different *ways* in which these 'things' or 'objects' concern us.[18] Such concerns surely play a part in Heidegger's ultimately abandoning the terms 'subject-' and 'object-correlate', and indeed 'constitutive' 'correlation' too, as Sec. 2.4 will discuss; but they also find a natural articulation through the crucial but difficult

---

[14] This is clearly part of the rationale for BT's taking as its starting point an analysis of our 'everydayness'.

[15] Cf., e.g., IPPW 37, PRL 240, 241, etc.

[16] Schear (2007: 129) and Cooper express similar thoughts: to retain 'a sense of Being' is 'to retain a sense of... the many ways of revealing and encountering things' and a failure to retain that sense is 'equivalent to "the oblivion of Being"' (Cooper 1997: 120).

[17] Cf., e.g., PIE 77: 'having ≠ theoretical apprehension-comprehension'.

[18] Compare Heidegger's scare-quoting of 'kinds' in the passage from FCM 275 quoted in Section 1.3.

Heideggerian notion of 'the Theoretical Attitude'. Through it, Heidegger points again to a crudity in our thinking about the Being of entities being sustained by a crudity in our thinking about subjectivity: *very* roughly speaking, by assimilating our dealings with all entities to their contemplation or disinterested observation, we assimilate all entities to those we contemplate or disinterestedly observe.

This notion, which raises a number of important difficulties that are set out at the beginning of Chapter 3, looms large in Heidegger's understanding of how he broke with Husserl—the latter supposedly remaining in that Attitude's grip. Whether that charge is just is a difficult question; I offer some brief comments on this in the Appendix, but cannot hope to settle the matter there. Instead I will offer an illustration of the present section's vision of 'phenomenological reflection' and its philosophical significance. I will examine one of the forms of experience that seem to have struck the young Heidegger as most forcefully calling for phenomenological analysis, and as exposing as narrow Husserl's perspective: 'the specific experience of the finding of God' (PRL 231). This exploration is, in some respects, not the most representative of Heidegger's 'constitutional analyses'; it is also less than fully followed through, and my own discussion of it will be brief.[19] But it is of interest from an interpretive point of view, as it reveals in vivid terms how he conceived of his philosophical work in the early years leading up to BT. The notion of 'constitution' is to the fore and its relationship to the Theoretical Attitude apparent, helping us to obtain a clearer impression of what that Attitude first meant for Heidegger.

1.2 The project illustrated: The objecthood of God and the 'how' of Christian faith

As early as his 1916 supplemental conclusion to his *Habilitationsschrift*, Heidegger declared that 'the theoretical attitude is only *one* kind of approach', only one of 'the wealth of directions of the formation of the living spirit' (DSTCMC 66). Heidegger developed this awareness in part through an intense engagement with what one might call an 'anti-theoretical'

---

[19] I discuss it at much greater length in my (forthcoming-c).

tradition in theology—a tradition represented in the nineteenth century by Harnack, Kierkegaard, Overbeck, and Schleiermacher, and running back through Luther and St Augustine to St Paul, as we will see soon.[20] That tradition identifies 'a theorizing, dogma-promoting influence' in our reflection on God which 'severely endanger[s] precisely the immediacy of religious life, and forg[ets] religion in favour of theology and dogma' (PRL 238). If philosophy of religion is not to become 'a rationalistic construction detached from life' (DSTCMC 68), it must turn its attention away from 'theory' and 'dogma', which represent only one 'direction' of 'living spirit', and return to the touchstone of the 'immediacy' and 'involvement' of the religious life in its 'wealth of directions'. Heidegger's own appropriation of this call for a recovery of our understanding of our 'life' or our 'experience'[21] and, in particular, those aspects of our life that are obscured by what one might well label a 'Theoretical Attitude', seems to have played a crucial role in giving sense to the notion that that Attitude is, firstly, indeed simply an *attitude*—'something one must so to speak "place oneself into" [*hineinstellen*]' (HCT 113) and not a reflection of the character of subjectivity as such—and, secondly, simply *an* attitude—only *one* of 'the wealth of directions of the formation of the living spirit'.

These concerns emerge in explicitly 'constitutional' terms. If we are to 'sharply divorce the problem of theology'—with its 'constant dependency' on 'theoretical consciousness'—from that 'of religiosity', we must look to '[t]he basic kinds of fulfilment of religious experience'—'"revelation", "tradition", "congregation"'—and recognize their 'constitutive character... in the essence of religion' (PRL 235, 244).[22] We must recognize 'the independence of religious experience and its world', and the religious life as 'an entirely originary intentionality with an entirely originary character of demands' (PRL 244). This broadening of our understanding of understanding also promises to deepen our understanding of the '*object*' of that understanding too. If we can recover our awareness of this 'original region of

---

[20] My (forthcoming-c): sec. 1, documents Heidegger's study of this tradition. Heidegger's own religiosity is a difficult but now quite frequently discussed topic. For biographical detail, cf. Ott 1994: Part 2 and Safranski 1999. For other interesting studies of Heidegger's thought in relation to religion and theology, cf., e.g., Crowe 2006 and McGrath 2006.

[21] Cf. PRL 50, 97, and 233.

[22] For other early remarks on 'constitution', cf. e.g. PRL 39, 41, and 44, and for the concept of 'fulfilment', cf. Sections 5.1 and 5.2.

life . . . in which religion alone realizes itself as a certain form of experience', then we may recover 'the specifically *religious* constitution of "God"' (PRL 243, 245). In asking the question of 'constitution', 'the holy' emerges as 'correlate of the act-character of "faith"' (PRL 252). By placing such 'subject-correlates'—such 'modes of access'—first in our thinking, we may shake off the temptation to begin our efforts to 'determine the sense of the objecthood of God'—'[t]he sense of the Being of God'—under the influence of an 'analogy with the theoretical and the constitution of the object of cognition' (PRL 222, 67, 84, 232). Such influence creates a distorted picture of our 'experiential comportment to God' as a theoretical 'holding-as-true',[23] and encourages us to regard the 'object' of Christian faith as 'simply a special object' (PRL 149). By reflecting on 'subject-correlates' such as prayer, we resist such an assimilation and uncover 'the constitution of an originary objectity [*Objectität*]', that of the 'recipient' of prayer (PRL 252).

Heidegger puts flesh on these bare bones in, for example, his examination of St Paul, whom Heidegger sees as struggling to free his congregation from the influence of what one might call 'the Theoretical Attitude'. Heidegger sees St Paul's reflections on the Last Judgement, for example, as pointing to a confusion and an irreligiosity in concern with the question of when that Judgement will take place. In one sense, there is no anticipating such an event because it 'comes like a thief in the night' (1 Thess. 5.3–7, New English Bible). But St Paul singles out 'the speculators and chatterboxes' who 'dwell upon and speculate about the "when" of the *parousia*' as those for whom that event is 'sudden', 'all at once' (PRL 110, 74, 107).[24]

Heidegger believes that in presenting such an 'objective determination' as a 'false concern' (PRL 110), St Paul is asking us to think about what the relevant 'subject-correlate' of the Last Judgement is, about what it is to 'comport oneself towards' *that particular event*. A concern with the 'when' of the Last Judgement reveals a particular sense of why that event matters—of the meaning and identity of that event. In particular, the knowledge that

---

[23] Interestingly, Kisiel (1993: 88) reports that the particular note from which I quote here is the only one in the collection to which Heidegger appends a signature. Since Heidegger accuses Catholicism of falling into a conception of faith as 'holding-to-be-true' (PRL 236), might this have a bearing on his own personal conversion to a form of Protestantism and his well-known remarks to Krebs about the '*system* of Catholicism' (BH 96)?

[24] Strictly speaking, '*parousia*' refers to the Second Coming, which in principle need not be accompanied by a Last Judgement. But I use the terms interchangeably here—a use which seems to reflect Heidegger's concerns in the lectures in question.

'the speculators and chatterboxes' seek is of the period in which we will not be subject to God's judgement. For this to be the 'preparation' one seeks, one's concern is the day by which one must have gotten one's house in order. But to 'prepare' in this way is to look at God's judgement as something to be 'escaped', 'overcome', or 'saved from' (PRL 107). Such an individual lacks a 'fundamental comportment to *God*' (PRL 110) and instead makes another concern fundamental: namely, her 'peace and security' (1 Thess. 5.3–7), which must be protected *in the face of* God's judgement.

What then is it to 'comport oneself towards' the Last Judgement as 'righteous judgement' (2 Thess. 1:5, quoted at PRL 98)? 'Paul's answer to the question of the When of the *parousia* is...an urging to awaken and to be sober' (PRL 74). To 'expect' the Last Judgement—as the specific event that, as a Christian, one must take it to be—is to want to be a certain way, not merely to want to be-a-certain-way-when-the-crucial-time-comes. What corresponds to the 'actual or possible acts of consciousness' (Smith, quoted above) that are 'correlated' with this event is 'not some ideational "expectation", [but] rather...serving God' (PRL 79). Genuine Christian 'hope' 'and mere attitudinal expectation [are] essentially different': the former is not poring over calendars or looking for portents with 'the speculators and chatterboxes', but is instead 'faithful, loving, serving expectation in sadness and joy' (PRL 107). This is the distinctive 'subject-correlate' of the *parousia*, in which that event is 'constituted' as the religious event that it is—the form of '*Verhalten*' or '*Haben*' that distinguishes the subject who genuinely 'intends' that particular event.

1.3 Further 'original havings'

The above discussion does, of course, raise a host of philosophical questions, on some of which I touch below.[25] There are also obvious echoes of this discussion in Heidegger's reflections on authenticity in BT, and on the notion of 'Being-towards-death' in particular.[26] But an exploration of these matters must be left to another occasion. My concern here has been to show

---

[25] Cf. Section 8.5, Chapter 8 n. 20, and Chapter 9 n. 19.
[26] Gadamer, Pöggeler, and van Buren have also suggested that we glimpse here an early instance of the notion of am 'historical destruction'—the sense being in this case that we need to break back through an over-layered 'Hellenism' (see below) to recover the experience of 'primal' Christianity. Cf., e.g., van Buren 1994: 151, 167.

how this discussion illustrates a kind of 'constitutional' analysis in which the young Heidegger engages. Many other such attempts to 'unearth' 'original' 'havings' are to be found there, including intriguing reflections on how we 'have' values and 'have' history.[27] But probably the best known of all of Heidegger's 'constitutional analyses' is that of tools. The sciences of geology and metallurgy have their historical roots in our successes and failures in using rocks, and then more complex hammers to shape other entities we find around us to suit our needs. But, Heidegger maintained, we caricature our understanding of the tools we use in such activities if we attempt to construe it as itself arising out of a form of theoretical reflection on, or distanced observation of, those tools; instead our relationship to those tools is one of use: 'The genuine relation to [a tool] is to be occupied with it in using it' (HCT 191). Correspondingly, we understand those tools not as entities with a particular construction or chemical composition, but as things that can be used for a variety of purposes: what makes what I hold in my hand a hammer is its usefulness for hammering, and to be that is to occupy a particular place in the practical life of *Dasein*. Tools are not 'objects for'—do not present themselves before—a '"knowing" [of] the world theoretically'; rather they are 'what gets used, what gets produced, and so forth' (BT 95 (67)). Such an analysis is 'constitutive' in the sense I have presented in that it reflects at least in part on how *we* must be in order to encounter such entities. To encounter tools we must not only be capable of using them—since they are 'those entities that are used or which are to be found in the course of production'—but also must have a certain *interest* in them: they 'become accessible when we put ourselves into the position of concerning ourselves with them in some such way' (BT 96 (67)).[28]

---

[27] PIE Part 1's analysis of different notions of how we 'have history' reveals a range of different 'subject-correlates' and 'object-correlates'—different forms of 'having' and different 'histories' so 'had'. Another early concern of Heidegger's—which vanishes only to reappear in the later LH—is to point out that '[i]t is one thing to *declare something a value*, another to *take something as a value in a "worth-taking"*' (IPPW 40). Heidegger suspects that 'value is already the product of theorization' (PRL 12, cf. also PRL 27), and we need to ask prior forgotten questions. Some entities may 'become[] theoretically known, but an ought?' 'How does an ought give itself at all, what is its subject-correlate [*Subjektskorrelat*]? (IPPW 37).

[28] The prominence in BT of Heidegger's discussion of tool use might encourage one to think that he offers a picture of *Dasein* as fundamentally 'a 'practical agent'; such a picture, which would replace one 'subject-correlate' that we take to be somehow fundamental (the Theoretical Attitude) with another ('practical engagement' or similar), has played a powerful role in the literature on Heidegger's work, and there certainly is some truth in it, though quite what that truth is is a difficult question which will concern us in what follows.

Heidegger finds such 'constitutional' issues present elsewhere in philosophy. They are present—almost pervasively—in a negative way, in philosophers' failing to attend to such issues and having their thought profoundly shaped by that failure. For example, Descartes takes a notion of mathematical determinability as definitive of the reality of entities that stand outside of us; this leads him to conclude that

[i]f anything measures up in its own kind of Being to the Being that is accessible in mathematical knowledge, then it *is* in the authentic sense. (BT 128 (95))

But what of a positive awareness of the diversity of 'subject-correlates' and of the influence our understanding of those 'correlates' might have on our understanding of their 'object-correlates'? Although Husserl describes '[p]ure phenomenology' as 'an essentially new science' which 'only in our days presses toward development' (1982: xvii), Heidegger sees positive 'constitutional' concerns at work throughout the history of philosophy, though as especially vivid in the work of those who populate his favoured philosophical pantheon.

The 'anti-theoretical' theological tradition of which the previous section illustrated Heidegger's appropriation is often seen as marked by a certain 'anti-Hellenism', by a suspicion that efforts by theologians to elucidate the message of the Gospels in terms drawn from Greek philosophy resulted in a distortion of that message—a 'disfiguration of Christian existence' (PIE 72). This theme is most prominent in Harnack, and in Luther's 'hatred of Aristotle' (PRL 67). But it is precisely in Aristotle that Heidegger comes, in the early 1920s, to see a profound appreciation of the importance of 'constitutive analysis'. He returns again and again[29] to the 6th book of the *Nicomachean Ethics*, where Aristotle distinguishes 'intellectual virtues'—forms that subjectivity takes that correspond to different regions of Being:

Where objects differ in kind the part of the soul answering to each of the two is different in kind. (*Nicomachean Ethics* VI, 1, 1139a 9–10, quoted and translated at PS 20–21)

Aristotle distinguishes five 'modes of disclosure' or 'uncovering' which 'answer' to 'diverse regions of Being which are disclosed in the various modes of *aletheuein* [disclosure]' (PS 16). To mention just four, Aristotle

---

[29] Cf., e.g., BBA 226–30 and the long 'introductory part' of PS.

distinguishes the scientific 'mode of disclosure' (*Episteme*), a 'mode' that reveals the ultimate principles and concepts upon which scientific thought draws (one of the roles of *Sophia*), a 'mode' through which we relate to that which we produce or manipulate (*Techne*), and a 'mode' through which we relate to ourselves (*Phronesis*). In doing so, he insists, for example, that the latter 'is not a mode of *aletheuein* which one could call theoretical knowledge' (PS 39).[30]

Heidegger also comes to see such constitutive concerns in Plato too, for instance, in his reflections in the *Phaedrus* on rhetoric, where Plato asks whether there is one or many 'possible mode[s] of psychic comportment' (271a6f, quoted and translated at PS 233). '[Y]ou see here a clear preparation for Aristotle's entire research' (PS 233), which in turn, for Heidegger, is a clear preparation for his own. Ultimately, emerging from his earlier anti-Hellenism, he comes to celebrate 'the intention of the Greek concept of truth'—'truth as uncovering'—as that of not 'prejudg[ing]' that 'uncovering has to be by necessity theoretical knowledge', that truth must 'conform' 'to a determinate concept of scientificity' (PS 17). Though it is also from out of that Greek concept that the Theoretical Attitude will subsequently emerge (PS 17), Heidegger sees a return to that 'original' 'intention' as key to undoing the baleful power of that attitude.

From our own perspective we can also see that 'constitutional' questions are certainly not unknown to philosophers working in the analytic tradition. For example, one might compare Jane Heal's recent reflections on our ascription to others of intentional states with Heidegger's examination of another significant 'subject-correlate': our *Mitsein*, our Being-with-others (BT 65 (41)). Heidegger insists that 'in the act of love I live "in" the beloved, in such a way that the beloved in this act is not an object in the sense of an apprehended object' (HCT 98)—'in itself, it is, indeed, monstrous to designate love a "consciousness-of-something"' (IPR 44)—and that 'friendship' is 'a resolute and thus mutually generous way of siding with one another in the world' (HCT 280). A failure to appreciate such 'subject-correlates'— which identify what it is to relate to an entity as another person—conjures up pseudo-problems, such as the 'pseudo-problem of empathy:

---

[30] Aristotle is also a key inspiration for Heidegger's notion of 'Being-in-the-world': 'What are crudely designated...as "faculties of the soul", "perception", "thinking", "willing", are for Aristotle not experiences, but ways of existing of someone living in his world' (IPR 223).

It is assumed that a subject is encapsulated within itself and now has the task of empathizing with another subject. This way of formulating the question is absurd, since there never is such a subject in the sense it is assumed here. (HCT 243)

Similarly, Heal argues that we will inevitably be led to other minds scepticism if we take as our starting point a conception of other people as 'devices which we try to operate', and a conception of what it is to understand other people as the capacity to predict how they will behave, in combating that conception, Heal offers a 'reminder' of what it is to deal with the kind of entities we call 'other people', of what their 'subject-correlate' is: 'fellow human beings' are entities 'with whom we talk, with whom we co-operate on shared projects, from whom we ask help when we are muddled and with whom we seek to forge a jointly created and growing understanding' (2004: 194).

Heal's proposal could be seen as illustrating what Cavell calls his 'colourful' proposal that analytic philosophy has not 'discovered the other as a philosophical problem' (2004: 280). Cavell emphasizes the role of what he calls 'acknowledgement' in our dealings with others—a willingness to see others as capable of making claims on our consideration; from his perspective, scepticism about other minds presupposes a distorting vision of ourselves and our involvement with others; it is a distorting fantasy of, and for, knowledge, through which we imagine the minds of others as—to echo PRL 149 quoted above—'simply' rather 'special objects'[31] and the problem that others pose for us as one specifically of knowing them, with both that 'knowledge' and those 'objects of knowledge' robbed of their distinctive features and instead understood on the basis of crude models based on other forms of 'knowledge' and other 'objects of knowledge'. A Heideggerian way of articulating what Cavell does is as making us rethink the 'subject-correlate' of other minds—just what it is that 'knowing another person' looks like; the yet broader upshot of such an investigation is a deeper appreciation of the 'Being' of 'other persons'.

To return briefly to one last Heideggerian example, I would suggest, but cannot argue in any depth here,[32] that we read Heidegger's reflections on authenticity as attempting to show—adapting the words of Cavell—that

---

[31] Fodor distinguishes himself by being explicitly aware of having adopted that attitude—'It's gotten hard to believe that there is a *special* problem about the knowledge of other minds (as opposed to knowledge of anything elses)' (Fodor 1994: 292)—but clearly does not see in it the significance that Cavell, Heal, or Heidegger do.

[32] Sections 6.4, 7.2, 8.5, and 9.2 will return to the topic of authenticity, though a proper treatment will require a work of its own.

philosophy has not discovered the *self* as a philosophical problem. The 'constitutional' question here is: how do we 'have' ourselves? Heidegger claims that 'modern epistemology' prides itself in its care over this issue, in its discovery 'that at first only the ego is given'; in doing so, it 'believes itself to be eminently critical' but is, in fact, 'uncritical' (WDR 162, 163):

> It is based on the presumption that consciousness is similar to a box, where the ego is inside and reality is outside. But natural consciousness knows nothing of all this. (WDR 163)[33]

This 'presumption' not only distorts our understanding of what the self is; it also conjures up a confused picture of what kind of feat 'understanding the self' is. One might say either that the way in which we 'have' the self is not a matter of knowledge or that 'self-knowledge' is importantly ill-suited to the model which other forms of 'knowledge' suggest to us: to adapt words of Cavell's, the relation is 'not that of knowing, [or] anyway not what we think of as knowing' (1979: 241).[34] Either way, when we reflect on 'self-knowledge' we end up looking for the wrong *kind* of thing. For example, Heidegger sees the Theoretical Attitude at work in Jaspers' deployment of the 'non-prejudicial attitude of mere observation'; in adopting this apparently 'eminently critical' attitude towards the self, we must 'adopt, and acquiesce in, certain basic approaches to the way in which life and the self are to be intended' (KJPW 7). Heidegger argues that when such an approach 'reveals' to us 'a realm of "psychical" processes that occur, the "soul" has been eclipsed in a fundamental sense' (KJPW 26).[35]

So how do we 'have' the 'soul' or self? In his response to Jaspers, Heidegger sounds two themes familiar from the later discussion of authenticity. He proposes that *Dasein's* 'own basic experience of having itself' is having itself 'in an *anxiously concerned* manner' and that 'the experience of having-myself in fact extends historically into the past of the "I"' (KJPW 26,

---

[33] Cf. MFL 187–8 on 'the misguided view that the most presuppositionless approach is the one beginning with a worldless subject', and BT 46 (24–5) on how Descartes' 'radical' 'new and firm footing' left the status of the Subject 'undetermined' and 'indefinite', simply applying to it the medieval ontological category of the '*ens creatum*'.

[34] To put these words in context, the 'truth' or 'moral' of scepticism, according to Cavell, is 'that the human creature's basis in the world as a whole, its relation to the world as such, is not that of knowing, anyway not what we think of as knowing' (1979: 241).

[35] Cf. also IPR 33 and OHF 5.

27). This returns us to an issue mentioned at the beginning of this section—the question of how we 'have' history:

> This past is not like an appendage that the 'I' drags along with itself; rather, it is experienced as the past of an 'I' that experiences itself historically within a horizon of expectations placed in advance of itself and for itself... [T]he historical is not merely something of which we have knowledge and about which we write books; rather, we are ourselves it, and have it as a task. (KJPW 27, 29)[36]

Just as the understanding which corresponds to tools differs in form from that which corresponds to the objects of natural science, self-understanding comes in yet another form. By the same token, we cannot model *failure* of self-understanding on some kind of general and indeterminate 'disconnection' of a 'Subject' and the 'object' of its would-be 'knowledge'. Instead, this brand of 'ignorance' too must be—as Heidegger might put it—worked out afresh for *Dasein*: lacking self-knowledge impinges on one's life in a 'qualitatively' and not merely 'quantitatively' different way from our lacking knowledge of the height of Mount Blanc or of how to use a hammer; my suggestion—and it can be no more than that here—is that Heidegger's discussion of authenticity and inauthenticity can be seen as attempting to articulate what that different way is, what this kind of 'knowledge' and its absence are like:

> Self-understanding should not be equated formally with a reflected ego-experience but varies in each case with the mode of Being of the *Dasein* and in fact in the basic forms of authenticity and inauthenticity. (BPP 175)[37]

From this perspective the philosophical mainstream appears to be uncritically fixated on understanding our dealings with life in terms of knowing—or 'anyway... what we think of as knowing', as one might instead be ready to say when one looks back from the perspective to which Heidegger leads us, and from which the real diversity of things called 'knowledge' is apparent. In this fixation, the philosophical mainstream has also failed to discover not only 'the problem of the other' (as Cavell argues too) but also

---

[36] Cf. also PRL ch. 3, PS 7, n. 29 above, and Kisiel's discussion of GP (1993: 122 and 130).

[37] Cf. also Heidegger's declaration, in the midst of the discussion of Being-towards-Death, that 'the evidential character which belongs to the immediate givenness of Experiences, of the "I", or of consciousness, must necessarily lag behind the certainty which anticipation includes', 'anticipatory resoluteness' being a distinguishing feature of the authentic (BT 310 (265), 352 (305)).

'the problem of the self'; it has failed to recognize the distinctive character of the self and of the challenge of 'knowing the self'—a failure which 'constitutive' reflections on how one 'has' a self may perhaps expose.

One question I have not attempted to answer is whether the different 'havings' discussed here really are 'original', really constitute modes of engagement with entities that cannot be 'resolved' into modes of engagement that other 'havings' embody. I will touch on what demonstrating such a fact is like in Section 9.2, but for now I simply wish to note what is at stake in such a task. Showing that the idea of a diversity of 'original havings' has content—showing that the Theoretical Attitude is *just an* attitude, one which we might or might not adopt and which has no claim to being peculiarly fundamental to what subjectivity is—is a difficult task because it is, in effect, the flip-side of 'the Question of Being' itself. Our efforts to understand the Being of entities is simultaneously an effort to grasp the basic ways in which we 'have'—'comport ourselves toward'—such entities; the suspicion that there might be an issue about the former—which we have largely 'forgotten'—is at the same time a suspicion that there might be an issue about the latter—which we would also seem to have forgotten; as Heidegger put it at the end of the 1920s:

[W]ithin entities there are certain *fundamentally diverse 'kinds' of entities* which prescribe certain contexts in respect of which we take up a fundamentally *different position*, even if we do not become conscious of this diversity as a matter of course. (FCM 275)

Heidegger's attempt, through 'constitutional analyses', to reawaken our awareness of the diverse forms that understanding takes—of the different 'positions' we take with respect to different kinds of entity—is at the same time an attempt to reawaken our awareness of the diverse forms of Being. Establishing that there is content to notions of there being a forgotten 'Question of Being', a diversity of 'original havings', and a Theoretical Attitude, is then one and the same task.

2
'Constitution' and the Categories

In this chapter, I will explain how our discussion of 'constitution' sheds light on other central concerns of the early Heidegger and bears on some related, and more familiar, philosophical issues. In particular, Heidegger's 'constitutive' reflections can be seen as standing in a long-standing tradition of concern with the categories, and an examination of a central issue that the categories raise will provide a framework upon which I will draw in later discussion of Heidegger's attempt to reject both idealism and realism. But we will see that the basis of that rejection also serves to raise the suspicion that talk of 'constitutive correlations' and 'subjective-' and 'objective-correlates' may itself be misleading. The chapter will end by considering one last radical ramification of this discussion: Heidegger's 'constitutional' reflections on understanding ultimately raise the question of the 'subject-correlate' of philosophy itself.

2.1 Con-formity and the 'application' of the categories

The above discussion could be seen as standing within a broader tradition of reflection on what have been called 'the categories', and that concept seems closely tied to that of 'constitution' in the young Heidegger's work.[1] In his *Topics* 9, 103b and *Categories* 4, 1b, Aristotle singles out ten 'categories' (substance, quantity, quality, relation, place, time, position, possession, activity, and passivity). That these categories do not suffice to capture the

---

[1] Cf., e.g., DSTCM 80, 107, and 108. Cf. also Crowell 2001 for an excellent examination of how issues associated with categories play a crucial role in the emergence of Heidegger's philosophy. Cf. also Kisiel 1993: ch. 1 and van Buren 1994: ch. 4.

diverse forms that objects take is a Husserlian and neo-Kantian staple,[2] and one might see that concern as running through the previous chapter's discussion, where we saw Heidegger striving to show that there are kinds of entity that will not fit within the concepts with which the philosophical tradition has largely operated. Failure to recognize this results in our 'speaking about *one* reality in categories and ways that are all taken from *another* reality' (BBA 231), and this in turn conjures up a host of perplexing, but actually pseudo-, problems. But what I want to consider in this section is another issue that the categories raise. It is one which will help us come to understand why Heidegger ultimately abandons notions such as 'constitution' and 'subject-correlate', and set in place a framework for our later discussion of his understanding of realism and idealism.

Oswald Külpe, whose work Heidegger alludes to on a number of occasions in his very early published work,[3] describes the 'business' of 'the fundamental science of ontology' as 'the discussion of the most general concepts of the understanding (categories)' (Külpe 1897: 16). On the face of it, this is a peculiar remark: why, one might ask, should ontology concern itself with the understanding? Are categories meant to be 'features' of things—and so fall within the remit of an ontology of such things—or of thoughts—and so fall within the remit of a reflection on 'the most general concepts of the understanding'? That Külpe seems to want to say 'Both' is not, however, a peculiarity of his outlook; the history of the discussion of categories is marked by such equivocations. Aristotle's categories, for example, have been understood as types of predicate, kinds of predication (roughly, the manner in which a predicate is ascribed to a subject) and highest genera: as we ascend through higher genera—horses falling under mammals, mammals falling under animals—the highest of all are the categories.[4] But, put very roughly, we can identify two principal tasks that have been assigned to categories: that of demarcating the most general kinds of things that there are—a task performed by what one might label 'objective categories'—and that of demarcating the most general

---

[2] However, as McManus (unpublished) discusses, Aristotle himself must still be credited with a deep awareness of such diversity and of the danger of overlooking it. 'Aristotle's commonest complaint against other philosophers', G. E. L. Owen observes, 'is that they oversimplify', 'fail[ing] to see that the same expression may have many different senses', with the 'arch-deceiver' being 'the verb "to be", "*einai*"' (Owen 1986: 259). Instead we must recognize that '[b]eing is said in many ways' (*Metaphysics* Γ 2 1003a33).

[3] Cf. PRMP 41 and DSTCMC n. 3, 5, 6, and 9.

[4] Cf. R. Smith 1995: 55–6.

kinds of idea that one might entertain—a task performed by what one might label 'subjective categories'. But what, then, is the relationship between 'subjective' and 'objective categories'? How do these seemingly quite different tasks come to be fused in our talk of 'the categories'? What follows is one possible answer to these questions.

Characteristically, post-Cartesian philosophy orients itself around sceptical questions concerning whether we really have knowledge of the external world, other minds, the past, and so on. But arguably, when we worry that our thoughts about the external world, say, might be false, we presuppose an answer to a certain question about what one might call the 'intelligibility' of those thoughts: how must our thoughts and that world be for it to be possible for the former to represent or misrepresent the latter?

One of the most basic thoughts of philosophy can be seen as an answer to that question: thoughts and the world share 'forms', with the 'intelligibility' of thought envisaged as something like a fit, an isomorphism, between the 'form of thought' and the 'form of the world'. The latter refers not to the particular way in which, as a matter of contingent fact, the world happens to be, but instead to something that might be called the world's 'logical' or 'metaphysical possibilities': the objects that happen to exist within it, as well as those that could happen to exist in it, belonging to certain fundamental kinds, possessing certain very fundamental or essential properties, and standing to one another in certain very fundamental or essential relations. In the relevant senses of 'form' and 'correspondence', the 'form' of the thought 'There is a black pen on the table in front of me' would 'correspond' to the 'form' of the world in which there happens to be a blue pen on the table in front of me in that that thought embodies a false but nonetheless intelligible claim about that world: that thought articulates another way in which the world might have been, reflecting, in some sense, the kinds of object that might be found in that world, the kinds of property that they might have, and the kinds of relation in which they might stand.

I have elsewhere labelled this conception of intelligibility 'intelligibility as con-formity'.[5] To ask how exactly one ought to understand the key notions it involves—'contingency', 'logical' and 'metaphysical possibility', 'kind', 'being fundamental', and 'being essential'—is obviously to raise fundamental philosophical questions. But I take it that anyone familiar with a little philosophy

---

[5] Cf. McManus 2006: 5.

has a rough sense of how these notions are meant to be understood here. The same ideas have been returned to again and again in the history of philosophy, and, as will have been apparent, are often articulated in different terms: another formulation would draw on the notion of 'categories', and would articulate 'con-formity' in terms of a correspondence between the 'subjective' and 'objective categories'. The story retold in the roughest outline is that I can think that there is a black pen on the table in front of me, a state of affairs in which certain objects possess certain properties and stand in certain relations to one another, because my thoughts are made up of constituents—one might call them 'ideas' or 'concepts'—whose functions are to represent objects, qualities and relations: the 'subjective categories' under which my ideas fall—by virtue of possessing the different functions just mentioned—correspond to the 'objective categories' under which the things that there are fall—'object', 'quality', and 'relation'.

If one adopts a con-formist conception of intelligibility one immediately confronts a second question: how do thought and world come to have common forms? Or, in categorical terms, how do 'subjective' and 'objective categories' come to correspond?[6] To ask this question is not to ask how a thought comes to be true of a particular fact, but rather how a thought comes to be the kind of thing that is capable of being true or false of a particular fact: an answer to the latter question would provide an account of the seemingly manifest fact that we *can* think about the world.[7]

Answers to this second question come in two very broad kinds. Those that one might call 'realist' state that 'objective categories'—or the form of the world—(somehow) dictate 'subjective categories'—or the form of thought; those one might call 'idealist' state that 'subjective categories'—or the form of thought—(somehow) dictate 'objective categories'—or the form of the world. Heidegger finds in Kant a vivid awareness of the problems that these alternatives face. In the *Logik* lectures, Heidegger examines an early letter of Kant's which, Heidegger believes, identifies

---

[6] Both Friedman and Käufer invoke a similar picture in building cases for seeing Heidegger's work as profoundly shaped by neo-Kantian concerns. Cf. Friedman 2000: 33, 40, and 62 and Käufer 2003: 79 (on the question of why or how 'logic'—which 'tells us about [judgements] forms'—and ontology—which 'tells us what [judgements] can be about'—'coincide'). These issues are given a particularly striking formulation in Kant, as I am about to show; but Heidegger clearly sees them as ancient.

[7] McManus 2006 sec. 8.6 raises reservations about whether this 'seemingly manifest fact' is quite what it seems—reservations which Section 2.3 below will echo.

'the problem of the *Critique of Pure Reason*—better: [Kant's] whole philosophy' (L 115). Kant recounts there his discovery of 'the key to the whole secret, the key to metaphysics which until then, had remained hidden to itself':

> I asked myself namely: on what basis rests the relation to the object of that which, in ourselves, we call representation? If the representation contains merely the way in which the subject is affected by the object, it is easy to understand how it corresponds to the object, as effect to cause, and how this determination of our mind can represent something, i.e. how it can have an object... Similarly, if that in us, which is called representation, were active with respect to the object, i.e. if the object itself were produced by it, in the same way as divine knowledge is imagined as the prototype of things, the conformity of the representation to its object would be intelligible.[8]

But what, then, of 'the pure concepts of the understanding', which Kant will 'with Aristotle, call *categories*' (Kant 1961: A80, B105), concepts which 'may not... be abstracted from the perceptions of the senses', but which also cannot be seen as themselves 'productive of the object' (1968: 112)?

> The problem... is how, then, a representation which is related to an object can otherwise possibly exist, without being affected by it in some way... [I]f such intellectual representations rest on our inner activity, whence comes the agreement which they are supposed to have with objects, the objects not being originated by this activity[?] ... [T]he question is, how is the understanding to construct for itself entirely *a priori* concepts of things, with which the things are necessarily in agreement; how is the understanding to draw up real fundamental principles about their possibility, with which experience is necessarily in faithful agreement, and yet are independent of it; this question always leaves behind an obscurity with respect to the faculty of understanding: whence comes the agreement with things. (1968: 112–13)

Two questions naturally arise here. Firstly, is this worry over 'the agreement with things' a worry over the truth of certain claims or the meaningfulness of certain concepts? There are surely suggestions of both here; but Heidegger's identifies as the deeper worry that over 'how [a representation] can have an object', can be 'object-oriented' (L 318); Heidegger calls this deeper worry 'the meaning' of the more superficial one:

---

[8] Letter to Herz, 21 February 1772, in Kant 1968: 111–12.

How are content-oriented assertions about entities possible, when what is expressed in those assertions does not and cannot come from experience and is not taken from the givens of experience? ... How can an assertion express something about a specific entity not by drawing what it expresses from the entity[?] ... That is the meaning of the question: How are synthetic *a priori* judgements possible? (L 318)

Secondly, is this problem really peculiar to 'pure concepts of the understanding'?[9] Heidegger would seem to have reason to think that it is broader than that, and in a way which rules out the notion, expressed in the first passage quoted from Kant, that our representations might 'contain[] merely the way in which the subject is affected by the object'.[10] Heidegger identifies in the first *Critique* itself the proposal that 'all comportment toward entities carries within it an understanding of the manner and constitution of the Being of the entities in question' (PICPR 16). Our capacity to recognize an object of type x *as* an x presupposes, the argument would go, an understanding of what it is to be an x. But this immediately raises a problem: how can one acquire a mastery of the concept of an x, this capacity to recognize something as an x? And what basis does this mastery have? It cannot be gathered *a posteriori*: we cannot acquire an understanding of what an x is by encountering an x unless we are able to recognize an x as an x, which is precisely the capacity for which we are seeking to account. As another twentieth-century Kantian, Wilfred Sellars, puts it:

[I]nstead of coming to have a concept of something because we have noticed that sort of thing, to have the ability to notice a sort of thing is already to have the concept of that sort of thing, and cannot account for it. (1956 sec. 10)

This realization might prompt one to claim that the understanding in question is instead something that arises from *within us*—that it is, in some sense, innate.[11] But this understanding is meant to be an understanding precisely *of* things which are not themselves our creation—insight into that which we, as finite creatures, encounter as coming 'from without', as 'other than' us, or, as Kant puts it, as 'independent of' and 'not being originated

---

[9] One would have reason for thinking it is if one thought—as Käufer suggests Kant did—that 'we derive empirical concepts from experience by abstraction, generalization, and reflection': 'Since [empirical concepts] derive from the objects they apply to, their applicability is never in question' (Käufer 2003: 82, 83). But I think one would struggle to find such a view in Heidegger.
[10] Kant eventually comes to a similar conclusion. Cf. Gardner 1999: 30.
[11] Cf. BPP 74.

by' any activity of ours. So why should an understanding which 'arises within us', which 'rest[s] on our inner activity', have any bearing on such things, an understanding which—as Heidegger puts it using a motif that will be important for us later—has not been 'measured beforehand against things' (L 318)? Kant articulates this worry by presenting the insight in question as specifically a *synthetic* kind of *a priori* insight: it seems to be a substantial 'anticipation' of the ways of the world, though not one derived from acquaintance with that world.

Let us consider finally Kant's other suggestion in the first quoted passage. Heidegger elaborates on that suggestion in the following way. The divine intellect 'does not seek and pursue entities but *qua* intellect first of all truly produces them, that is, first makes them possible at all, makes them as possibilities' (L 115); but

> [a]s a finite entity—*substantia finita (creata)*—the human subject has not produced the world that is out there. Rather, it itself has been produced along with other entities, and has been placed into the world along with them. To the degree that these things have a relation to intellect, they have it primarily only because they have been created. They have such a relation of essence only to the *intellectus archetypus*, since they did not bring themselves before that intellect, but just the opposite. (L 116)

Heidegger's IPR lectures trace in Aquinas, and in some detail, this very line of thought, that what accounts for the 'con-formity' of the intellect with the objects about which it thinks is the fact that both 'have been created'. Our ideas have the capacity '*adaequatio ad rem*'—to match or fail to match up to a thing—by virtue of that thing itself having been created to match an idea, an idea of God's (IPR 140).[12] Section 5.4.4 will present this discussion in more detail. But for now, let us simply note Kant's reaction to this proposal—his assessment of it as 'countenanc[ing] every whim and pious or speculative figment of the imagination' (Kant 1968: 114).

So we face a dilemma. Realism attracts us because it preserves the 'independence' of the objects we judge; the problem with realism is that

---

[12] As presented here, this account would need to be supplemented with one according to which we finite subjects share, in some way, in the ideas of the divine intellect. For example, Kant proposes that '*Plato* accepted a past spiritual intuition of Divinity as the original source' of our concepts (p. 113). Though that reading of Plato has a long history, it is far from clear that it is correct. Cf., e.g., Rich 1954. For a useful discussion of other interpretations of these ideas, cf. Craig 1996.

it also renders our understanding of those objects a mystery. Idealism at least recognizes this difficulty;[13] and its 'solution' is to bite the bullet and sacrifice the status of that understanding as of entities which are truly *other than* us. For many philosophers, however, that sacrifice, which would make room for an *a priori* understanding, is too great to make, as would be the quasi-idealist solution—an idealism at one remove—that postulates a creator god.[14]

2.2 Constitution and idealism

Heidegger claims to endorse neither realism not idealism. For example, he claims that his notion of 'knowing as a mode of Being-in', which we will discuss below, 'stands neither this side nor on the far side of idealism and realism, nor is it either one of the two positions': '[i]nstead it stands *wholly outside of an orientation to them and their ways of formulating questions*' (HCT 167).[15] But many philosophers have made this neither–nor claim, and they typically disappoint; they normally turn out, despite their claims, to be mired in a species of realism or idealism after all. Is Heidegger any different? A reason to think that he is not is that the notion of 'constitution' may seem less than neutral with respect to the previous section's concerns.

Realism sits uncomfortably even with the minimal Husserlian notion of 'constitution' identified in Section 1.1. Certainly, the idea that our subjectivity might be structured in such a way as to 'constitute' objects of type x as a

---

[13] Hence, one might say, as BPP 167 puts it, that idealism 'pose[s] the problems of philosophy more fundamentally, more radically than any realism does'.

[14] How have these forms of realism and idealism manifested themselves in the thinking of particular philosophers? And how do these forms of realism and idealism relate to the diverse other views to which philosophy has given those same labels? Though Heidegger's historical writings give us plenty of clues, I will not comment further on these questions here but for noting that Heidegger's own stance would seem to be an attempt to recapture the Greek perspective, for which, he insists, 'there is no such contrast' (IPR 6). (Cf. sec. 1 of my (forthcoming-b).) Nor will I worry over whether our discussion covers all the forms that realism or idealism might take: convincing contemporary realists and idealists that the critical perspective set out here is relevant to them would require a demonstration that they are committed to something like con-formism—a task that would have to be undertaken on a case-by-case basis. One also ought not expect, I think, to find con-formism espoused—certainly in contemporary philosophical work—as an explicit commitment, but instead to find it operating on what Goldfarb has called the 'proto-philosophical level', as a 'way of looking at things that we tend to adopt at the start, without noticing that a step has been taken', but which serves to establish 'an agenda of further questions', 'to be asked and answered by philosophical theorizing' (1997: 78). (Cf. also his 1983.)

[15] Cf. also PIA 73, BT 57 (34), 228 (183), and 250 (206).

result of encountering objects of type x is confused, inasmuch as it is only if our subjectivity is already so structured that we can recognize objects of type x as such. But the mere idea of such a 'constituting' stance, a 'how' prior to any particular perception of a 'what', may seem—irrespective of Husserl's own intentions and his own understanding of 'constitution'—to raise con-formist questions which demand an idealist answer. Smith writes:

> [T]he meaning content of the act [of consciousness] projects a certain structure in the projected object, and so the object-as-intended is constituted with the projected structure. (D. W. Smith 2007: 300)

Without suggesting that either Husserl or Smith think that this is the way such ideas ought to be understood, they invite, on the face of it, the following question: 'That may be the structure that the meaning content of this act of consciousness projects in the object, but how is it *really* structured?' This question makes us wonder whether there is a correspondence of structure— one might say 'form' or 'category'—between consciousness' 'projection' of objects and 'objects out there in the world', and how such a correspondence might be expected to come about. One might respond by pointing out that the above question overlooks the facts that the 'object' in which the structure is projected is 'the projected object', and that it is 'the object-*as-intended*' that 'is constituted with the projected structure'. But emphasizing these features of Smith's formulation simply invites questions about the relationship between 'the projected object' and 'the object-*as-intended*', on the one hand, and actual objects out there, so to speak, on the other: 'What philosophical significance does "the structure of the 'the object-as-intended'" have if it does not have implications for the structure of the object full-stop? How can the former have implications for the latter unless some kind of underlying idealism is in place?'[16]

Moreover, despite his claims to the contrary, there are plenty of remarks that suggest that Heidegger himself did ultimately embrace a form of idealism. About Being, he states:

> [O]nly as long as *Dasein* is ... 'is there' Being. (BT 255 (212))[17]

---

[16] The image of 'projection' is central too in BT, and how it is to be understood will be an important theme in what follows.

[17] Cf. also BT 228 (183): '[B]eing "is" only in the understanding of those entities to whose Being something like an understanding of Being belongs.'

And about truth, he states:

'There is' truth only insofar as Dasein is and so long as Dasein is. (BT 269 (226))

Indeed, Heidegger explicitly expresses a certain kind of sympathy for idealism, talking of an 'advantage in principle' that idealism retains over realism:

If what the term 'idealism' says, amounts to the understanding that Being can never be explained by entities but is already that which is 'transcendental' for every entity, then idealism affords the only correct possibility for a philosophical problematic. (BT 251 (208))[18]

[T]o this very day I am unaware of any infallible decision according to which idealism is false, just as little as I am aware of one that makes realism true ... Instead we have to ask what this idealism—which today is feared almost like the foul fiend incarnate [*den leibhaften Gott-sei-bei-uns*]—really is searching for. (BPP 167)

An outlook with idealist leanings may also seem to be suggested by ideas that Section 3.4 will discuss: Heidegger's attack on a conception of the non-human world as fundamentally made up of 'present-at-hand' objects and his insistence instead on the primacy (in some sense) of the 'ready-to-hand'—objects such as hammers and spanners whose identity is seemingly determined by their place in human practices. In what follows I will refer to this attack and this 'primacy' claim collectively as the 'Primacy of Practice Claim'.[19]

However, I believe the accusation of idealism to be ill-founded for reasons that Part III will present. But to begin this process of rereading, let us look first at a formulation that might itself prompt idealist thoughts but which, suitably understood, can lead us towards a recognition of how, as Heidegger seems to propose, both realism and idealism might be abandoned, towards a sense of what it might mean to 'reject realism and idealism'.

2.3 'Living in the categories'

A form of words which spring to mind when we consider the difficulties with which Section 2.1 closed—a form of words which one finds in the

---

[18] In its original context, Heidegger follows these remarks with an identification of another sense of 'idealism' that he straightforwardly rejects.

[19] I follow Blattner (2007) in using the expression 'primacy of practice', but I do not claim to be using it in the same way.

young Heidegger—is that we must simply '*live in* the categories'.[20] We have seen realist responses founder on the fact that we cannot make sense of reading categories off the world, since we must already have them at our disposal to 'read' the world at all—indeed, to engage in any kind of thinking activity. If so, there is no 'coming to' those categories: like a fish in water, the categories are a medium within which the thinker can and must always already live. But the notion that we 'live in the categories' is less than transparent, and this section will present two possible interpretations of it.

The first interpretation responds to the difficulties raised by Section 2.1 by saying that the meaningfulness of our thought is, in some sense, unsurveyable—its possibility ungraspable—by us. What the above difficulties demonstrate, according to this view, is that we live, as it were, in the midst of, bathed in, meaning, and can never step outside of it so as to see that, or how, it is. That fact, like the fact that the world is one fit for our comprehension, is one so fundamental as to be unjudgeable. Analogously, perhaps we should conclude that the intelligibility of our thought and talk stands as an unsurveyable condition on our thinking and talking as we do. That our thought and talk is intelligible is something that one cannot come to see happens to be the case; it is something in which I 'move and have my being',[21] in that it is a condition of the intelligibility of every thought or proposition I might entertain.

Now, can we make sense of this view? One obvious worry is: if the existence of meaning is such an ineffable fact, how have we managed to say so much about it in the last couple of paragraphs? But rather than explore such problems further,[22] let us note that there are grounds for thinking that Heidegger was sympathetic to this problematic view.[23] Cooper sees Heidegger as believing that

---

[20] For the presence of this motif in the work of some of Heidegger's formative influences, cf., on Husserl, Kisiel 1993: 371, 393; on Lask, Crowell 2001: ch. 2, Kisiel 1993: 27, 34, 226, and 516, van Buren 1994: 98–9; and on Eckhart, van Buren 1994: 99. For a variety of earlier uses of the 'living in' construction, cf., e.g., DSTCM 99, 115, 123, and 148.

[21] Cf. Anselm's adaptation of the Platonic image of a 'supreme and unapproachable light': '[W]hatsoever I see, I see through it, as the weak eye sees what it sees through the light of the sun, which in the sun itself it cannot look upon...O supreme and unapproachable light!...Everywhere thou art, and I see thee not. In thee I move, and in thee I have my being; and I cannot come to thee.' (1926: ch. 16)

[22] For such an exploration, cf. McManus 2006: sec. 8.5.

[23] For example, in the later essay, 'The Way to Language', he proposes that '[i]n order to be who we are, we human beings remain committed to and within the Being of language, and can never step out of it and look at it from somewhere else'; for that reason, 'we cannot know the nature of language—know it according to the traditional concept of knowledge defined in terms of cognition as representation' (OWL 134).

our thought 'is embedded in a form of life, a way of Being-in-the-world, which shapes—and so cannot be measured against—the world we are in' (1997: 109); he then goes on to embrace what seems to be a version of the first interpretation of the notion that we 'live in the categories': he argues that we find in Heidegger 'wonder that we and the world are so fitted for one another that anything can, as it were, be a *something*, an identifiable thing present for us in thought and speech' (p. 113).[24]

I will argue, however, that the early Heidegger gives us reason to doubt whether we really have a sense of what it is at which, according to this first interpretation, we can merely wonder: the 'con-formity of thought and world', rather than merely being something we cannot 'measure', is a 'feat' to which we simply have not assigned sense. Our first interpretation naturally draws on a certain picture, which McDowell has articulated as one of 'a view-from-sideways-on';[25] that interpretation seems to deny that we can adopt such a view, while believing that what would be so seen is something at which we might 'wonder'. The second interpretation I will offer instead takes the 'view from sideways-on', *and* that which would supposedly be viewed from 'there', to be illusions.[26] On this interpretation, the metaphor of an 'external perspective' serves only to *articulate* the illusions in question: we believe we glimpse the possibility of 'seeing' and perhaps 'evaluating' (or 'measuring', as Cooper says) how particular activities of ours happen to 'work'; our 'ordinary' or 'pre-philosophical' 'perspective' now takes on the air of being an 'internal perspective' which contrasts with the 'external perspective' that we believe we might strive (perhaps unsuccessfully) to adopt. To find out that such an external perspective is an illusion is then to see that the notion of 'working' in question was actually a confusion; such 'working' is not something of which we might

---

[24] The above view may also have some similarities with that which Kisiel (1993) ascribes to Heidegger in seeing him as probing conditions of meaningful thought and talk that are ultimately ineffable. I will not here consider that view, nor the more complex position that Cooper sets out in his 2002.

[25] Cf., e.g., McDowell 1981: 207–8.

[26] I do not wish to discount the possibility that the notion of wonder has an important part to play in Heidegger's thought (and, as Cooper's discussion shows, a focus on the notion of 'measure' may naturally lead there). (Cf. also Phillips 1999, whose discussion of Wittgenstein makes both notions prominent.) But my sense is that it is marginalized in his thought of the 1920s by the anti-con-formist reflections I will identify below and by Heidegger's sense that the real challenge that meaning poses to those who have mastered the 'disclosure' of entities is the continuing 'appropriation' of that 'disclosure' through what he calls 'authenticity'—a notion on which I will touch at several points below. An account of the abandonment—or, I suspect, transformation—of that notion, and of the emergence—or perhaps re-emergence—into prominence of a kind of wonder, would seem to be part of the story of the emergence of the later Heidegger. (Cf. also Chapter 5 n. 31, and Chapter 7 n. 30.)

strive to catch a glimpse or indeed something of which we might regret being unable to catch a glimpse; rather, it was a notion to which we had assigned no clear sense in the first place, as indeed is the point of view from which it might have been 'glimpsed'.

According to this interpretation of the 'internal/external' metaphor as merely *articulating* the illusions in question, an 'external standpoint' on something on which we come then to think of ourselves as 'normally' or 'ordinarily' having an 'internal standpoint' is what the illusions in question are illusions *of*. If so, it is these 'standpoints' being *illusory*, rather than their being 'external', that makes them troublesome.[27] Moreover, the *lack* of regret, of a sense of 'something one cannot do' (Wittgenstein 1967: sec. 374), is important here: in recognizing that there is no such 'external', 'view from sideways-on', we ought also to recognize that there is no corresponding 'internal' 'view' either. One might say that these illusions result in our feeling that we occupy a *merely* '*internal* perspective' on some matter; but, at bottom, the illusion is that we merely have a *perspective* on that matter, that there is something we may not be able to 'see' or 'measure'.

Although there are intimations in his work of the first interpretation, I will suggest that Heidegger's understanding of the confusion of con-formity fits the second better. The root problem with con-formity is not that it helps itself to an 'external perspective', but rather that it confusedly succumbs to the illusion of a perspective. Heidegger's response to the difficulties sketched at the end of Section 2.1 is not, in any straightforward sense, to attempt to solve them: rather, as we will explore in Part III, they are to be exposed as confusions. He declares that '[t]here is no problem in seeing how Descartes' position shines through the problematic' within which these difficulties are found; as Section 5.3 will show, it does so in the presupposition there of a 'content with the character of being prior', which 'resides first of all and fundamentally within the subject' (L 318):

> Here ... we can see ... how Kant remained imprisoned in this way of posing the question: How does the subject in its knowledge come out [*kommt ... hinaus*] to the object? (L 318)[28]

---

[27] McManus 2005 discusses some of the tricky issues here in more detail in the context of their relationship to Wittgenstein's philosophy.

[28] Cf. also L 333 and PS 342.

Heidegger's diagnosis would seem to be that the problem of the correspondence of 'subjective' and 'objective categories' arises out of the adoption of a flawed ontology of the subject—one which creates the illusion of a perspective from which one might contemplate, on the one hand, 'subjective categories', and on the other, 'objective categories', and then go on to consider how they correspond. Heidegger seems to have hit upon this diagnosis as early as the supplemental conclusion that he added to his (1916) *Habilitation*; there he insists that if we reflect not on 'the epistemological subject' but instead on 'the concept of living spirit', then 'the problem of the "application" of categories no longer makes sense' (DSTCMC 66).

I will argue below that 'constitutive' thoughts lead Heidegger to the conclusion that one does not have the subject clearly in view as long as one views it in isolation from the world about which it thinks and the objects that populate that world: subjectivity is a way of 'being-amidst' those objects and, hence, no sense can be assigned to the notion of a relation of correspondence or fit between 'subjective' and 'objective categories', which we might strive to assess or measure or, for that matter, at which we might feel we can simply wonder. But, as we will see, the same considerations also provide a basis on which one might come to feel the need to abandon concepts such as 'constitutive correlation' and 'subject-'and 'object-correlate'.

2.4 Intimations of 'Being-in-the-world' and the vanishing of talk of 'constitution'

The concept of 'constitution' leads Heidegger to reflect on how the subject must be in order to encounter different kinds of object; in doing so, he sees himself as pursuing that reflection further than Husserl had himself, considering a broader range of 'subject-' and 'object-correlates'. But his application of these notions ultimately leads Heidegger to the conclusion that they themselves are potentially deeply misleading. So, for example, in Section 1.2's asking of the Husserlian 'constitutional' question of the 'correlation' of God with 'a system of meanings that present [Him] in various possible ways in actual or possible acts of consciousness' (Smith, quoted above), what corresponds to 'acts of consciousness' are the 'directions' of the 'living spirit' of the religious life. With such 'acts'—'"revelation", "tradition", "congregation"'—before us, we obtain a sense of how Heidegger felt able to call his concept of 'constitution' 'radical' (PRL 96), but also of why he ultimately came to see a distortion in the very notion of 'constitution' and its associated terms.

Heidegger comes to see 'havings' as taking forms that notions like 'subject-' and 'object-correlates' disguise. Once one has come to consider 'subject-correlates' such as tool-use, let alone 'faithful, loving, serving expectation in sadness and joy', one's conviction that what one is considering are essentially structures of *consciousness*—or even, one might say, *subjectivity*—must be under threat. In response, and in order to make room, as it were, for these anti-Cartesian thoughts, Heidegger introduces a term in place of 'subject' and 'thinker'—terms our use of which serve, he fears, to reinforce trains of thought that he wishes to challenge. That term is '*Dasein*', and perhaps the most important feature that Heidegger comes to ascribe to *Dasein* is its character as 'worldly'.

To illustrate this process, consider the way in which, in describing the 'subject-correlate' of tools, one ends up describing, to use an idiom Heidegger later adopts, a way of *Sein-bei* tools. Macquarrie and Robinson translate this expression as 'being-alongside' but this misleadingly suggests a 'being next to'; '*bei*' corresponds to the French '*chez*', giving '*Sein-bei*' a connotation of 'being at the place of' or 'being at the home of'; but for the stronger claim on the expression by Heidegger's '*Mitsein*', 'being-with' might be a good translation; overall, of the possible alternatives, 'being-amongst' or 'being-amidst' (Dreyfus' suggestion, 1991: xi) seem the most apt. These expressions draw attention to the fact that the image of, on the one hand, a 'subject-correlate', and on the other, an 'object-correlate' fails to register that—in the tool case—what the former actually refers to is a way of being with (amongst, amidst) the latter: in describing the former, one refers to the latter, and in describing the latter, one refers to the former, precisely in such a way that talk of a 'correlation' also becomes misleading. Only if one were already confused might one *stumble upon* a 'correlation' between hammers and hammering—*discover* a 'fit' between this 'subject-correlate' and this 'object-correlate'—because in describing hammers one will have been referring throughout to the actions of a hammerer, and vice versa. (This observation will be of importance in Chapter 6.) The idiom of a 'constitutive' or 'subject-object correlation', on the other hand, suggests a correspondence of two distinct worlds, an alignment of the contents of a subjective, 'inner' sphere with that of an objective, 'outer' one. As the *Logik* lectures say of what I have called 'con-formity', '[t]here is no problem in seeing how Descartes' position shines through the problematic' here (L 318, quoted above).

A parallel shift might emerge out of reflection on another 'experience' upon which the young Heidegger focuses: the 'environmental experience' (IPPW 59). The 'constitutional question' here asks:

How do I live and experience the environmental [das Umweltliche]? How is it 'given' to me? (IPPW 74)

To think of the *Umwelt*, the surrounding world, as 'had', 'lived', 'experienced', or 'given' in much the same fashion as the objects we find 'within it'— thinking of it as a very large object that includes all the others, say—would allow one to imagine the world as an object that we might find or lose as we might find or lose objects we find within the world. But, as Heidegger emphasizes, one can only find or lose something *within* a world; so the world cannot itself be something that one might find or lose.[29] But this does not only have consequences for the ontology of the world; it also clearly has implications for how we understand ourselves too. As entities capable of finding or losing entities, we must already have a world in which to search; 'having a world' is not some 'spurious contingency' (IPPW 74) that such subjects can be conceived of as possibly lacking. Instead we are 'worldly' creatures: 'experience itself has a worldly character' and, as an experiencing entity, 'I am as such always attached to the surrounding world' (PRL 10).

But this, of course, also raises a worry about the formulation of our initial 'constitutional' question. One might express the above critical thoughts by saying that the environmental world is 'given' through a distinctive 'subject-correlate'. But, Heidegger suggests, 'for something to be *given* is already a theoretical infringement': the world is part of the very fabric of the Being of creatures such as ourselves but, when I think of it as 'given', '[i]t is already forcibly removed from me' (IPPW 74). Indeed, even the more catholic idiom of 'having' might seem misplaced; with the environing world, we encounter an 'object' which one might say—to adapt words from a 1922 letter to Jaspers—'we do not have but *are*' (HJC 34). Or, as Heidegger will

---

[29] Cf. Section 7.2 for another take—or perhaps another interpretation of the above take—on Heidegger's critique of external world scepticism.

later put it, *Dasein's* mode of Being is 'Being-*in*' a world, the very same world that the entities with which it engages populate; rather than 'being given', 'having' or 'correlating-with-', *Dasein* 'resides' or 'dwells' 'amid' [*bei*] that world of entities (BT 80 (54)):

> When *Dasein* directs itself towards something and grasps it, it does not somehow first get out of an inner sphere in which it has been proximally encapsulated, but its primary kind of Being is such that it is always 'outside' amidst [*bei*] entities which it encounters and which belong to a world already discovered. (BT 89 (62))

I suggest that, since expressions such as 'subject' and 'object' draw our attention away from this 'primary kind of Being', Heidegger abandons them and, with them, talk of 'subject-' and 'object-correlate' and of the 'constitution' of the latter through its 'correlation' with the former.[30]

My suspicion is that Heidegger came to see 'constitution' then, just as he came to see 'subject' and 'consciousness', as simply too misleading, as too ready to insinuate into our thinking ideas under whose influence we then fall but of whose presence we remain unaware. Like those terms, it has an historical baggage and a contemporary use from which Heidegger wants to distance himself: an example of the former is the Kantian notion of objects as '"constituted" when the unconceptualized data of sense are organized or framed within the *a priori* logical structures of judgement itself' (Friedman 2000: 27), and an example of the latter is Natorp's 'radicalization of the idea of constitution', which Heidegger saw as precisely 'maintaining' 'the predominance of theoretical consciousness within the whole problematic of spirit and reason' (PIE 106, 109). Despite Natorp's specific desire to avoid 'objectifying the subjective' and revive an appreciation of its distinctive mode of Being, Heidegger saw at work in his thinking a notion of constitution as '*constitution in consciousness*', which issued in a '*non*-considering of

---

[30] Something analogous can be seen in the development of Wittgenstein's philosophy. In his later work, Wittgenstein came to the conclusion that his earlier self had been unwittingly committed to a narrow conception of language—one which blinded him to the fact that '[t]here are many things... which we may or may not call propositions; and not only one game can be called language' (1979: 12). (McManus 2006: appendix A discusses these issues.) Crucial to recognizing this diversity was a recognition of the different roles that these propositions play in our lives. But that very mode of reflection suggests something about language, something that Wittgenstein flags with his term, 'language-game': 'the term "language-*game*" is meant to bring into prominence the fact that the *speaking* of language is part of an activity, or of a form of life' (PI 23). Wittgenstein came to the conclusion that 'to imagine a language means to imagine a form of life' (PI 19), and I think it reasonable to suspect that recognizing the diversity of *Dasein's* 'comportments' encouraged a similar change of mind in Heidegger.

"consciousness" from the constant view point of *constitution*!' (PIE 77, 100, 103, second italics added). Through this notion, 'the theoretical relation of apprehension' is instead 'firmly predetermined'; and 'only from it' do '"soul", "God", "life" receive their sense', a 'thingly-ness in the broadest sense' (PIE 89, 88, 109, 110).

Must one understand 'constitution' in this way? Clearly not, as Heidegger's own talk of 'radicalizing' the notion shows;[31] and one might take the time and trouble to distinguish *one's own* concept of 'constitution' from everyone else's; but one also might wonder whether such distinctions are really heard and whether one might not be better off—as I believe Heidegger concluded— leaving such terms behind.[32] So in place of talk of 'consciousness', we find talk of 'comportment' or 'having to do with'; in place of talk of 'subjectivity', we find talk of 'life' and, later, '*Dasein*'; but what is retained from Heidegger's 'constitutional' reflections is a sense that philosophical clarity about the world that we find calls for us to reflect on how we 'have' that world.[33]

2.5 The 'subject-correlates' of science and philosophy

All questions of philosophy are, at bottom, questions about the How— strictly understood, questions of method. (PRL 62)

---

[31] Cf. PIE 115 and PRL 96, quoted above.

[32] It is also clear that there are further ways of understanding 'constitution' and further issues that those ways raise. I suspect that Moran is right when he says that '[i]n a sense, the whole problem of phenomenology comes down to the problem of constitution' (Moran 2000b: 164).

[33] Section 5.4 will present an argument that sets out a motivation for some of the basic claims that make up Heidegger's notion of Being-in-the-world. But is not such an argument what we have just seen? And did not our reflection on tool-use provide us with another way to that same idea? I think that the above argument, the argument of Section 5.4, and our reflection on tool-use are, in fact, related, but I also think that it is eminently plausible that Being-in-the-world is an overdetermined notion for Heidegger—one to which he is led by several routes. Following on from n. 30 above, one might ask of Wittgenstein which came to him first—the recognition of the diversity of language, or the recognition that language's 'medium', so to speak, is 'life'? I suspect that the answer is probably neither, that each step towards a recognition of each nudged Wittgenstein closer to a recognition of the other. I suspect that Heidegger's development also takes that form. For similar reasons, I do not think there is anything particularly incongruous about his expressing the worries about the notion of 'constitution' that this section discusses during the very same period in which he also seems to find that notion the most natural for the articulation of his own thoughts. As Heidegger later observed, '[n]obody can in just one single leap take distance from the predominant circle of ideas' (OWL 36).

Finally in this chapter, I turn to another far-reaching question that the notion of 'constitution' raises, concerning the 'subject-correlates' of science and philosophy itself. A *bête noire* of the story so far is the Theoretical Attitude; but, as Chapter 3 will explore, quite what the status of that Attitude is for Heidegger—and quite what might be wrong about adopting it—is less than obvious. Is it just that it is one 'attitude', one 'having' among many, and that we need to listen, as it were, to those others too? Or is it actually ill-suited to revealing how things are—even the particular kinds of things that one might suppose were its distinctive 'object-correlate'? Heidegger's reflections seem to suggest, to say the least, that theoretical consciousness rests upon other modes of intentionality, and for that reason, the perspective that theoretical consciousness provides us with is apt to mislead us. But how, exactly?

These worries also threaten our comfortable attachment to two 'activities' that might seem paradigmatically theoretical: science and philosophy itself. If we need to reevaluate the Theoretical Attitude, ought we now to ask what the sciences *can* tell us, about what limits their distinctive 'attitude' might impose on what they can reveal? Or perhaps whether the 'illumination' that they provide is something quite other than that which we are apt to think 'theoretical knowledge' embodies. And what of philosophy? Ought we now to ask whether philosophy should be seeking a theoretical form of understanding? Might the philosophical tradition, when it acknowledges its true calling, pose a quite different kind of challenge to us to that which items of theoretical knowledge can meet?

Heidegger's own assessment, in the 1920 PIE lectures, is that the 'endangering of the predominance of the theoretical' by the phenomenological exploration of 'different possibilities of lived experience' 'could not in the long run leave the structure of the philosophical problematic unaffected'; with an awareness of 'the opposition between living experience... as atheoretical and the knowing of it' 'as theoretical apprehension', 'philosophy itself is in question' (PIE 17, 28). Indeed, once one has come to consider the possibility that 'the prevailing of the theoretical attitude' has 'distorted' our understanding of 'lived experience', one must wonder whether 'a consideration of living experience that does not immediately and necessarily theoretically disfigure it is possible at all', whether philosophy might not be 'condemned to violence' (PIE 18, 29). So, for example, Dahlstrom has argued that Heidegger's philosophical reflections cannot be understood as theoretical in nature. He identifies a particular reflexive problem that Heidegger seems to face in articulating his fundamental ontology—a problem that Dahlstrom calls 'the paradox of thematization'. As we will see in the next chapter, there are some grounds for ascribing to Heidegger the view that theoretical assertions can reveal only one kind of entity: the *Vorhanden*.[34] If that is so, then Heidegger cannot use theoretical assertions 'to indicate, specify, and communicate' the other forms of Being that he seems to insist we must acknowledge (Dahlstrom 1994: 778). Dahlstrom's 'paradox' arises because that is precisely what a work like BT appears to do. Therefore, those appearances must be deceptive.[35]

Though, as we will see below, there is reason to doubt the force and relevance of Dahlstrom's 'paradox' to Heidegger's work, it does provide an understanding of an intriguing theme that runs through his reflections in the 1920s, even if it received relatively muted expression in BT itself. This is a recurrent worry of whether philosophy ought to be seen as a science,[36] and indeed, at some points, whether its insights should be seen as expressible in propositions at all. In the *Beiträge*, Heidegger proposes that

> In philosophy...what is 'true' is not a proposition at all and also not simply that about which a proposition makes a statement. (CP 10)

But earlier too, Heidegger voices suspicion of the notion that philosophical insights can be captured in propositional form. For example, he rejects the notion of an answer to the Question of Being being 'a free-floating result', 'what it asserts propositionally...just passed along' (BT 40 (19)), as something 'petrified' (HCT 87), 'procured like a coat and hat' (MFL 17). He warns that

> [w]henever a phenomenological concept is drawn from primordial sources, there is a possibility that it may degenerate if communicated in the form of an assertion. (BT 60-1 (36))[37]

---

[34] As will also become apparent there, there are also plenty of reasons to doubt this ascription, of some of which Dahlstrom is aware. Cf. his 1994: 778 n. 9 and 2001: 202–6 and 355–6.

[35] Cf. also Dahlstrom 2001: 17, 207f, 235–65, 352–69, 392f, and 433f. Cf. also Lafont's identification of 'Heidegger's self-posed problem of how assertions, the objectifying tools par excellence, can be used to thematize the unobjectifiable' (Lafont 2002: 233).

[36] Cf. Sections 9.1–9.2 below.

[37] Cf. also, e.g., HCT 139, 308–8 and FCM 300.

The notion that Heidegger's insights might not be propositional in form is one of which some commentators have made much. So, for example, in the light of the 'paradox of thematisation', Dahlstrom has suggested that Heidegger's ontological proposals might need to be seen as forming parts of a 'ladder' that is 'climbed and thrown away' (1994: 787–8), as Wittgenstein declares those who understand him ought to treat the propositions of his *Tractatus* (1922 sec. 6.54).[38] While some have seen such as expedient as 'desperate' (Okrent 1988: 292), that Heidegger might need to use a strategy of something like this form is one which has received support from a variety of quarters.[39] The worry that it ushers in 'windy mysticism' (Ryle, quoted above) is understandable enough though, and in Chapter 9 I will offer my own construal of this theme—a construal which, I hope, is reasonably non-mysterious.[40]

---

[38] Cf. also Dahlstrom 2001: 208 and 252.
[39] Cf., e.g., Priest 2002, Witherspoon 2002, Moore 2012; and discussions of the notion of 'formal indication' in Kisiel 1993, van Buren 1994, and Crowell 2001.
[40] I do not mean to suggest here that Heidegger's attitude toward mysticism was hostile, nor indeed that ours should be. Heidegger clearly took the mystical tradition seriously, and valued it, for example, as a 'counter-movement' to 'a theorizing, dogma-promoting influence' in religious reflection (DSTCMC 68). There might perhaps be grounds for connecting the view I will offer with such mysticism; but the view remains, I would still insist, un-'windy'.

PART II

3
Vorhandenheit

In Heidegger's discussions of 'constitution' and the tendency to force the Being of entities into categories to which they do not belong, the Theoretical Attitude emerges as the villain of the piece. For example, by succumbing to an 'analogy with the theoretical and the constitution of the object of cognition', we come to regard the 'object' of Christian faith as the 'object' of such cognition: God emerges as 'simply a special object' (PRL 232, 149). But there is another way in which Heidegger presents the Theoretical Attitude as less than 'fundamental' or as 'narrow', incapable of surveying all that this is; that is, by suggesting that the theoretical is—in a sense to be examined—'founded' in other forms of 'comportment'. One crude picture of this relationship—a picture we will challenge—presents the theoretical as a mode of relating essentially embedded within—and which we enter into only when there is a 'breakdown' in—our pragmatic dealings with the world around us. Quite what sense and what truth there may lie obscured in this picture will be a central question in what follows.

What makes that question more complex still is the fact that Heidegger sees this 'founding' as a feature not just of the theoretical; it characterizes a whole group of other phenomena with which Heidegger thereby associates the theoretical. For example, he talks of 'the proposition [*Satz*], the *theoretical* assertion [*Aussage*]' (PS 174) as if they were one and the same thing. We have already seen, in Chapter 1, Heidegger seemingly happily running together the 'constant dependency' of theology on 'theoretical consciousness' with a 'dogma-promoting influence' and a fixation on 'the object of cognition' (PRL 235, 238, 232, quoted in Section 1.2); and a similar sliding occurs in L 9–11, where Heidegger talks of the sense of truth that has 'real priority' in 'modern logic' as that which is 'oriented to propositional assertions' [*Aussagesatz*], 'cognitional truth', and 'truth as theoretical apprehension':

[T]he determination of truth gets oriented, primarily and in principle, to this kind of speech, the propositional assertion [*Aussagesatz*]. The act of uncovering entities in such assertions is what is true, and so the truth of theoretical–scientific knowledge has become the basic, original form of truth as such. Cognitional truth [*Erkenntniswahrheit*] achieves a universal priority. (L 11)

But is the truth of 'propositional assertions' the same thing as 'cognitional truth', and that, in turn, the same as 'truth as theoretical apprehension'?

Indeed, these are not the only phenomena seemingly swept up together with Heidegger's interest in the Theoretical Attitude; he associates the Theoretical Attitude with intuition, contemplation, and 'just looking'.[1] He also, of course, associates it with the mode of thinking that characterizes science and, in particular, the natural sciences; but here too it is not clear that he means to pick out 'theorizing'—where that means formulating general principles under which we subsume particular observations and/or less general principles—as opposed to, for instance, the making of observations. Certainly, Heidegger seems to have no particular interest in the theory/observation distinction as that is typically understood in contemporary philosophy of science. Let me also add one more uncertainty: when he links the Theoretical Attitude to theorizing or assertion, does he connect it with them as they actually are or as we may be inclined to understand them? When we contemplate the Theoretical Attitude, are we contemplating assertions and/or the theoretical? Or are we contemplating confused fantasies that we may have of what assertions and/or the theoretical are?

So what exactly is at stake when Heidegger talks of the Theoretical Attitude and its 'founded' character? There is another association that one might hope will bring us some clarity: the Theoretical Attitude is seen as revealing what seems to be a particular kind of entity, the *Vorhanden*. Through this connection the 'founding' of the Theoretical Attitude is connected to what I labelled in Section 2.2 the 'Primacy of Practice Claim', Heidegger's depiction of the *Zuhanden* as, in some sense, 'prior to' the *Vorhanden*. These are very familiar ideas for readers of Heidegger and the Heidegger literature; but, as we will see, this relation of 'priority' and indeed its relata raise significant difficulties.

---

[1] Cf., e.g., BT 99 (69).

3.1 Themes in the discussion of *Vorhandenheit*

'*Vorhandenheit*' figures as a pivotal term in BT, and yet the idea it expresses is complex, and perhaps even incoherent. Macquarrie and Robinson note that the literal meaning of '*vorhanden*' is 'before the hand', that it can be used in ordinary German usage to refer to 'the stock of goods which a dealer has "on hand"', or to the "extant" works of an author', and, in philosophical work, 'as a synonym for the Latin "*existentia*"' (BT 48 (26), translators' note). It is introduced as the latter in BT (BT 67 (42)), though also as picking out a mode of '*existentia*' that specifically contrasts with *Dasein's*.[2]

But, as commentators have noted,[3] there are many other notions that the term '*Vorhandenheit*' seems meant to tie together. The following list includes notions that Heidegger explicitly connects with *Vorhandenheit*, as well as ones to which commentators repeatedly turn in translating or explaining the term:

1) presence[4]
2) thing[5]
3) mere thing[6]
4) object[7]
5) substance[8]
6) nature[9]
7) the objective[10]
8) reality[11]

---

[2] Cf. also BT 71 (45) and 79–82 (54–6).

[3] Cf., e.g., Fell 1992 and Christiansen 1997: 80.

[4] Cf., e.g., BT 48 (25–6), Philipse 1998: 135 and 148, and Stambaugh's sense (35) below.

[5] Cf., e.g., BT 245 (201) and Gorner 2007: 153: 'the Being of things or substances: presence-at-hand (*Vorhandenheit*)'. A problematic passage is BT 254 (211).

[6] Cf., e.g., L 158, Blattner 2006: 64 ('the kind of Being of mere things') and Gorner 2007: 81 ('the Being of mere things (presence-at-hand)').

[7] Cf., e.g., Guignon 1983: 101 and Richardson 1986: 47.

[8] Cf., e.g., BT 122 (88), 245 (201), 365 (318) and Dreyfus 1991: 71: 'occurrentness as the way of Being of isolated, determinate substances'. (On 'occurrentness', cf. sense (34) below.) Cf. also Guignon 1983: 144, Schear 2007: 128, and Carman 2007: 112: 'occurrent (*vorhanden*) entities, that is... *substances*'.

[9] Cf., e.g., L 63, BPP 28 and n. 51 below. But, cf. the distinctions drawn at BT 100–2 (70–2), 254 (211) and L 314–15. Cf. also Käufer 2002: 171, Schear 2007: 128, Fell's 'third sense' (1992: 71) and his discussion of the relation between 'nature' and 'the natural scientific' (pp. 67, 72–3).

[10] Cf. Philipse 1998: 52, Heim's translation as 'objective thing' (e.g. MFL 127) and Stambaugh's sense (35) below.

[11] Cf., e.g., BT 245 (201), 228 (183) ('presence-at-hand ("Reality", "world-actuality")') and L 62: 'a thing's being-actual, its realness (its being-there-on-hand)'

9) the material[12]
10) the thematic[13]
11) a mere *that!*[14]
12) things that are not *zuhanden*[15]
13) a thing with properties ('*decontextualized* features' as opposed to 'aspects' or 'situational characteristics' (Dreyfus 1991: 77–78))[16]
14) the isolatable/de-contextualised[17]
15) a 'what' as opposed to a 'who'[18]
16) as 'brought to the fore' by 'conspicuousness, obtrusiveness, and obstinacy' (BT 104 (74)—with 'obtrusiveness' revealing that which is 'just present–at–hand and no more'; BT 103 (73))[19]
17) as revealed by the Theoretical Attitude[20]

---

[12] Cf., e.g., BT 79 (54), L 63 and 314.

[13] Cf., e.g., BT 414 (363) and Richardson 1986: 49.

[14] Cf., e.g., Fell 1992: 75 on 'sheer that-being' and the evidence associated with senses (31) and (32). As we will see below, one way of looking at Rouse and Blattner's reading of Heidegger is as arguing that, given his other commitments, the *Vorhanden* can be no more than 'mere thats' and as such cannot be seen as objects we might understand, though this is offered as a critique rather than an exposition of Heidegger's view. (I will not discuss here Lafont's suggestion that one might think of the *Vorhanden* as that which is picked out through direct reference (cf. her 2000: 242). Among the interesting philosophical possibilities that this raises is that of a notion of the *Vorhanden* as bare thats but as, nonetheless, intelligible 'objects of thought'. This is not, however, a proposal well-founded in Heidegger's text, nor do I suppose Lafont ultimately sees it as such.)

[15] Cf., e.g., BT 227–8 (183). Gelven 1989: 61 ('things independent of their function or use (i.e . . . "present –at-hand": *vorhanden*)'), Rouse 1998, sec. 1 ('shorn of their practical significance'), Blattner 2006, below, on 'things that are not assigned to roles in human activity' (p. 64) (cf. also p. 55), and Gorner 2007: 153: 'For the most part the account of presence-at-hand is negative, in the sense that it is what readiness-to-hand is not.' Cf. also Preston 1998: 534 n. 15, Philipse 1998: 136, and Turetzky 1998: 184. But cf. also BT 100 (70).

[16] Cf., e.g., BT 122 (88) and 200 (158). Cf. also Rouse 1985: 202, Kaufer 2002: 173 ('We first have to de-contextualize our familiarity with the world in order to arrive at pure natural properties'), and Fell 1992's 'third sense' (p. 71).

[17] Cf., e.g., NUAS 173f, Guignon 1983: 157, Richardson 1986: 48 and 72, Rouse 1987: 74, Dreyfus 1991: 71 quoted in n. 87 above, Lafont 2000: 50, and Fell's 'third sense' (1992: 71). A similar thought might be seen at work in Beck's 2005 interpretation of *Vorhandenheit*, but I will not discuss his complex—though very interesting—proposal here.

[18] At BT 71 (45), Heidegger refers to this as 'presen[ce]-at-hand in the broadest sense' but Section 8.3 will identify a different notion which Heidegger picks out with the same expression.

[19] Cf. also HCT 211–12 where the 'obstructive [and] unserviceable' is described as 'merely a thing, not a thing in the theoretical sense'. Cf. also Fell's 'second sense' (1992: 71).

[20] Cf., e.g., BT 175 (136), 177 (138), 209 (166), L 104, and IPPW 62. Cf. also Guignon 1983: 202 ('the present-at-hand of theoretical reflection'), Richardson 1986: 47, Rouse 1987: 97, Friedman 2000: 48, Mulhall 2005: 41 ('present-at-hand, the object of theoretical contemplation'), and Dahlstrom's argument presented in Sec. 2.5.

18) as revealed in knowledge[21]
19) as revealed in 'pure beholding'[22]
20) as revealed by 'intuition'[23]
21) as revealed by 'just looking', by 'fixed staring'[24]
22) as revealed by natural science[25]
23) as revealed by mathematics[26]
24) as revealed by interpretation[27]
25) as revealed by assertions/statements [*Aussagen*], sentences/propositions [*Sätze*], judgements [*Urteil*] or propositional attitudes[28]
26) as revealed by 'going through' the *Zuhanden*[29]
27) as revealed by a 'change-over' (BT 409 (357)), or a 'prescinding', from engagement with the *Zuhanden* (L 314)
28) as revealed by 'devivification'[30]

---

[21] Cf., e.g., Moran 2000: 48: 'the specific kind of Being, presence-at-hand (*Vorhendenheit*), displayed by the objects of cognitive acts'. Cf. also Turetzky 1998: 183–4 ('A hammer... is at-hand insofar as properties such as its shape and composition are observed.').

[22] Cf. following note.

[23] At BT 187 (147), Heidegger talks of 'the priority' of 'pure intuition [*puren Anschauen*]' which 'corresponds noetically to the priority of the *Vorhanden* in traditional ontology'. (Cf. also BT 246 (202).) But at BT 215 (171), Macquarrie and Robinson translate '*reinen Anschauung*', which would be quite naturally rendered as 'pure intuition' too, as 'pure beholding'. I give two separate 'entries' here because, when viewed in context, there may be two distinct ideas in play here—a possibility on which Macquarrie and Robinson seem to be taking a stand, whether or not intentionally.

[24] Cf., e.g., BT 88–9 (61–2) and Käufer 2003: 85 on 'pure occurrence' (cf. sense (34) below) as 'nothing more than something for staring-at' (p. 85).

[25] Cf., e.g., BT 415 (363) and Philipse 1998: 64.

[26] Cf., e.g., BT 122 (88) and 129 (96): 'mathematical knowledge is exceptionally well suited to grasp' 'constant presence-at-hand'.

[27] Cf., e.g., BT 89 (61–2).

[28] Cf., e.g., BT 89 (61–2), 200–1 (157–8), and 209 (166). But cf. also Mulhall 2005: 91–3 and Fell 1992's 'third sense' (1992, 71). I do not distinguish here between notions which, for various reasons, other philosophers do distinguish, because Heidegger himself seems unconcerned with these distinctions (cf., e.g., BT 257 (214) and PS 174 quoted in the introduction to this chapter). Translators have happily, and without obvious distortion, used 'assertion' or 'statement' for '*Aussage*' and 'proposition' or 'sentence' for '*Satz*'. 'Propositional attitude' is an expression whose introduction postdates BT; but his remarks on judgement would obviously have a bearing on what that expression is taken to denote, as, in all likelihood, would those on assertions/statements and sentences/propositions, since Heidegger does not seem overly concerned with these as linguistic phenomena, as distinguished from what one might call the 'mental states' that they express. (Where such a concern does emerge is in his 'diagnosis' of certain confusions about the 'gap' between thought and its objects, cf. Sections 4.2.2 and 7.4.) For the reason just given, Schear has suggested that 'judgement' is a more appropriate label for Heidegger's concern in his discussions of '*Aussagen*' (2007: 129–31). While I am tempted by that view, I have decided to stick with the term 'assertion', simply because there is a more natural term, '*Urteil*', that Heidegger could have used but chose not to.

[29] Cf., e.g., BT 121 (88).

[30] Cf., e.g., IPPW 71 and 75.

29) as revealed by 'de-' or 'unworlding'[31]
30) as revealed by anxiety[32]
31) as the unintelligible[33]
32) as the strange[34]

To this already long list one ought perhaps to add the following four, which are the preferred translations of *Vorhandenheit* adopted by Macquarrie and Robinson, Dreyfus, Stambaugh, and Hofstadter respectively, and which, as any translation is liable to do, seem to introduce ideas not obviously present in the original—in this case ideas in addition to, or sometimes combining some of, those listed above:

33) the present-at-hand
34) the occurrent[35]
35) objective presence[36]
36) the extant[37]

There are yet more trails that run from *Vorhandenheit* and which one might follow,[38] but the above will suffice for now.

---

[31] Cf., e.g., BT 94 (65), HCT 217–18, Guignon 1983: 157, Rouse 1985 and Blattner 1995's criticisms of Dreyfus, and Fell 1992: 70–1 on where 'all referentiality fails' and entities reveal themselves without '*any* involvement *whatsoever*' (BT 393 (343)).

[32] Cf. Fell's 'first sense' (1992:71) and what he presents as supporting evidence (p. 70).

[33] Cf., e.g., BT 193 (152) on the *Vorhanden* as 'absurd [*widersinnig*]', 194 (153) on their 'essential unintelligibility [*Unverständlichkeit*]', HCT 217–18, and Fell 1992: 76 and 77.

[34] Cf. Fell 1992: 69, 70, and 75.

[35] Macquarrie and Robinson themselves begin to make a case of sorts for 'occurrent' in their note to BT 141 (106) regarding '*vorkommen*'. Cf. also L 156 n. 131 ('what is there, what occurs [*Vorhandenes—Vorkommendes*]'. For other invocations in the secondary literature of 'occurrence' as explaining *Vorhandenheit*, cf. Blattner 2006: 52 ('what "merely occurs" (*vorkommt*)' and 'occurrent or present'), Gorner 2007: 4 ('the Being of things and their properties which simply occur'), and Philipse 1998: 133, 166 and 29 ('things that are *Vorhanden* (simply exist and occur, are extant))'. A question emerges here, of course, about quite what the force of these 'merely's and 'simply's is; one possibility sends us back to sense (12) above; another is suggested by Moore's proposal that '"whats" that are present-at-hand [are] of no intrinsic value' (Moore 2012: 472).

[36] In her introduction to TB, Stambaugh instead translated *Vorhandenheit* as 'things of nature' (TB vii).

[37] Hofstadter also translates *Vorhandenheit* as 'the at-hand' (cf. BPP).

[38] Cf., e.g., Fell's '*fourth* proper sense' (1992: 76). I also leave out of account here Heidegger's identification of *Vorhandensein* with 'the presence of *phusis* in the broadest sense' (L 77) and the possible shaping influence on Heidegger's thought of the Aristotelian notion that *episteme* does not reveal the *archai* (cf., e.g., BBA 227). Such parallels can only illuminate if we have in place a proper assessment of just what the Greek proposals mean and what Heidegger takes them to mean, which would require a study all of its own. (For some discussion, cf. Taminiaux 1991: 118–22 and 127–9.) To give a brief indication of the difficulties here, BPP explores the notion that, in its Greek roots, the *Vorhanden* ought

Many of these proposed senses of the term '*Vorhanden*' themselves raise questions of interpretation: 'object', for example, is anything but a transparent notion in philosophical discussion.[39] Is it here meant in something like a Kantian sense?[40] Or a Fregean sense?[41] Or some further sense? But it is when we come to the issue of the connections between these many different senses that the range of questions that press upon us expands exponentially. Taking any two and claiming that they in some way pertain to the same phenomenon would seem to call for philosophical clarification and argument. For example, Heidegger himself explicitly links (7) and (10) when he says that '[t]hematizing objectifies' (BT 414 (363));[42] but are there other ways of 'thematizing'? Can one only 'thematize' the 'objective'? As Haugeland (2005: 428) notes, Heidegger surely would not have seen 'historical entities' as 'occurrent' (sense 34) but, nonetheless, describes 'historiology' as a science and declares that '[e]very science is constituted primarily by thematizing' (BT 445 (393)).[43] Also, what are we to make of occasions on which Heidegger seems to *distinguish* that which is 'thematic' from that which is 'thematic for theoretical understanding'—as he does at L 154, for example—and 'objectification' from 'theoretical consideration'—as he does at MFL 129?[44]

Am I being unnecessarily pernickety here? I do not think that Heidegger, if presented with these worries, would think so. At BT 72 (46) he remarks on the need to understand the 'ontological origin' of 'Thinghood' if we are to understand what we mean by calling for an 'un-reified' conception of the subject: the worry is that we may not be sufficiently clear about what a

---

be understood as 'the produced' (cf., e.g., BPP 101, QCT 160, and n. 252 below). My suspicion is that this exploration suggests a growing awareness on Heidegger's part that this concept is more problematic than his handling of it in BT might suggest.

[39] Cf. PRL 25 where Heidegger insists 'Object [*Objekt*] and thing [*Gegenstand*] are not the same.'

[40] Cf. Haugeland 2000: 45: '[E]ntities that can be known in explicit, theoretical judgements—paradigmatically, the knowledge attained in natural science'.

[41] See below.

[42] Cf. the discussion of Dahlstrom in Section 2.5. There are also, of course, many contexts in which Heidegger emphasizes the connection between ideas on our list without invoking the term, *Vorhandenheit*, as an intermediary. Cf., e.g., BPP 201 on the connection of judgement (sense 25) with the idea of Being as objectivity (sense 7).

[43] Cf. also Blattner 1995: 323–4, Schear 2007: 149, and BT 413 (361): 'The ready-to-hand can become the "Object" of a science without having to lose its character as equipment'.

[44] '[I]n our direct dealings it is the with-which that is thematic ... But while it is thematic, it is not thematic for theoretical understanding' (L 154); '*Objectification, or even theoretical consideration*, does not necessarily belong to being-amidst [*Sein-bei*]' (MFL 129, italics added).

thing, a *res*, is to make 're-ification' a substantial and determinate charge.[45] To deny that *Dasein* is a thing seems just daft if 'being a thing' means 'being real' or 'occurring', in some non-technical sense. So, if not that, then what? And why think that more refined conceptions of 'objecthood' or 'thinghood' (or 'reality') are all that 'the thematic' can reveal? One would be pushed towards a similar conclusion—that the subject of a first-order, non-quantifying assertion can only be an object—if one were to adopt, for example, a Fregean notion of 'objects' as that which singular terms pick out.[46] But—and this is all that matters about the analogy here—the charge of 'reification' would then look very different, in fact almost trivial from the perspective of one committed to a more substantial notion of 'objecthood'. In PRL we read:

An 'object as such' means only the 'to which' of the theoretical attitudinal relation. (PRL 42)

If 'the thematic' were 'the thematic for theoretical understanding', then this would assign a straightforward but trivial sense to 'thematizing objectifies' (setting aside worries about the relationship between 'objectivity' and 'objects'). And if, as passages such as L 154 seem to suggest, 'the thematic' *cannot* be equated with 'the thematic for theoretical understanding', then the question remains: why think that 'thematizing objectifies'?

The term '*Vorhandenheit*' enters Heidegger's vocabulary relatively late in the years that lead up to BT,[47] and, as a result, it must be conceded, he never explicitly links that term to, for example, the notion of 'devivification' (sense 28). Also, the diversity of uses identified above might prompt one to conclude that 'not all presence-at-hand is the same', and that instead '[t]here are different kinds of presence-at-hand' (McNeill 1999: 83).[48] While there is some truth in that, Chapter 8 will suggest a way of seeing a unifying concern in that diversity. It is clear, I think, that a cluster of ideas exists in Heidegger's pre-BT work—a cluster that evolves but retains some continuity and which corresponds to the majority of our 36 senses above. The term around which that part of the cluster that persists into BT cluster is

---

[45] Cf. also BT 487 (437) on the question, 'what does... "reifying" signify?'.
[46] For discussion, cf. Brandom 1994: 360f. Heidegger makes Fregean noises in HCT 65's discussion of the connection of 'nominalization' and 'thematizing'.
[47] Cf. Kisiel 1993: 332 and 508.
[48] I will not explore McNeill's own complex discussion here.

'*Vorhandenheit*'; but Heidegger is running many of these themes together before he introduces that term, and ultimately it is that running together, that clustering, that I want to explore.[49]

If that clustering lacks an underlying principle or non-arbitrary set of principles, then we must regard Heidegger's reflections around the term '*Vorhandenheit*' as a mess. In the following sections I will illustrate the challenges that we face by considering some central associations of the *Vorhanden*, including its association with assertions (Section 3.2) and with science (Section 3.3); Section 3.4 will sketch some of the difficulties we face in understanding the supposed 'priority' of the *Zuhanden* over the *Vorhanden* before Chapter 4 explores in detail the most influential attempt to understand that relation: namely, Dreyfus'. In these discussions I will raise yet more worries about whether there is an intelligible order to Heidegger's discussions. But I will suggest in Part IV an account of what that order might be.

3.2 *Vorhandenheit* and assertion

Heidegger labels as 'the speciality of assertion' its 'levelling of the primordial "as" of circumspective interpretation to the "as" with which *Vorhandenheit* is given a definite character' (BT 201 (158)). But why ought all assertions to be taken to reveal the *Vorhanden*? The '"as" structure', we are told, 'gets pushed back', 'dwindles', 'no longer reaches out into a totality of involvements'; this seems an accurate phenomenological description in that, while contemplating the fact that 'the hammer is heavy', we are not consciously reflecting on the uses to which the hammer may be put and for which a heavy hammer in particular may be appropriate or inappropriate. But that certainly does not seem to imply that we are considering the hammer as—to take only a handful of notions from the list of Section 3.1—a 'mere thing', a natural phenomenon, a material thing, a mere *that*, merely occurent, as 'isolated' or 'de-contextualised' or something specifically *not zuhanden*, or that such consideration is 'pure beholding', a 'fixed staring', a de-worlding,

---

[49] It should also be noted, for example, that Heidegger does not always sharply distinguish the *Vorhanden* from the *Zuhanden*: as we will see in connection with assertions (*Aussagen*), Heidegger sometimes seems to see the difference between the *Vorhanden* and *Zuhanden* as one of degree, with these two concepts as 'extremes'.

a de-vivifying, somehow mathematically articulated or under the influence of the Theoretical Attitude. Indeed, if Heidegger is right about the '*derivative*' status of assertion (BT 200 (157)), the person who understands the assertion 'The hammer is heavy' *must* appreciate the 'totality of involvements' in which the assertion and its talk of 'hammers' and 'heaviness' have their 'life'.[50] If when we 'occupy ourselves with' such an entity, it 'lets shine through as such this totality of involvement relations' within which it is what it is (EP 77), why does it not do so when it is the subject of an assertion? We may not be consciously reflecting on that 'totality' or that 'life'; but it is one of Heidegger's concerns to show that 'conscious reflection'—'explicit preoccupation' (EP 77)—is not the only way in which we may be said to grasp an object or appreciate a state of affairs.

Heidegger's own discussion is also more nuanced than the 'headline-grabbing' claim that assertions *as such* reveal the *Vorhanden* suggests.[51] In the *Logik* lectures we read:

There are various levels between a functional involvement with something, on the one hand, and a pure determining on the other. However, our analysis deals chiefly with the two 'extremes'.

1. assertions [*Aussagen*] in and for a practical function
2. a determining that describes one's specific lived world
3. a determining *qua* assertion about what is there, what occurs. (L 156 n. 131)[52]

Indeed, BT's own discussion is prefaced by the warning that it 'stick[s] to certain limiting cases of assertion which function in logic as normal cases and

---

[50] Cf. Gorner 2007: 41–2.

[51] Schear 2007 makes the same point. In his useful challenge to the 'virtual consensus among commentators that judgement is correlated with present-at-hand entities' (p. 136), Schear questions several ways in which Heidegger's texts might be thought to provide philosophical justification for such a 'correlation'. In doing so, he is casting doubt on the connection between several of the notions that I list above as associated with 'presence-at-hand'. But Schear takes the notion of presence-at-hand itself to be reasonably well understood, whereas I am arguing that it—and the cluster of 'correlations' that its various uses seem to presuppose—need to be subjected to scrutiny too. So, for example, Schear combines my senses (5), (6), and (13) and/or perhaps (14), in proposing that 'Present-at-hand entities, such as the rock, are paradigmatically substances and their properties that inhabit nature' and that '[c]haracteristic of substantial entities is their ontological independence'. One aspect of the latter is that 'being a substance is possible independent of being in any relation to other substances', which Schear notes is a theme in early modern philosophy (pp. 128, 133, 133 n. 23). However, while it may be the case that 'the being of natural substance *seems* relatively clear' (p. 135, italics added), it was a lesson of the work of Leibniz and Spinoza that it is not: in particular, making sense of natural objects, such as rocks, as 'ontologically independent', and hence as substances in that very sense, proves impossible.

[52] Cf. also BPP 210 and 213.

as examples of the "simplest" assertion-phenomena' (BT 200 (157)), and Heidegger proposes that there are 'many intermediate gradations' between those and 'the kind of interpretation which is still wholly wrapped up in concernful understanding', including

Assertions about the happenings in the environment, accounts of the ready-to-hand, 'reports on the Situation', the recording and fixing of the 'facts of the case', the description of a state of affairs, the narration of something that has befallen. (BT 201 (158))

'We cannot', Heidegger continues, 'trace back these "sentences" to theoretical assertions'—one of the notions with which *Vorhandenheit* is associated—'without essentially perverting their meaning'. But why then fixate on the 'headline' and think that Heidegger believes that assertions *as such* reveal the *Vorhanden*?

Moreover, the content of the claim that 'assertions reveal the *Vorhanden*' depends, obviously enough, on the sense of *Vorhandenheit* we have in mind; and even if we understand by 'assertions' Heidegger's 'extreme cases' of 'theoretical assertions', it is unclear that there is a claim here that is both non-trivial and plausible. If 'the *Vorhanden*' means 'objects revealed by theoretical assertions', then the claim is tautological: 'theoretical assertions reveal objects revealed by theoretical assertions'. If 'the *Vorhanden*' means natural phenomena, things specifically *not zuhanden*, or perhaps even material things, then the claim may not be obviously false; but it is still problematic, and lacks intuitive appeal. For example, if we recall Haugeland's comment above, the claim would seem to commit us to rejecting the idea of historical theories. But certainly, if 'the *Vorhanden*' means 'mere things', mere *thats,* things merely occurrent, 'isolated', or 'de-contextualised', then it is very unclear what the claim means or that it is plausible. For example, in understanding the object before us as a particular mass of hydrocarbons and iron, we may be 'dimming down' its character as a hammer (BT 177 (138)) and 'isolating' it from the context in which hammers have a use; but that does not entail that the assertion 'dims down' our recognition of this object *as* a particular mass of hydrocarbons and iron or 'isolates' it from the space within which one finds it or the space of forces that make its constituents hydrocarbons and iron; and the assertion certainly does not seem to reveal mere *thats*.

Instead, the most that can be said, it seems to me, is that a certain thoughtless engagement with the assertion *may* allow one to succumb to the impression that one does appreciate the 'totality' and the 'life' that make the object of one's assertion what it is, when in fact one does not. Heidegger remarks that '[t]hat which is put forward in the assertion is something which can be passed along in "further retelling"', and that through this retelling, 'what has been pointed out may become veiled again' (BT 197 (155)). What Heidegger seems to touch on here are themes from his discussion of inauthenticity, and in particular, 'idle talk'. But the fact that one might engage with an assertion inauthentically does not entail that assertions *as such* serve to—in some way—blind one to the 'ontological origin' of assertions in a broader understanding or narrow one's understanding of the Being of entities. I will touch on this connection with authenticity in Chapter 8, where I will offer my own perspective on how best to make sense of Heidegger's invocation of the notion of *Vorhandenheit*.

3.3 *Vorhandenheit* and science

This section will begin our discussion of Heidegger's understanding of science, pointing to some of the key textual evidence, introducing some of the most influential interpretations, and offering a preliminary clarification of its relationship to the *Vorhanden*.

Let us begin with the following question, which echoes one posed in the chapter's introduction. When Heidegger associates science with revealing the *Vorhanden* and with the Theoretical Attitude, does he take the Theoretical Attitude itself to be an accurate reflection of what it is like to do natural science, or does it reflect a particular and powerful misconstrual of that too? Does he think that science reveals the *Vorhanden*, or is this how we are apt to misunderstand what science reveals? There is an important equivocation in the expression 'the scientist's understanding of Being', because according to Heidegger the scientist is apt to fail to recognize the understanding of Being that she employs when she does natural science: does *Vorhandenheit* correspond to *that* understanding or to the way the scientist is apt to understand that understanding—that is, to her failure to recognize that understanding of Being? For example, the scientist may well be tempted to believe that when she does science, she 'purely beholds'. But that is a misunderstanding, and if that misunderstanding were to be adopted more widely it could not be seen as a matter of modelling the Being of entities on the Being of entities as revealed by natural science, because that is *not* how natural science reveals things as being.

Let us consider how Heidegger sees the understanding of Being implicit in natural science. One of the more conspicuous themes in Heidegger's comments on science is the notion of science as emerging out of a kind of withholding of action—something we might well call 'just looking'. Heidegger explores these 'passivist' themes, as I will label them.[53] But it is not obvious that he endorses them,[54] nor that he sees them as telling the whole story. So one might very well ask whether they present what Heidegger thinks scientists really do, or perhaps instead what he thinks philosophers and some scientists have thought scientists do. Two claims to be found in Heidegger's work strongly suggest the latter—that he does not think that the natural scientist 'just looks'. The first I will call the 'Prior Projection Claim':

Scientific knowledge presupposes a prior projection of the Being of the objects that scientific knowledge claims to describe.

The second one might call the 'Primacy of *Scientific* Practice Claim':

Scientific knowledge presupposes—is bound up with, is unintelligible without reference to—certain specific practices.

I have formulated this second claim in deliberately vague terms, but all of Heidegger's commentators agree that he wants to make a claim of something like this form.[55] Both of these Claims are problematic, because on certain readings they have radical consequences, apparently revealing *a priori* commitments implicit within the thought and practice of scientists—commitments which might seem to sit uncomfortably with the claims made for scientific knowledge that it represents objective knowledge or even knowledge at all.[56]

---

[53] Aristotle plays a part in leading Heidegger to both the 'activist' themes I am about to address and the above kind of 'passivism', the latter connecting to Aristotle's picture of science emerging out of a certain leisure. Cf. *Metaphysics* A 1 981b23 and, e.g., PS 65 and EP 168.

[54] Contrast, for example, the seemingly straightforward 'passivism' of BT 157–8 (200–1) with the much more nuanced BT 408–15 (357–64).

[55] Cf., e.g., Blattner 2006: 116: '[Heidegger] points out that... the cognitive and theoretical achievements of natural science depend on a set of scientific *practices*'.

[56] Carman 2003: 159 articulates a related point: 'Resistance to realism amongst readers of *Being and Time* seems to be driven by the suspicion that it must be incompatible with Heidegger's insistence on the existential groundedness of cognition'.

Heidegger proposes that 'the theoretical attitude is positive knowledge, i.e. knowledge of entities in themselves, making manifest for the sake of manifestness'; but 'what makes positivity possible as such . . . is the antecedent, unobjective, founding projection of the constitution of the Being of entities, which stakes out a field' (EP 199). Consider the following important passage from BT:

The classical example of the historical development of a science and even for its ontological genesis, is the rise of mathematical physics. What is decisive for its development does not lie in its rather high esteem for the observation of 'facts', nor in its 'application' of mathematics in determining the character of natural processes; it lies rather in *the way in which Nature herself is mathematically projected*. In this projection something constantly present-at-hand (matter) is uncovered beforehand, and the horizon is opened so that one may be guided by looking at those constitutive items in it which are quantitatively determinable (motion, force, location, and time). Only 'in the light' of a Nature which has been projected in this fashion can anything like a 'fact' be found and set up for an experiment regulated and delimited in terms of this projection. The 'grounding' of 'factual science' was possible only because the researchers understood that in principle there are no 'bare facts' ['*blossen Tatsachen*']. In the mathematical projection of Nature, moreover, what is decisive is not primarily the mathematical as such; what is decisive is that this projection *discloses something that is a priori*. Thus the paradigmatic character of mathematical natural science does not lie in its exactitude or in the fact that it is binding for 'Everyman'; it consists rather in the fact that the entities which it takes as its theme are discovered in it in the only way in which entities can be discovered—by the prior [*vorgängigen*] projection of their state of Being. (BT 413–14 (362))[57]

In articulating the Prior Projection Claim, Heidegger presents scientific observation and theorizing as another case of a 'comportment toward entities' that 'carries within it an understanding of the manner and constitution of the Being of the entities in question' (PICPR 16, quoted in Section 2.1). For reasons that Section 2.1 sets out, this proposal can seem to entail a form of

---

[57] Cf. also DSTCM 81, BPP 321–2, PICPR 21–3, and EP 185–90. Clearly this passage is also an important piece of evidence that any reading of the notion of *Vorhendenheit* needs to accommodate, in tying 'something constantly present-at-hand' to natural science, 'Nature herself', the 'mathematically projected' and 'matter', as well as conspicuously distinguishing it from the kinds of fact that one might imagine characterize 'mere thats' or 'bare facts'. I hope by now to have at least weakened any tendency that the reader might have had to take such invocations of the *Vorhanden* as transparent.

idealism, that presupposed understanding arising out of ourselves; why else, one might ask, would Heidegger describe it as a '*projection*'? But how can '[t]he prior [*vorgängige*], non-objective, field-demarcating projection of entities as Nature' (EP 196) be *of* Nature, and scientific knowledge that rests upon that 'projection' be a knowledge *of* the world as it is 'out there', if the *substantia finita* that is the human scientist 'has not produced the world that is there' (L 116, quoted in Section 2.1)? A less extreme but still deeply problematic reading sees the Prior Projection Claim as entailing that our scientific knowledge represents some kind of falsification of the world, a 'mere projection', its findings artefactual, creatures of an imposed framework without roots in that upon which it is imposed.[58] Less extreme again—indeed to some the sensible philosophical view to hold—is the claim that findings based on such 'projection' are revelatory of 'the-world-*for*-human-beings' rather than as it is in itself. This view has also been proposed as at work in passages such as BT 413–14 (362).

The latter view may seem to chime with the Primacy of Practice Claim (introduced in Section 2.2). As the following section will show, *Zuhandenheit* is not much easier to pin down than *Vorhandenheit*, but what seem to represent for Heidegger paradigmatic *zuhanden* objects are those he calls '*das Zeug*', which Macquarrie and Robinson translate as 'equipment' (BT 98 (69)). When introducing this term, Heidegger gives an illustrative list: 'In our dealings we come across equipment for writing, sewing, working, transportation, measurement [*Messzeug*]' (BT 97 (68)).[59] For objects to present themselves with this kind of Being, they must, in some sense, present themselves within practices, 'dealings', of ours: to present a paradigm case, we encounter things as hammers in the course of building or repairing. But Heidegger also insists that the experience of perceiving *vorhanden* objects is, in some sense, dependent on a background provided by our practices: the *Vorhanden* loom when the *Zuhanden* break or go missing, but also within the distinctive practices of doing science. This takes us to the Primacy of Scientific Practice Claim:

---

[58] This is a possibility that Nietzsche seems to entertain when he declares that '[t]o a world which is *not* our idea the laws of numbers are wholly inapplicable' (1986: 22). A rather different version of this worry would be that science presents as *vorhanden* everything upon which it focuses its attention. This is a theme to which we will return.

[59] Cf. also BPP 163 ('equipment for working, for travelling, for measuring') and 68 ('the instrument, the tool, the measuring instrument, the vehicular instrument').

[T]heoretical research is not without a *praxis* of its own. Reading off the measurements which result from an experiment often requires complicated 'technical' set-up [*'technischen' Aufbau*] for the experimental design. Observation with a microscope is dependent upon the production of 'preparations'. Archeological excavations, which precedes any Interpretation of the 'findings', demands manipulation of the grossest kind. But even in the 'most abstract' way of working out problems and establishing what has been ordained, one manipulates equipment for writing, for example. However 'uninteresting' and 'obvious' such components of scientific research might be, they are by no means a matter of indifference ontologically. The explicit suggestion that scientific behaviour as a way of Being-in-the-World is not just a 'purely intellectual activity', may seem petty and superfluous. If only it were not plain from this triviality that it is by no means patent where the ontological boundary between 'theoretical' and 'atheoretical' behaviour runs! (BT 409 (358))[60]

In light of these remarks it is tempting to say that the 'passivist' picture of science captures at best what we may think we do when we do science, with science as it is being instead the replacement of one kind of concerned involvement by another. I want to endorse that reading of Heidegger, but first want to consider another related view.

If 'theoretical research is not without a *praxis* of its own'—if 'the theoretical' has a 'primordially practical character' (EP 199)[61]—might that not entail that its peculiar objects would be fundamentally *zuhanden* after all? Rouse, for example, proposes that what Heidegger *should* have seen his overall outlook entailed for science was that 'science is an example of *Dasein's* everyday concernful absorption in the world' and 'discovers not the present-at-hand, but new ways...in which things around us can be ready-to-hand' (1985: 206, 203).[62] Blattner (1995) has developed this interpretation and, despite drawing very different philosophical morals, also seems to have shared it, Husserl arguing specifically 'against Heidegger' that the notion of an 'original motive...for science' lies in 'the motivation for a playful "intellectual curiosity"',

---

[60] In what seems to me an odd reading, Rouse sees this passage as showing that, for Heidegger, 'research practices...are only *associated* with theoretical cognition', which is itself a 'form of disengaged viewing' (1987: 76). I will be questioning the ascription to Heidegger of such a view—a view which is very similar to that which Heidegger attacks at BT 409–10 (358) (quoted below). Indeed, I believe that the view that Rouse himself espouses and *contrasts* with Heidegger's is much closer to Heidegger's than Rouse realizes—which is something to be borne in mind when I raise questions about claims that Rouse makes below.

[61] Cf. also PS 27: 'Episteme...is itself a *praxis*'.

[62] Cf. also his 2000: 24–6.

one that is not springing from any necessity of life... or from the context of the goal of self-preservation, a curiosity which looks at things, and wants to know things, with which it has nothing to do.[63]

In contrast, Dreyfus has argued that

For Heidegger, scientific theory is an *autonomous stance*. It is not... based on an interest in control. Science is *not* instrumental reason. Here Heidegger is more traditional than pragmatists such as Nietzsche, Peirce, or early Habermas. (1991: 80)

I think the textual evidence strongly supports Dreyfus' claim.[64] In the 1928/29 EP lectures Heidegger rejects a construal of science's objects as emerging through 'a mere widening of practical-technical expertise' beyond 'profitable use and working of the soil' and 'building houses and bridges' (EP 181–5). In the 1927/28 PICPR lectures he characterizes '*scientific* knowing' as 'solely aimed at entities themselves, in order to tear the entities from concealment'. In such a pursuit,

all those purposes of comportment are omitted which aim at employment [*Verwendung*] of what is uncovered and known; all those limits are omitted which hold the investigation within the planned technical intention [*technischer Absicht*]. (PICPR 18–19)

But we also find the same thought before BT, in the 1925/26 *Logik* lectures, for example, where Heidegger talks of knowing as often being fused with 'an involvement that is not merely and primarily cognitive' but also of its being able to free itself from that to become 'an autonomous way of being involved with' the world (L 212–13).[65] 'By looking at the world theoretically', BT itself tells us, we 'dim down' 'the specific worldhood' of the 'ready-to-hand' to 'the uniformity of what is purely present-at-hand, though... this uniformity comprises a new abundance of things' (BT 177 (138)).

Now, such evidence is compatible with Rouse and Blattner's view, which is that what Heidegger thought about science is one thing, and what he should have thought, given his broader philosophical outlook,

---

[63] An unpublished note translated and quoted in Moran 2000b: 183.
[64] I disagree with Dreyfus over other aspects of his interpretation of Heidegger as the next chapter will show. Also, Chapter 6 will argue that there is something misleading in saying that 'Heidegger never concluded from the fact that our practices are necessary for *access* to theoretical entities that these entities must be *defined in terms of* our access practices' (Dreyfus 1991: 253).
[65] Cf. also BPP 320, and PS 27 and 64 regarding Aristotle and the idea of an 'autonomous *episteme*'.

quite another. Rouse and Blattner believe that what Heidegger saw as necessary for encountering the *Vorhanden*, he also gave us reason to believe is impossible. For example, echoing Rouse's view of a 'decontextualized viewing' which allows us to 'merely look' (Rouse 1985: 203, 204), Blattner believes that, for a 'complete decontextualisation' that leaves us 'staring at some utterly decontextualised stuff', 'the entire enterprise of on-going coping would have to break down' (Blattner 1995: 325, 326). According to Rouse,

> [Heidegger] never forgot that even the discovery of the present-at-hand would presuppose the prior disclosure of the worldhood of the world. He only failed to realize that this dependence must undermine the very possibility of encountering the present-at-hand at all. (1985: 208)

On these grounds, the objects of natural science must be, like 'all objects', 'ready-to-hand' (Blattner 1995: 336);[66] Heidegger should have arrived at the view 'not only that science does not discover things present-at-hand, but that there is no genuine phenomenon corresponding to presence-at-hand' (Rouse 1985: 200).[67] It will be one of the concerns of Part III to challenge this way of looking at Heidegger.

3.4 *Vorhandenheit* and *Zuhandenheit*

Let us turn now to the proposal that the Theoretical Attitude and the revealing of the *Vorhanden* presuppose other forms of comportment—in particular, those embodied in our grasp of the *Zuhanden*. Like the association of *Vorhandenheit* with science, this is a familiar enough notion from the secondary literature. But the presupposition in question is difficult to bring into focus and to articulate without falling into claims that seem either obscure or just false. The following chapter will take as an example perhaps the best known attempt—certainly in the Anglophone philosophical world— to make sense of the Heideggerian notion that activities we might think of

---

[66] For similar conclusions, cf. Versényi 1965: 12 and Sallis 1986: 142.

[67] Compare Rouse 1987: 158: 'Electrons... count as electrons in much the same way that hammers count as hammers. The characteristics that specify this have to do with the ways we (must) take account of them in what we do.' What I will question below is whether this gives us grounds for thinking of electrons as 'ready-to-hand' in—as I will put it—any 'thick' sense.

as revealing the *Vorhanden* presuppose activities the mastery of which is best understood on the model of our mastery of the *Zuhanden*. I give this rather contorted formulation here because of general difficulties with the notion of *Zuhandenheit* which this final section of the present chapter will discuss.

Just about every commentator on Heidegger will agree, *in some way or other*, with the abstract claim that Section 2.2 labelled 'the Primacy of Practice Claim': the *Zuhanden* is prior to, or more fundamental than, the *Vorhanden*. How we fill out this claim is, however, a tricky matter. One interpretation needs to be identified and rejected immediately, though it is one which plenty of Heidegger's remarks encourage.[68] It is that the *Zuhanden* are, as Fell (1992: 66) puts it, 'chronologically' prior to the *Vorhanden*: we encounter them first in our experience of the world in that our scientific activity, for example, emerges out of our practical dealing with the world around us. But, as Fell has also argued, that kind of claim is neither contentious nor interesting; to make it seem either would seem to require a conflation of the *ordo cognoscendi* with the *ordo essendi* (Fell 1992: 72). A careless glance at phenomenology might well take that to be one of its congenital vices; but if we can avoid ascribing it to Heidegger, the principle of charity requires that we should.

We will return to this question of the 'priority' relation later, but for now I want to focus instead on the problems associated with the relata of the Primacy of Practice Claim. For what are now, I hope, familiar reasons, that claim must have a diversity of senses corresponding to the diverse notions of *Vorhandenheit* that we have considered: 'the *Zuhanden* are more fundamental than mere things', or 'the natural', the 'isolatable', that 'which is revealed in knowledge', and so on. But the *Zuhanden* raise some similar problems.

The *Zuhanden* have been identified in the literature as:

1) 'gear, equipment, tools' (Inwood 1999: 128)
2) 'use-objects' (Blattner 2006: 51)
3) 'things that have the character of the "in-order-to"' (BT 97 (68)) (Inwood 1999: 128)
4) things with which we are 'practically engaged' (Moore 2012: 469)
5) 'pragmatic entities' (Fell 1992: 65)
6) 'things that serve human purposes in some way' (Inwood 1999: 129)

---

[68] Cf. e.g., HCT 194–5.

7) things 'useable, employable in the pursuit of [*Dasein's*] purposes' (Mulhall 2005: 41)
8) 'entit[ies] defined by [their] involvement in our practices' (Blattner 2006: 55)
9) entities identified by their role in human life (see Blattner below)
10) entities whose Being is fixed by *Bewandtnis* (involvement, relevance, functionality) (Gorner 2007: 42)
11) entities which 'show themselves ... in our having-to-do-with-them' (Gorner 2007: 38)
12) entities whose Being is fixed by *Verweisung* (reference) and which 'belong to a system of references' (Gorner 2007: 42, 43).

Again, this is not a comprehensive list, nor does it point to all of the notions that are bound up with Heidegger's reflections on the *Zuhanden*.[69]

The feature of the above list that I wish to explore is the process of 'thinning' that takes us from its top to its bottom. But before turning to that, let us first note a step that is often made. It is from a 'priority' claim for *Zuhandenheit*—such as that '[c]ognition and knowledge [are] derivative from ("founded upon") ... everyday practical understanding' (Rouse 2005: 125)—to a 'fundamentality' claim for *Zuhandenheit*—such as that '[o]ur most fundamental forms of comportment are practically rather than conceptually articulated' (Wrathall 2005: 345) and that, according to BT, 'everyday practical purposive activity [is] the most fundamental setting for the disclosure of things in the world' (Rouse 1998 abstract).[70] The move is made, I believe, on the basis of an intuition that what the Primacy of Practice Claim shows is that our experience of tools is a good model of what it is to experience things in general.

The particular 'fundamentality' claims set out above have at least reasonably clear senses; but they are not obviously plausible: why think that 'everyday' or 'practical' 'comportment' or 'understanding' has the kind of fundamentality alluded to here? For instance, do we not have an equally fundamental experience of nature? At this point, however, Heidegger seems

---

[69] For reasons set out in n. 38, I leave aside in particular its association with Greek notions. Cf., e.g., Kisiel 1993: 239–40.

[70] Cf. also Käufer 2003: 84: '[J]udgments presume access to a shared world that is carved into possible subject-matters, possible "about–whichs". This carving is not a result of judgement; it happens at a more fundamental level, with practical involvement.' As the reader will see, this is a view that I find congenial but I believe the notion of 'the practical' that Käufer invokes needs scrutiny.

to give us a suggestion about how the *Zuhanden* might be generalized to include the natural:

> The wood is a forest of timber, the mountain a quarry of rock; the river is water-power, the wind is wind 'in the sails'. (BT 100 (70))

The proposal that the wood or the mountain is a tool would be peculiar to say the least, but there is something not implausible about the proposal that we might experience them through, as it were, their 'employment' or 'profitable use', through their relationship to our practical human purposes.[71] But why think of *this* 'nature' as fundamental, the nature addressed by *homo oeconomicus*, rather than, for example, the nature before which we feel awe? And how plausibly, and how far, can we extend the range of objects to which we relate through 'use' or 'employment'? What of works of art? Other living things? Other people? Along with these philosophical worries, there is also textual evidence that Heidegger rejected such a view and saw it as a misunderstanding of his intentions:

> [I]n *Being and Time*... I took my departure from what lies to hand in the everyday realm, from those things that we use and pursue... It never occurred to me, however, to try and claim or prove with this interpretation that the essence of man consists in the fact that he knows how to handle knives and forks or uses the tram. (FCM 177)

One option at this stage is to continue to 'broaden' or 'thin out' one's understanding of the *Zuhanden*:

> Heidegger... expand[s] the conception of the ready-to-hand far beyond equipment... [A] great many other things are involved in our activity without exactly being equipment: paintings and other forms of adornment, religious artefacts, copies of novels, and so on. We do not typically *use* these items for a specific purpose, but to say what they are we need to talk about their roles in human life and not just their physical properties. The paraphernalia of human life is ontologically distinguished by *being* what it is *assigned* to be by our practices; its Being is involvement. (Blattner 2006: 54–5)[72]

---

[71] Heidegger certainly does not leave unquestioned the above 'pragmatic' understanding of nature; cf., e.g., the retrospective remarks discussed in the introduction to Chapter 5, where the passage from FCM 177 that I cite next is also quoted in full.

[72] Cf. also Blattner 1999: 48 and 58.

The *Zuhanden* are now understood not as tools, not as things which we use, but as things with which we are 'involved'.

But even without accepting notions such as that 'science... is in itself practical' (EP 33), is not our relationship towards the objects of physical science an 'involvement'? Even according to familiar, realist understandings of scientific knowledge, these objects can be said to be ones which 'show themselves... in our having-to-do-with-them' (Gorner, quoted above);[73] and, of course, we can say this partly at least because these descriptions seem to say so little. Similarly, whether we say that these entities are 'involved in our activity' (Blattner, quoted above) will depend on how widely we construe 'activity'. Is science an activity? Is contemplation? And whether these entities are 'involved in our practices' will depend on how widely we construe 'practice'. When the 'the practical' refers to 'practical matters'—'profitable use', 'employment'—one might say 'No', but for reasons examined above we may not want to fix on such a 'thick' characterization. One might say 'Yes' if, for example, 'the practical' is as 'thin' as 'things we do'.

Blattner suggests that 'to say what [*Zuhanden* entities] are we need to talk about their roles in human life and not just their physical properties'. But is this a well-understood distinction? To introduce examples that will be important for us later, an object's length is something that is measured in the following way... its weight something measured in this other way... Is not that a matter of saying what these objects are by 'talk[ing] about their roles in human life'? Or one might propose that we have no grasp on such objects independent of some human conceptualization of those objects, that embodied in the human practice called 'doing physics'. In this sense they are entities which 'belong to a system of references' (Gorner, quoted above). Why is this 'involvement' too thin to count as involvement in a 'role in human life'?[74] It is tempting to draw the line once again by reference to particular *kinds* of 'role', 'involvement', or 'reference' in our lives. Rouse,

---

[73] For examples of Heidegger invoking such 'thin' senses, cf., e.g., BPP 162–3.

[74] But would we say that the Being of these entities is '*assigned*... by our practices' (Blattner 2006: 55, quoted above)? Although one might say that they are what they are by virtue of their relationship to the practice in question, it may indeed seem odd to talk of that Being being 'assigned' by them. But again, I am unsure whether the distinctions invoked here are well understood, and will draw the distinction Blattner wants to draw. For example, 'paintings... religious artefacts, [and] copies of novels' may be what they are by virtue of their relationship to the practice in which they figure; but are they 'assigned' their Being by those practices? It does not seem very natural to me to say that a piece of the True Cross, for example, is 'assigned' its Being by the practices in which it figures.

for example, talks of 'the references to the world of practical activity within which things have a place and make sense' (pp. 201–2). But such talk of the 'practical' places us back on the slippery slope down which we have slid once already. Rouse also invokes the idea of our 'everyday concernful absorption in the world'; but 'concern' and 'absorption' seem as elastic as 'involvement' and 'dealings'; and it is unclear quite what makes a form of 'absorption' 'everyday' or that the latter notion can by itself bear much philosophical weight.[75,76]

Another way to see the problem here is to note how closely the above specifications of our dealings with the *Zuhanden* now resemble specifications of the quite general 'relation' of *Being-in-the-world*. Heidegger talks of 'dealings', 'having to do with', 'dwelling with', 'being at home with' (BPP 208, BT 80 (54), PS 21, 191, 267, 21); Kisiel indeed translates *Sein-bei* as 'being involved with'.[77] The vanishing of this gap—between the 'involvement' that is characteristic of our relationship with the *Zuhanden* and the 'involvement' that is our Being-in-the-world—poses a particular problem for the 'passivist' notion mentioned earlier, that we 'prescind' from, or 'withhold', our 'involvement' with the *Zuhanden* when we adopt the 'scientific perspective' that reveals the *Vorhanden*. What, we want to know now, is the 'involvement' that is withheld or prescinded from and the 'involvement' that remains? How much distinctive content can we assign to the former, especially after it has been 'thinned' in the fashion described above?

Now, someone who wants to claim that science 'discovers...new ways...in which things around us can be ready-to-hand' or that 'all objects', including the objects of natural science, are 'ready-to-hand' (Rouse and Blattner, quoted in Section 3.3) might well say to the above worries: 'Precisely!'[78] The gap alluded to vanishes, and all dealings with entities are species of the 'involvement' that reveals the *Zuhanden*. Allowing the *Zuhanden* to swallow up all non-*Dasein* entities would undermine the

---

[75] The long and difficult history of the terms 'ordinary' and 'everyday' in Wittgensteinian scholarship seems to point in this direction.

[76] The worries set out in this paragraph may also raise some suspicion about Carman's attempt to distinguish his 'ontic realism' from 'deflationary realism' (cf. his 2003: 180–1). Though I touch on his discussion briefly again later (cf. n. 293), I will not attempt to do justice to its complexities here.

[77] Cf., e.g., HCT 266 and Section 2.4 above.

[78] Blattner's view here is compatible with his effort to hold the line above, inasmuch as the latter view is part of an exposition of Heidegger, whilst the former effort is part of a critique of Heidegger.

Primacy of Practice Claim: the *Zuhanden* is prior to, or more fundamental than... what, exactly? But one might bite that bullet, embracing that conclusion too. Rouse (2000: 23) does just that, though he understands that conclusion as a philosophical truth—as what Heidegger *ought* to have said, rather than as an accurate interpretation of what he *did* say.[79]

Nevertheless, what I think we should take from the above discussion is that we are not yet clear about the *Zuhanden*/non-*Zuhanden* distinction—and that we do not eliminate this lack of clarity by insisting that all objects fall on one particular side of that distinction. What I have presented above—and I think it is not unrepresentative in Heidegger commentary—is a pattern whereby we begin with a claim about 'profitable use', which is clear but pretty obviously false, progressively water this down, and end up with an unclear claim about 'dealings', 'having to do with', or the like, which might be true—but then, who can tell? The Primacy of Practice Claim and associated proposals are saved from straightforward falsehood, but their significance becomes moot. I will defend what may well seem from the perspective of those wedded to more pragmatist readings of Heidegger a rather 'thin' construal of claims about *Dasein*'s essential 'involvement' with its world; but I hope to give that construal a clear sense, which I think the 'thin' construals attacked here lack. My own construal is 'thin' in being driven by a relatively formal argument. It seems to me that the construals I attack are 'thin', because, to echo Austin, in setting them out '[t]here's the bit where you say it and the bit where you take it back' (1962: 2).

The above discussion has been, of necessity, relatively brief, and does not do justice to the readings of Heidegger upon which I have commented critically. So the next chapter offers a more detailed 'case study', taking as its subject the most influential attempt to cross this difficult terrain, examining Dreyfus' reading of Heidegger, and in particular, Dreyfus' concept of the 'Background'. Echoing worries set out in the present chapter, I will argue that it is very difficult to say quite what the 'Background' is supposed to do for us and, to turn to a question that echoes one raised earlier in this chapter, it is unclear whether that than which the 'background' is more fundamental is something real or a philosopher's myth. The arguments that Dreyfus uses to make a case for recognizing the 'Background' seem to make the most

---

[79] Cf. also the brief discussion of Rouse in Section 4.2.2.

sense if one assumes the latter; but that fits poorly with the ways in which Dreyfus characterizes the 'Background'—in particular, his description of it as a non-representational, third 'way of Being'. What I will go on to propose in Part III is that we start again, as it were, in our reflection on the *Vorhanden* and the *Zuhanden*, orienting our thinking this time to notions of 'constitution' which Part I explored.

4

Dreyfus's Concept of the 'Background'

Perhaps the most influential interpretation of the Primacy of Practice Claim is that presented in Hubert Dreyfus' reading of Heidegger. Central to that reading is the proposal that if we are to—in some sense—'make sense' of propositional attitudes, assertions, and other intentional phenomena, then we must recognize what Dreyfus calls the 'background'. Though Dreyfus has, over the years, put the notion of the 'background' to a variety of philosophical uses,[1] considerations familiar from the literature inspired by Wittgenstein's reflections on rule-following have played a central role in motivating the case for believing that we need to recognize the 'background' and thus also in identifying precisely what it is about the intentional that supposedly needs to be 'made sense of': Dreyfus calls on two different arguments that seem to show that what he calls 'representationalism' will land us with an unstoppable 'regress of rules'. But how, in the light of the problems that those arguments reveal, might our position be thought to be improved by our recognizing the 'background'? I will argue that if, through a recognition of the 'background', we are thought to have acquired solutions to those problems, then it is not at all clear that the supposed solutions that emerge work. An alternative interpretation is that that recognition forms part of an attempt to 'dissolve' those problems. In order to bring some clarity to that possibility I will consider a number of different ways in which Dreyfus' proposals might be interpreted by drawing on ideas set out by John McDowell, whose view of at least one of the 'regress' arguments

---

[1] For example, he has recently invoked it as a basis for understanding the notion of non-conceptual content in his 2001 and 2005. In the latter, Dreyfus explores how his ideas might provide a critique of McDowell's. I will touch on the recent exchange between the two (published as Dreyfus 2007a, 2007b, McDowell 2007a and 2007b) below.

Heidegger himself anticipates, as Section 4.2.2 will show. But if we do endorse these McDowellian readings of Dreyfus' proposals, it has some serious consequences. My overall aim in this chapter is to show that, on either interpretation, Dreyfus' notion of the Background faces serious philosophical problems and that we should seek an alternative interpretation of Heidegger rather than burdening him with these same problems.

4.1 What is the 'background' meant to do for us?

In Heidegger's discussion of 'Being-in-the-world', Dreyfus sees described 'a mode of awareness' (1991: 68, 1993: 34) that is intentional in that it 'reveals entities under aspects' (1991: 68) but which does not consist of having 'representations' (1980: 9). This 'background' is not a matter of 'mindless', 'mechanical' or 'zombie-like behaviour' (1991: 68, 1993: 34); but it is, nonetheless, 'non-mental' (1991: 76), 'non-cognitive' (1980: 9), 'unthinking activity' (1993: 35). Dreyfus can propose that the 'background' is neither 'mental' nor 'mindless' because he also maintains that the 'traditional' vocabulary of philosophy is inadequate for describing this 'background' (1991: 7):

The Cartesian/Husserlian ontology of the brute physical world and the intrinsic intentionality of individual minds just is not rich enough to explain how we are able to act. We may just have to grit our teeth and countenance body-intentionality and Being-in-the-world as a third way of Being. (2002c: 336)[2]

What is it then that a recognition of this 'third' 'background' way of Being is meant to do for us?

According to what Dreyfus calls 'representationalism', 'the mind is defined by its capacity to form representations':

On this view all that we know—even our general know-how for getting around in the world and coping with things and people—must be mirrored in the mind in propositional form... Representationalism assumes that underlying everyday understanding is a system of implicit beliefs. (1997: xvii)[3]

In opposition to this 'view of the mind and its relation to the world', Dreyfus proposes that:

---

[2] Cf. also 1999: 21 and 2000b: 302.   [3] Cf. also 1986: 99.

[R]elating to objects by way of intentional states such as desires, beliefs, perceptions, intentions, etc. [is] a derivative and intermittent condition that presupposes a more fundamental way of Being-in-the-world that cannot be understood in subject/object terms. (1991: 5)[4]

As Wrathall puts it, Dreyfus argues 'that intentional states can only have a content against a non-intentional or pre-intentional background' (2000: 93). These negative characterizations of this 'more fundamental way of Being-in-the-world' are filled out using a variety of different—though clearly related—notions that include 'skill', 'coping', 'know-how', 'body-intentionality', 'custom' and 'practice': 'For Dreyfus ... the background is a set of practices, skills, and activities' (Wrathall 2000: 93). Recognition of this 'background' is meant to have wide import, 'help[ing] us to see how phenomena as diverse as consciousness, intentionality, rule-following, knowledge, and representation presuppose skills, habits, and customs' (Stern 2000: 53).[5] What emerges is typically thought of as a novel 'account[] of intentionality' (Rouse 2000: 7).

As I have indicated, it is not easy to align Heidegger's *Zuhandenheit* and *Vorhandenheit* with categories such as those just used. But it should, I think, be clear enough how the above story presents us with a possible reading of the Primacy of Practice Claim, in presenting kinds of understanding that our grasp of the *Zuhanden* might be thought to exemplify—'skill', 'coping', 'know-how', 'practice', and so on—as presupposed by (being prior to, more fundamental than) kinds of understanding that our grasp of the *Vorhanden* might be thought to exemplify—'belief', 'perception', 'consciousness', 'knowledge', 'propositional attitudes', and so on.

But exactly what is it about the latter that needs accounting for, that needs to be 'made intelligible' or shown to 'make sense'? A natural way to approach this question is by working our way backwards from the arguments that have been presented as demonstrating the need for the Dreyfusian 'background'; in this way we come to see the needs that it is meant to satisfy and thus what it is that is supposedly in need of explanation. Although Dreyfus states that Heidegger does not try to prove his 'theses' (1991: 60, 120), in commentaries on Dreyfus'

---

[4] Cf. also 1999: 11.

[5] There is a visible looseness to what is presented here as presupposing and as being presupposed, and I will argue that this looseness is problematic; but—as I touch on in a moment—it does reflect the (at least apparent) looseness of Heidegger's own discussion of the *Vorhanden* and the *Zuhanden* which Chapter 3 explored.

discussion of the 'background', three particular arguments are attributed to him again and again. One is, in a recognizable sense, phenomenological, and is illustrated by the following passage:

Heidegger can and does claim to have given a concrete demonstration of his position, by showing that when we carefully describe everyday ongoing coping activity we do not find any mental states. (Dreyfus 1991: 86)[6]

A second consideration which is frequently cited is the claim that 'knowing-how is not reducible to knowing-that'.[7] Though there has been a recent revival of interest in this claim,[8] Stern has argued—plausibly, I think—that it is less than clear how this claim contributes to a case for the existence of a Dreyfusian 'background'. In particular, Stern argues that what support it provides seems best characterized in other terms, for example, as embodying a version of the 'phenomenological' argument above, or the observation that we have failed thus far to produce analyses of forms of knowing-how in terms of knowing-that. But neither construal leaves us with a compelling argument. The observation mentioned is compatible with the possibility that we might produce such analyses in the future; and the 'phenomenological' argument above invites the obvious response that our managing to deal skilfully and intelligently with the objects around us without entertaining explicit beliefs about them does not rule out the possibility that this feat rests on certain *implicit* or *unconscious* beliefs.[9]

So commentators seeking a compelling argument for the existence of the Dreyfusian 'background' have been forced to look elsewhere; and an argument to which commentators on Dreyfus repeatedly turn is one which focuses on what might be called a 'regress of rules'. As I will show, there are, in fact, at least two different arguments there to be unearthed; but, again, neither provides straightforward support for Dreyfus' claims.[10]

---

[6] Cf. also 1991: 93, 1993: 27–8, and 1997: xii–xiii.
[7] Cf., e.g., 1991: 85–6, 117–18, 1997: xi–xii, Preston 1993: 45, and Stern 2000: 63.
[8] Cf., e.g., Stanley and Williamson 1998.
[9] Cf., e.g., Stern 2000: 64. If we were to take Dreyfus' remarks at 1991: 85–7 (where he says that he sees little reason to think that the proposed analysis of the 'background' will be forthcoming (cf. also 1997: 265, 286)) as a reply to the above response, then that reply would seem to assume that the burden of proof lies with those who think the 'background' is unnecessary.
[10] Comments at 1997: xii and 285–6 show that Dreyfus' own perception of the relationship between, and relative fundamentally of, these 'phenomenological', 'know-how', and 'regression' arguments is complicated. There are also other considerations that one might offer in support of the need to recognize a Dreyfusian 'background'. (For example, one Searlian thought would turn on the possibility of cases in

4.2 A first 'regress of rules'

4.2.1 Rules for applying rules

Wrathall gives a brief but clear statement of the first argument:

[T]he application of rules itself depends on skills for applying rules. If we try to capture *those* rules in terms of the application of further rules, then ... (Wrathall 2000: 96–7, ellipsis in the original)

The philosopher who believes that one can explain a person's behaviour on the basis of, so to speak, 'rules alone' faces an explanatory gap that cannot be crossed; the system of rules envisaged would need to be 'capable of expressing how to apply its own concepts and rules'; however, as Rouse puts it, '[t]hat is not possible, because no rule or concept can determine its own correct application' (2000: 17).[11] We do indeed find something like this argument in Dreyfus; the philosopher of 'rules alone'

will either have to admit a skill for applying these rules or face an infinite regress. Or, if he says that one doesn't need a rule or skill for applying a rule, one simply does what the rule requires ... [then] why not just accept that one simply does what the situation requires, without recourse to rules at all? (1980: 8–9)[12]

The argument is perhaps best known today through its occurrence in Wittgenstein's rule-following considerations;[13] but the fact that the crucial notion upon which, as Dreyfus makes clear, the argument turns—the notion of one's needing a rule for applying a rule—will lead to trouble has been recognized at least since Kant, who, in a well-known passage (Kant 1961 A133/B172), cites the need to halt the regress described as revealing the need for the 'peculiar talent' he calls 'judgement', 'the power of rightly

---

which one would not be inclined to ascribe to individuals different rules, or different factual beliefs, but in which one finds, nonetheless, variations in application of the words whose use those rules are thought to govern; in more extreme cases of 'disagreement in judgement', we feel entitled to ascribe 'disagreement in definitions' too (to adapt Wittgenstein 1967: sec. 242), but that policy would generate an implausibly fine-grained taxonomy of intentional contents if applied to the cases alluded to. (I would like to thank Taylor Carman for drawing my attention to this concern.)) Most commentators on Dreyfus—including sympathetic ones like Stern and Wrathall—have, however, concentrated on the arguments picked out above, and I will follow that lead.

[11] Cf. also Stern 2000: 64.
[12] This argument also surfaces at 1997: 286–7.
[13] Cf., e.g., his 1967 sec. 185–90 and 198–202.

employing' rules, 'distinguishing whether something does or does not stand under a given rule'.

As the previous section made clear, Dreyfus sees the 'background' as providing a 'background' not only to rules but also to all intentional states; so how might the above argument about rules be generalized? Robert Brandom—another important reader of Heidegger—sets out what might be a suitable generalization in the following reflection, which turns on an analogue of the crucial notion about rules set out above; the analogous notion here is that one's grasp of the 'representational purport' of a belief might itself come in the form of a belief:

> Taking something as a representation must not be parsed in terms of the adoption of explicitly contentful attitudes or intentional states such as belief. If being a consumer of representational purport, taking something as a representation of something, is understood as believing of it that it correctly represents (or equally if the purport is understood as intending that it do so), then an infinite explanatory regress is generated by the possibility of querying the nature of the representationalist purport ('that...') and success ('of...') such a belief exhibits. There must be some way of understanding something as a representation that consists not in interpreting it (in terms of something else understood as a representation) but in taking, treating, or using it *as* a representation. (1994: 74)

Without the further, 'supplementary' kind of understanding to which the argument seems to point, a representation seems to stare back at us as 'just another bit of worldly furniture, like what it represents': 'Why is not confronting a map as well as terrain just adding one more thing to be baffled about?' (1994: 74) But before considering whether Dreyfus' 'background' ought to be understood as such a 'supplement' to 'representations', let us examine whether the need for such a 'supplement' is quite what the above argument demonstrates.

4.2.2 A problem to be solved or dissolved? The 'master thesis' and 'depicturization'

Consider a second formulation of the generalized form of the argument— one which Stroud offers in an attack on the notion that 'thinking, or intentional phenomena generally' might be 'accounted for or even fully described by speaking exclusively of "representations" or "intentional contents"... present to the mind':

It seems obvious that 'representations' alone are not enough because, at the very least, the person also has to ... 'grasp' the 'content' that is represented there. That suggests that thinking involves both 'representations' or 'contents' and a grasp or an understanding of them ... To say that [those graspings or understandings] too consist of nothing more than the presence before the mind of ... 'representations' would lead eventually to a regress. (Stroud 1991: 245)

What Stroud's presentation begins to make apparent is that this argument turns on a very particular understanding of 'representations'.

Certain crucial questions arise here which, for the sake of simplicity, I will phrase in terms of rules once again. What understanding of a rule entails that one 'needs a rule or skill for applying a rule'? Why not say instead that what it is to know a rule simply *is* to be able to apply it? In saying that only someone who has 'grasped' the rule can apply it, what is it that the addition of a 'supplementary' 'grasp' is meant to bring? And *to* what exactly?

In our first 'regress' argument we are being asked to imagine someone who in some sense 'knows the rule' but at the same time does not 'grasp' it: as Stroud puts it, it is 'present before the mind'. But what kind of thing is this 'rule' that it can be 'known' in this way? To reject the notion that what it is to know a rule just is to be able to apply it seems to involve embracing a notion of 'knowing a rule' as 'having present before one's mind' something like a string of signs whose meaning remains to be established—a version of what McDowell has called the 'master thesis':

[T]he thesis that whatever a person has in her mind, it is only by virtue of being interpreted in one of various possible ways that it can impose a sorting of extra-mental items into those that accord with it and those that do not. (McDowell 1993: 270)

Just as one might feel that one must not only have a rule 'before the mind' but also 'grasp' it, or that *real* mastery of a rule requires that one also master a rule for applying that rule to the world, Brandom's argument turns on 'the possibility of querying the nature of the representationalist purport ("that ... ") and success ("of ... ") [that] a belief exhibits'. But this 'possibility' seems to rest on the 'master' notion—the 'extraordinary idea', as McDowell puts it—that one can 'have' a thought' before the mind' without also 'having before the mind' the kind of worldly situation that that thought represents. In opposition to this 'possibility', McDowell proposes that 'a thought, just as such, is something with which only certain states of affairs would accord' (McDowell 1993: 270).

Now although it is easy to suspect—because it may be true—that our first 'regress' argument is often read into Heidegger's work by readers familiar with it in Wittgensteinian or Kantian guise, we do actually find a version of it in the 1925 lecture course, HCT; but what is striking about its presentation there is the attitude that Heidegger adopts towards it. What we find there is a rejection of that argument and an anticipation of McDowell's diagnosis of why it should be rejected.

In the passage in question (HCT 42–3), Heidegger attacks 'efforts...to take the apprehension of a picture as the paradigm by means of which... any perception of any object can be illuminated'. Heidegger insists that the 'real reason' for rejecting this proposal is that 'it does not correspond to the simple phenomenological findings', though he does throw in a further 'difficulty' which he will 'only mention without exploring'. 'If knowledge in general is an apprehension of an object-picture as an imminent picture of a transcendent thing outside', then we face not only the familiar, protosceptical question, 'how then is the transcendent object itself to be apprehended?', but also a puzzle about why confronting the object-picture as well as the transcendent object is not, to echo Brandom, 'just adding one more thing to be baffled about':

If every apprehension of an object is a consciousness of a picture, then for the immanent picture I once again need a picture-thing which depicts the imminent picture for me, etc. etc.

But Heidegger continues to insist that this is a 'secondary factor' and not 'the main thing':

It is not because we fall into an infinite regress, and so explain nothing, that the infrastructure of the consciousness of a picture for the apprehension of an object is to be rejected. It is not because we arrive at no genuine and tenable theory with this infrastructure. It is rather because this is already contrary to every phenomenological finding. It is a theory without phenomenology.

Exactly what we are to make of the charge with which this paragraph ends is a difficult question.[14] But a natural construal of his point here is that the 'infinite regress' alluded to only arises if we first endorse a theory which, as

---

[14] We will return to it in Section 9.2.

Heidegger puts it, 'goes against all the plain and simple findings'; those in the grip of such an 'extraordinary' theory fail to recognize that

[c]onsciousness of a picture is possible at all first only as perceiving, but only in such a way that the picture-thing is actually apprehended beginning with what is pictured on it.

To actually think of something as a picture—to 'apprehend' a 'picture-thing'—is to 'begin with what is pictured on it'. To 'have a picture before the mind' is to have before the mind something which—as McDowell puts it, 'just as such'—is something which 'shows something, [namely] what is pictured itself': '[i]n perceiving [a picture-thing], I see through it what is pictured' (HCT 42). Heidegger's explanation of how we come to our 'infinite regress' is that it emerges only through a prior 'depicturization' (HCT 44), through our beginning with the 'extraordinary' notion that a picture is 'a thing like a natural thing or another environmental thing' (HCT 42);[15] the argument does not lead us to, but instead *begins with*, the 'master' notion that a picture is just another piece of 'terrain . . . to be baffled about'.

This diagnosis can be found at work elsewhere in Heidegger's work, as Section 7.4 will show. It suggests that it is only if one first embraces what McDowell calls the 'master thesis' that one comes to believe in a 'gap' between rules and representations, on the one hand, and the world, on the other—a gap which a 'supplementary', *non*-representational 'grasp' or 'judgement' would bridge. But if the 'master thesis' is a confusion, the puzzle to which it seems to lead is an illusion, and so is the 'grasp' which seems necessary if that puzzle is to be solved: that 'grasp' would meet an illusory need.

So how, then, does Dreyfus see things? Is his invocation of the 'background' part of a confused attempt to *solve* this first 'regress' problem? His remarks about the need to 'grit our teeth and countenance . . . a third way of Being' suggest that the 'background' plays something like the 'supplemental' role sketched. By embodying 'a mode of awareness' which is itself non-representational but which 'reveals entities under aspects', the Dreyfusian 'background' would seem to fit the job description of something that would bridge the 'gap' which, according to our first 'regress' argument, 'representations' leave us facing. In this way, the postulation of the 'background' could be presented as 'accounting for intentionality', the need for such an

---

[15] Cf. also L 370.

'account' emerging from the 'fact' that—as Dreyfus does at one point state—'rules are, by themselves, meaningless' (1991: 118): but, as I have made clear, the Heideggerian/McDowellian response would be that only an 'extraordinary' idea of rules would lead one to think that.

Another reason for adopting this *critical* Heideggerian/McDowellian reading of Dreyfus is that it would provide an explanation of how he comes to feel driven to claim that 'everyday skillful engagement with familiar things' does not involve 'representations', a claim which, Christiansen has argued plausibly, we can in no way take literally:

Surely, when I am routinely hammering away, I do see that or how the nail is going as it should, namely, straight, as I intend. Surely, I quite literally perceive, come the appropriate moment, that the nail has been hammered in as required, so that it is time to stop hammering. (Christiansen 1998: 66)[16]

If Dreyfus were, on some level, under the influence of the 'master thesis' and saw his 'background' as playing the 'supplemental' role that our first 'regress' argument 'reveals', that would explain why he might feel the need to deny Christiansen's seemingly truistic claims. The first 'regress' argument may seem to show that our most immediate dealings with the world must be *non*-representational: the final step whereby one recognizes, for example, that a spade before one is indeed a spade would seem to be something that a further 'supplemental' 'skill' has to make possible, despite the fact that we would ordinarily talk quite happily of '*seeing that* the object was a spade'. But, from the Heideggerian/McDowellian perspective, this inclination to withhold a perfectly normal use of the propositional attitude idiom arises out of a residual commitment to a 'depicturizing' or 'master' understanding of propositional attitudes such as perceiving that... recognizing that... and so on. It is only on that understanding that those attitudes leave us confronting the 'gap' described. If one rejects that understanding, then the gap evaporates, and with it, the need for non-representational 'skills' to step in and assume roles that we would ascribe—in 'ordinary language'—to seeings that... perceptions that... and so on.

Now ordinary language could, of course, be confused, and we might find that we need a new descriptive vocabulary. But the Heideggerian/McDowellian diagnosis we have examined offers an alternative, and I think more

[16] Cf. also Searle 2000: 77–80 and Schear 2007: 143–6.

appealing, explanation of how and why that 'need' might seem to arise, of how and why we may find ourselves driven to view with suspicion utterly natural ways of describing utterly familiar activities of ours. According to that diagnosis, in ascribing a hitherto unappreciated and wider role to 'the *non*-representational', an earlier 'move in the conjuring trick' (Wittgenstein 1967 sec. 308)—an earlier confusion about 'the representational'—has influenced us: our descriptions of familiar phenomena have become forced and peculiar, as we wedge 'the non-representational' into areas which we—in our 'depicturizing' confusion—see 'the representational' as having forfeited but which we—with what remains of our good sense—will still naturally want to describe in the representational terms that 'ordinary language' presents to us. This diagnosis also suggests a critical interpretation of what might seem a rather similar proposal that Rouse offers in arguing that we should 'undo' the distinctions that Dreyfus wishes to draw between a 'background' and that which it supposedly 'founds' (Rouse 2000: 23). Rather than conclude with Rouse that the latter should 'be regarded as exemplifying, rather than contrasting to, practical coping' (p. 19), the above diagnosis suggests that there may be something awry with our understanding of both of the notions involved: 'representation' *and* 'coping'.[17]

But might one yet argue instead that Dreyfus' remarks on the 'background' are precisely meant to point out how 'extraordinary' some of our thinking about rules and representation is? He observes that:

The essential characteristic of representations according to the tradition is that they are *purely* mental, i.e. that they can be analysed *without reference to the world*... Heidegger rejects this traditional interpretation of the mental. Even deliberation is not the pure detached theoretical reflection described by the tradition. (1991: 74)

---

[17] McManus 2008: 440 sets out parallel Wittgensteinian worries about Dreyfus' phenomenological case for thinking that 'expertise' is 'a way of coping in which reasons play no role' (2005: 53, cf. also 1986). A point I would now add is that Heidegger's reflections, though recognizably phenomenological, also point out limitations on the significance of some phenomenological seemings, such as the absence from experts' reflections of 'analysis and comparison of alternatives' (Dreyfus 2005: 53). By analogy, neither the functional context within which our expert use of a tool is possible, nor the need for such expertise to be acquired, figure in the conscious awareness of the expert at work: as Heidegger puts it, '[e]xplictness and awareness do not decide on theses matters' (HCT 196). (Ironically, Dreyfus 2007a: 358 could be seen as making an analogous point.) I draw on this thought in my (forthcoming-b) in arguing that the intuitive plausibility of certain pro-sceptical thought experiments is exactly what Heidegger's anti-sceptical outlook entails.

In remarks such as these, Dreyfus seems to be distinguishing representations as they really are from what those in the grip of a 'depicturizing' myth think they are, from 'the sort of self-sufficient entities philosophers since Descartes have supposed', '*self-contained* representations' (1991: 74–5). So might we instead read Dreyfus as making precisely the Heideggerian/McDowellian point? Perhaps we can, but at a price.

Firstly, the first 'regress' argument would no longer give us any reason to propose that 'everyday skilful engagement with familiar things' does not involve 'representations'; the 'gap' that that argument exposed is between the world and 'master' 'representations', not representations as they actually are.

Secondly, the Heideggerian/McDowellian reading affects how we ought to hear the claims that Dreyfus makes, and are made on his behalf, about having revealed 'conditions of'—having 'accounted for'—the 'possibility' of intentionality. On this reading, the only sense in which we have established 'how intentionality is possible' is by recognizing how a confused,'extraordinary' idea made us think that it was *im*possible.[18] According to the present, more sympathetic reading, Dreyfus does not explain how real, non-'master' 'representations'—representations as they actually are—'are possible': no *question* of 'possibility' was ever successfully raised about *them*. Rather, he shows how a fantasy of representation seems to uncover the need for a 'supplementary' 'grasp' which would then make those (fantastical) 'representations' 'possible' once again.

The idiom of 'grounding' and 'presupposition' that is so characteristic of Dreyfus (and Heidegger) can still play a part in reflection that is meant precisely not to provide 'constructive' explanations, but to show that our demand for such explanations is confused.[19] So, for example, one might still articulate the point of the preceding paragraph by saying that a 'background' is 'presupposed' by 'the representational' (1991: 5). If we took 'the representational' to refer to the 'master' myth, we cannot take the 'presupposition' in question to reveal an explanation of how *that* is 'possible' or is 'founded', because, as a myth, it is neither. But one might instead say that

---

[18] According to McDowell, when, in rejecting the 'master thesis', one comes to state that 'a thought, just as such, is something with which only certain states of affairs would accord', one is returning to an overlooked piece of common sense rather than completing a piece of 'constructive philosophy' (1994: xxiii).

[19] Compare the discussion of the early Wittgenstein's talk of 'elucidation', 'internal properties', and 'internal relations' in McManus 2006.

that myth presupposes a 'background' in that those who are in its grip, if they are to *believe* that they can make sense of intentionality, must take for granted further forms of understanding which will 'reach outside' the mythical 'closed' 'inner space' that is the home of the 'representations' that the 'master thesis' conjures up. Such a sense of having discovered further *non*-representational forms of understanding would be the natural way for one still in the grip of that thesis to react; but ultimately, they ought to recognize and reject that thesis, and recognize that both sides of the representational/non-representational distinction are ill-understood when we are in the grip of the 'master' thesis.

If we adopt the previous paragraph's interpretation of the 'presupposition' in question, what emerges with the 'background' is not a novel and coherent 'account of intentionality'. If the 'inside' by reference to which such a 'reaching outside' is defined is a confusion, so too is the imagined need to 'reach outside' and the 'capacities' or 'skills' that we imagine meeting that need. The point of showing that this myth needs to be supplemented in the way described would then be to show that it is indeed a *myth*, and the puzzle to which it seems to lead an illusion. In the light of that puzzle, intentionality had seemed '*un*accountable for' and the 'job description' emerged for something that would provide that 'account' and solve that puzzle—a description which a hitherto unacknowledged 'background' was believed to fit. But if the puzzle is an illusion—an instance of what Heidegger calls 'sham problems' (HCT 162)—then that undermines at least one reason for seeing intentionality as needing 'accounting for' and for believing that there is a real task for the envisaged 'background' to perform. So a third critical consequence of this more sympathetic, Heideggerian/McDowellian reading is that our first 'regress' argument gives us no reason to think that representations as they actually are need to be supplemented by a *non*-representational 'background' that illustrates a *third* way of Being. Indeed, it is in our thoughts about the 'second' 'way of Being'—about 'the intrinsic intentionality of individual minds'—that our confusion lies, and what we need to do is identify and eliminate that confusion—the 'depicturizing'/'master' myth—not add a 'third way of Being' to our ontology.[20]

---

[20] The arguments developed in this chapter were originally sketched in my 2008—an article which was written prior to the exchange between Dreyfus and McDowell at the 2007 APA meeting. Although Chapter 7 n. 9 will touch on an issue that this exchange raises, I will not explore that exchange in detail here. But my sense is that it broadly confirms my proposal that the two thinkers operate with different

I will end this section with the suggestion that on this reading a recognition of what is right in Dreyfus' remarks might require a recognition of what could be called their 'reactive' or 'dialectical' character. For example, in saying that 'deliberation is not the pure detached theoretical reflection described by the tradition', we need to recognize that actually *nothing* is 'pure' or 'detached' in the way that 'the tradition' imagines; when we think with 'the tradition', we have no determinate notion of 'purity' or 'detachment' in mind. But if this is so, saying that deliberation is *not* 'pure' or 'detached' ought *not* to be our final conclusion, and instead we need to recognize that we are operating with confused notions of 'detachment' *and* 'involvement', 'purity', *and* 'impurity'. The insistence that deliberation is not 'pure' or 'detached' ought to be treated perhaps as Dahlstrom suggests in his comparison of Heidegger's claims with Wittgenstein's 'ladder', as needing to be 'climbed and then thrown away'. Dreyfus seems to see Heidegger's supposed 'prioritizing of doing over knowing', his 'reversal' of the tradition's 'usual priority' (1991: 49), as requiring similar treatment, but not the core proposals he himself wants to make about the 'background'; the more sympathetic Heideggerian/McDowellian reading suggests that perhaps he should.[21]

4.3 A second 'regress of rules'

4.3.1 *The impossibility of 'spelling out' 'ceteris paribus rules'*

Despite its heritage, its familiarity, and its invocation by Dreyfusian commentators and—on occasion—Dreyfus himself, our first argument is not the 'regress of rules' argument that Dreyfus typically offers. Consider the following passage:

When I am acting transparently—for example, making a promise—I do not need any rules at all. I have learnt from imitation how to promise, and I am a master promiser. But if something goes wrong, I may have to invoke a rule—for example, the rule that one must keep one's promise. But the important thing to notice is that this is not a strict rule

---

conceptions of the mental, and that the viability of McDowell's poses a significant problem for Dreyfus' attempts to identify his 'Background'. (Cf., e.g., McDowell's discussion of 'the Myth of the Disembodied Intellect' (2007a: 349).) It also becomes clear that they operate with different conceptions of what it is to be guided by reasons, which has a bearing on my criticism of Dreyfus mentioned in n. 17.

[21] I return to Dahlstrom's proposal and related issues at the end of Section 7.5.

whose conditions of application are stated in the rule itself. It is a *ceteris paribus* rule. In the case of an unfulfilled promise there are allowable excuses, such as I was sick, or I saw that what I promised would hurt you. The rule 'always keep your promises' applies 'everything else being equal', and we do not, and could not, spell out what everything else is nor what counts as equal. Moreover, if we tried to define each exception, such as being sick, we would again have to bring in further *ceteris paribus* conditions.[22]

He continues:

These *ceteris paribus* conditions never capture, but rather presuppose, our shared background practices. These practices are an aspect of our everyday transparent ways of coping. Thus, understanding is not in our minds, but in *Dasein*—in the skilful ways we are accustomed to comport ourselves. Thus even when mental content such as rules, beliefs, and desires, arise . . . they cannot be analyzed as *self-contained* representations as the tradition supposed. Deliberative activity remains dependent upon *Dasein's* involvement in a transparent background of coping skills. (1991: 75)

This passage has a number of interesting features. First of all, the crucial issue does not seem to be one with rules as such. Dreyfus distinguishes 'a strict rule whose conditions of application are stated in the rule itself' from '*ceteris paribus* rules', and his point would seem to be that the majority of the familiar rules we follow in life cannot be identified with, or translated into, the former. In principle, the passage above seems to allow that some (real enough) rules could be 'strict' in the above sense and could be 'spelt out'; if so, when Wrathall proposes that if 'the application of rules itself depends on skills for applying rules', then '[i]f we try to capture *those* rules in terms of the application of further rules, then . . . ', *pace* Wrathall and his ominous ellipsis, no endless regress will result—at least according to this second argument—as long as we come eventually to 'strict' rules. Dreyfus' point seems to be that he does not think that that will happen when we consider 'rules for applying' familiar rules such as 'one must keep one's promises'.[23]

---

[22] Cf. also 1986: 80–1 and 1997: 56–7.
[23] Where the first excerpt does suggest something like the first 'regress' argument is in its allusion to the possibility of 'spell[ing] out what everything else is [and] what counts as equal'. If one needs rules to guide the kind of basic judgements of similarity and dissimilarity, sameness and difference, that one makes when one subsumes or refuses to subsume objects under concepts, then clearly further rules will be needed when one comes to apply the concepts using which such rules are articulated. But this does not seem to be the line of thought that Dreyfus is following up in the contexts in which he presents the above argument.

To begin the task of evaluating this argument, a natural worry that might be expressed at the close of the first quoted excerpt is: 'So how on earth *do* we manage?' What kind of response to this worry does the second excerpt embody? As it stands, one can imagine it eliciting just more worry: 'Is Dreyfus just saying that we just *do* manage? If he is, then this misses the real worry, which is: *How* do we manage?' When Dreyfus proposes that 'our common-sense understanding... is not a propositional knowing-that... but rather consists of dispositions to respond to situations in appropriate ways' (1991: 117) and invokes 'a direct way of responding appropriately to the solicitations of the environment in which the agent is inextricably embedded' (2000b: 302), it is easy to hear some sense in the response, 'But *how* can there be such things?' To cite 'know-how', 'sensitivities', forms of 'awareness', 'skill' and 'familiarity', thanks to which we do supposedly manage to 'manage' or 'cope' will strike some as merely giving a (rather misleading) statement of what the problem is. So in what way does the citing of the 'background' provide us with more than a 'We just can!' response?[24]

We face a similar worry if we understand the argument as a *reductio ad absurdum* of a certain ontological austerity, the project of making sense of intentionality by reference to 'representations alone'. The implications of the fact that such a project cannot work are unclear; it might be seen as showing that we must have certain further 'capacities' or 'skills'; but to be told in this way that 'there must be more' will strike many as—again— simply identifying our difficulty, not eliminating it.

One also might take the above argument to be simply shifting the burden of proof onto representionalists, making clear that they have an awful lot of explanatory work to do and that the prospects do not look good. Though there may well be something to be said for this proposal and there are points at which Dreyfus seems drawn to it,[25] it, by itself, entitles us to no stronger conclusion than that both sides in this debate might be equally stumped. But I believe that Dreyfus' overall view is meant to be more positive than that, his invocation of the 'background' being meant to help us resolve—in *some* way—the problems that our second 'regress' argument raises.

---

[24] Other passages that it is easy to imagine eliciting this response can be found in, e.g., 1986: 28, 88, 1991: 103, and 1997: xxiii, xxiv, xxviii, 263: 'We are masters of our world, constantly effortlessly ready to do what is appropriate.'

[25] Cf. 1991: 86–7, 117 and 1997: 285.

4.3.2 *A problem to be solved or dissolved? 'Closure' and the 'view from sideways on'*

One option is that one might hope to be able to fill out one's story of 'skills' and 'familiarities' in such a way as to provide a substantial *solution* to the problem identified above. So what precisely is the problem that the second 'regress' reveals? The representationalist seems to be committed to a 'spelling out' of the demands embodied in the rules that we follow that requires a kind of 'closure' that cannot be secured. This problem, which is, once again, one familiar from the rule-following literature,[26] is also sometimes articulated using the concept of 'relevance: if the conditions that bear on whether a particular concept or rule should be applied are open-ended in the way described, then there would appear to be no end to the task of determining whether 'all relevant considerations' have been taken into account, because that set of 'considerations' is open-ended.[27]

Any attempt to fill out the story of the 'background' must address a version of the 'We just can!' complaint: there seems very little reason to think that 'skills' or 'familiarities' have any prospect of achieving a kind of 'closure' that cannot be achieved with rules. For example, one way in which the first excerpt might make one worry about our capacity to 'manage' is by raising the question of why I ought to believe that 'I have learnt from imitation how to promise' rather than—to echo Kripke (1982)'s 'quus'— qu-omise, a practice quite like promising, but for failure to keep a qu-omise being excusable if it was made on 5 May 1973. Since this might turn out to be a clause buried in the imagined web of yet-to-be-articulated certeris paribus clauses, why ought I to think that I *am* indeed familiar with—skilled in—promising rather than qu-omising? Reference to clear instrumental skills, such as riding a bike, may provide us with a comfortable sense that, with skills, what constitutes mastery is not a difficult issue. But it is actually unclear why skills are any more able to deal with such 'gerrymandering' worries (to use Brandom's term (1994: 28)) than dispositions are typically

---

[26] It has been cited as, for example, a reason for thinking that intentional states cannot be understood as dispositional states. (Cf. Boghossian 1990, Miller 1997, 1998, 2003 and, for critical discussion, McManus 2000a.) Despite his occasional talk of 'dispositions' in characterizing the 'background' (such as 1991: 117 cited in the previous section), Dreyfus clearly does not see himself as advocating anything like dispositionalism as that position is understood in the rule-following literature, not least because that position—far from requiring us to recognize a third way of Being—claims to make possible a parsimonious denial of the need for a ('second') way of Being that is distinctively intentional.

[27] Cf. Dreyfus 1991: 118–19, 1997: xviii, xxi, Preston 1993, and Christiansen 1997.

thought to be.[28] (Later I will consider the possibility that the invocation of 'skills', and so on, is precisely not meant to bring 'closure'. The question then will be: how can we drop this demand?)

In considering these matters, an issue that arises is quite what kind of 'filling out' the 'background' story needs, and what *kind* of thinker—which university department, as it were—is to provide it. Dreyfus has indicated that he saw the emergence of neural networks as a promising development for those interested in his issues, but also that that optimism has waned. His reasons for both reactions are interesting.

His initial enthusiasm seems to have been prompted by the notion that neural networks might in some way provide an explanation of our senses of sameness without an (apparently doomed) recourse to rules. (Neural nets represent a possible answer to the question, 'If not symbols and rules, what else?' (1997: xiv-xv).)[29] Suitably trained networks will respond appropriately to examples of a category with which they have never been presented, and this may seem to suggest that such networks have mastered the similarity in question without their 'containing' anything that might be thought of as a representation of a rule that articulates what that similarity is.[30]

One way of articulating Dreyfus' later pessimism is as arising from the realization that such nets can be expected to produce the appropriate responses only as long as one restricts the inputs with which it is provided to ones sufficiently similar to those using which it was trained. However, if one steps outside of that domain—as we humans who are 'able to project our understanding into new situations' can (1997: xxiv)—one has no grounds for expecting the net to generalize in the way in which we intuitively would. This problem, I suggest, is the familiar gerrymandering problem: any sequence of examples that one might provide—any 'history of training input–output pairs' (1997: xv)—is consistent with any number of

---

[28] Parallel gerrymandering problems have been raised for accounts of intentionality founded on the idea of biological function (cf., e.g., Davies 2000), and it is not obvious why they could not be raised, not only in connection with 'skills', but also in connection with the notions of 'know-how', 'embodiment', 'empathy', 'style', 'involvement', and our being 'guided' by our 'needs' that Dreyfus also sometimes invokes (cf. 1997: xxvii, xx, xxv, 276, 291, 1986: 16, 40, etc.). Cf. also n. 31.

[29] Cf. also 1986: 92–3, 109.

[30] Cf. 1997: xxxv–vi and 2005: 54–5. Articulating the point here is difficult because of issues analogous to those discussed in Section 4.2 above: for example, one might ask why we ought not to say that the network in question 'contains' a representation of the rule if it is capable of marking the distinction that the rule articulates. But I will not pursue that point here.

different generalizations. ('Everything', Dreyfus notes, 'is similar to everything else in an indefinitely large number of ways' (1997: xxvi).) Thus, similarities between the ways in which two nets are disposed to respond to a particular range of inputs do not give us reason to expect that they are disposed to respond in the same way to all inputs.[31]

What is interesting about Dreyfus' disappointment here is that it seems to show that what he thinks we need is a theory that *will* solve problems such as the gerrymandering problem. But, given that we do not have such a theory, it is unclear now why he still feels happy to say, for example, that 'background sensitivities... determine what counts as similar to what' (1997: xxix). In his *Being-in-the-world*, we read:

> Referring is a shared social skill, and *Dasein* is socialized into this practice of pointing. We can either stop with this claim and do empirical work in developmental psychology to find out how people get socialized into a practice, or we can attempt to lay out the general structure of the phenomenon. Heidegger, of course, chooses the latter approach. (1991: 270)

One might propose that Dreyfus' talk of 'background sensitivities' is a contribution to the latter project too, and his interest in neural nets essentially an interest in the former.[32] But if problems such as the gerrymandering problem are laid at the door of that 'empirical' project, then it is unclear what philosophical work the 'laying out' project is to be expected to do, and why the most just assessment of what it is that 'determines what counts as similar to what' is not that 'background sensitivities' *do* but that neither representationalists nor their Dreyfusian opponents can say. Both camps would then, again, be revealed as equally stumped.[33]

Following on from the previous section's treatment of the first 'regress' argument, might we instead see a citing of the 'background' as part of an attempt to *dissolve* the 'spelling out' problem. One 'dissolving' approach I will consider—and there certainly could be others—argues that the sense that we face a puzzle in seeing how we 'manage' with capacities such as

---

[31] The same would seem to be true of other systems that Dreyfus has discussed which might be seen as possible 'fillings-out' of the 'skills' story, such as Freeman's theory of 'attractor landscapes' (cf. 1999: 6–8 and 2005: 49–50) and models of the brain as 'function[ing] holographically' (cf. 1986: 61 and 91–2, though Dreyfus has since described the latter models as 'not convincing' (1997: xiii)).

[32] Cf. also 2005: sec. II.

[33] Something like this note is sounded by Dreyfus at 1986: 36 and 69 and 1997: xliv.

promising turns on a very particular and questionable—one might say 'extraordinary'—understanding of what 'seeing how' must involve; one might argue, for example, that that sense of puzzlement precisely presupposes that 'seeing how' will come in the form of an account using which someone who has no mastery of the concept of 'promising' could still identify what counts as 'a promise that must be kept'. McDowell's plea for 'modest' theories of meaning and his rejection of the need for 'a view from sideways-on' is a rejection of such a demand.[34] Might we understand Dreyfus' views in a similar way?

Such a reading would offer an interpretation of, for example, Dreyfus' proposal that Heidegger 'can only *point out*' and 'cannot *spell out* the background practices in so definite and context-free way that they could be communicated to any rational being or represented in a computer' (1991: 4), Heidegger's view being, according to Dreyfus, no worse off for that. Such a reading would also seem to chime with Dreyfus' proposal that the 'background' is 'so pervasive in everything we think and do that we can never arrive at a clear presentation of it' (1991: 32)[35]—a proposal which Dreyfus' commentators have hitherto struggled to interpret as embodying a specific (and plausible) argument against representationalism;[36] and the reading might also offer a way of understanding Dreyfus' remarks about what one might call the 'embedded' character of the capacities that make up the 'background'—remarks to which I will turn next and which would otherwise elicit particularly animated versions of the 'We just can?!' response.

Dreyfus suggests that our judgements of sameness are indeed a mystery if we imagine ourselves 'stood outside the world' (Dreyfus and Dreyfus 1986: 88).[37] But rather than our being overwhelmed by the open-ended range of potentially relevant considerations that might influence whether one affirms or denies a claim such as 'This is a promise that one ought to keep', '[h]uman beings are somehow already situated in such a way that what they need in order to cope with things is distributed around them where they need it' (1997: 260); our situation is '*always already*... permeated by relevance' (2005: 49), 'organized from the start in terms of human needs and propensities which give the facts meaning' (1997: 262). In such a situation in which 'man is at home' (1997: 260):

---

[34] Cf., e.g., his 1994 and 1997.
[35] Cf. also Dreyfus 1991: 22, 155, and 200.
[36] Cf., e.g., Stern 2000: 61–2.
[37] Cf. also Dreyfus 2005: 49.

[O]ur present concerns and past know-how always already determine what will be ignored, what will remain on the outer horizon of experience as possibly relevant, and what will be immediately taken into account as essential. (1997: 263)

Now, it is not hard to imagine a reader who would be exasperated by the above remarks: if the story concerning how 'concerns' and 'know-how' can do this 'determinative' work has to take for granted the fact that the world—'the human world'—'is prestructured in terms of human purposes and concerns' (1997: 261), then the pressing question simply now becomes 'How does it come to be so prestructured?'

Clearly we do not want to 'account for' the 'harmony' between thought and world—and undermine our gerrymandering worries—through a hopelessly idealistic vision of objects somehow electing to present to us those aspects of themselves that correspond to the concepts we happen to use. So might we hear Dreyfus' remarks on the 'human world' here as part of an attempt to *reject* any attempt to explain such a 'harmony'? Dreyfus' rejection of the attempt to see—from 'sideways-on'—what it is about an 'inhuman' world that calls forth our 'human' responses would then be a rejection of an 'immodest' attempt to understand the world in terms other than those that we use so as to explain why those terms are somehow suited to, or fit for, that world.[38] Section 6.1 will suggest that Heidegger's 'prioritizing' of the *Zuhanden* over the *Vorhanden* might serve to make a similar point. If so, the above response to the second 'regress' argument would have been—after the fashion of Section 4.2.2—Heidegger's response too.

But what price is there to be paid if we read Dreyfus' proposals in this spirit? For many philosophers of language, explanation just *is* immodest explanation; and McDowell agrees to the extent that he sees modest theories which, 'by design, start in the midst of content', as unable to 'contribute to [the] task of representing content as an achievement' (1987: 105).[39] A McDowellian reading of Dreyfus here requires us once again, I suggest, to hear in a different way the claims that Dreyfus makes, and are made on his behalf, about having revealed 'conditions of'—having 'accounted for'—the 'possibility' of meaning and intentionality.

---

[38] This would also be one way of construing remarks such as that 'the everyday world...cannot and need not be made intelligible in terms of anything else' (1991: 122). Dreyfus has since qualified this claim—in 2000a—but not in such a way as to encourage immodest theories of meaning.

[39] Section 7.2 will raise some doubts about this formulation.

One might still articulate the McDowellian point by saying that the impossibility of the envisaged 'spelling out' reveals that a 'background' is 'presupposed' by 'the representational' (1991: 5), *if* one takes the latter to be something that can be understood 'immodestly' and the mode of 'presupposition' (as explained in Section 4.2.2) as once again one that makes clear the 'architecture' of what is, in fact, a confusion. The impossibility of such an immodest 'spelling out' could be said to reveal that we cannot stand outside of, and survey, our ways of making sense: at any stage in the project of 'foregrounding'—by attempting to 'spell out'—our understanding, there could then be said to remain a residual 'background' of understanding which we presuppose and have not 'spelt out'. But what is crucial here is not a mistaken fixation on 'representation' at the expense of the '*non-representational*', of a 'third way of Being' (such talk might be best heard, echoing the discussion at the end of Section 4.2.2, as 'reactive' or 'dialectical'); rather it is the confused notion of an immodestly 'spelt out' understanding of representation, of 'the second way of Being'.

It is by reference to that illusion of understanding that a challenge of explaining how representation 'is possible' seems to emerge. If one accepts that challenge, then, as has been argued above, it is unclear why the invocation of a background of 'skills', 'familiarities', and so on, ought to help us meet it; if one rejects the challenge, then it seems misleading to describe what one has done as revealing the 'conditions of'—or having 'accounted for'—the 'possibility' of intentionality. In particular, one will not have provided a theory—based on 'familiarities' or 'skills', rather than, or in addition to, 'representations'—that will provide us with an explanation of how the world happens to succumb to human thought, or that is better placed to explain what immodest representationalist theories cannot. What has been revealed to us is not, as it were, limitations of representation but the structure of a confusion about representation and of a wrong-headed explanatory project of 'accounting for' the 'achievement' of representation that that confusion inspires. On this reading and that presented in Section 4.2, what both 'regress' arguments fundamentally show is that—and how—our thoughts are informed by some crude notions about representation: when we attempt to think through these crude notions, we run into the regresses described, but that should lead us to recognize the crudity of those notions of the representational, of the 'second way of Being'. Dreyfus' postulation of a hitherto unrecognized, *non*-representational, third 'way of Being' does not, it seems to me, help clarify our confusion here.

But, in any case, it is not clear to me that Dreyfus does really reject 'immodest' demands. As was shown above, his disappointment with neural networks seems to be that they fail to explain a feat that 'immodest' theorists characteristically seek to explain.[40] Indeed my overall suspicion is that Dreyfus is confused, drawn towards all of the ideas that Section 4.2 and the present section have articulated—'solving' *and* 'dissolving': that is to say, there is significant textual evidence in support of all of the four readings considered—two critical and two more sympathetic—even though these 'dissolving' and 'solving' readings are incompatible with one another.[41]

In this chapter I have argued that, were one to abandon 'immodesty' and the 'master thesis', one would spare oneself the 'regress' problems described. But that, in itself, does not prove that those notions are actually confused. (And nothing has been said here that leads, I think, in any clear way to a dissolution of, for example, the qu-omising worry set out in Section 4.3.2.) But it is not at all clear to me that Heidegger really does set out to deal with these difficulties; and, if he does not, then I suspect we will struggle to understand his remarks on the *Zuhanden*, the *Vorhanden*, and the former's 'priority' over the latter by reference to those difficulties. I have indicated, however, how Heidegger views the first regress, and will, in what follows, pursue a reading according to which he provides specific reasons for rejecting a 'view from sideways on'. That reading takes its bearings not by worries such as those raised by the second regress, but by a notion by which Dreyfus passes closely when he declares that it makes no sense to imagine 'background coping' 'failing', and that it is not even best thought of as a 'relation' (1991: 249, 347). Understood in this way, it makes no sense to

---

[40] In his (1999), Dreyfus would seem to sanction an 'immodest' hope when he accepts the intelligibility of 'the *logical* question... what *constitutive conditions must be satisfied* for the sounds coming out of peoples' mouths to count as language?'—a question that would help 'provide a theoretical explanation of language' and is asked from 'an external perspective from outside the world of linguistic meaning' (1999: 13). But quite what Dreyfus has in mind in these brief remarks is unclear to me, so I will not explore them further here. One might also think that Dreyfus' views on artificial intelligence commit him to 'immodesty'. For some brief critical comments on that thought, cf. McManus 2008: 449–50.

[41] A sketchy but important objection to the sympathetic, McDowellian readings of Dreyfus presented here is that the broadly 'therapeutic' spirit of those readings is at odds with Dreyfus' overall sense of the kind of work he is doing, which is instead a matter of 'doing phenomenology' or 'doing ontology'. McManus 2008 makes some brief suggestions about how this objection might be addressed, touching on themes which Section 9.8 will also explore.

imagine an account of how such 'skills' come to have 'traction on' the world, and in this specific sense there is no deep 'explanation of intentionality' on offer that would 'represent content as an achievement'. But I believe we will best appreciate the character of these claims if we take our bearings by the 'constitutional' concerns that Part I of this book presented.

PART III

5

The Measure of Truth

> *Metrein*, to take measure, is the mode in which *Dasein* makes something intelligible. (PS 87)

In the 'constitutional' reflections upon which Part I focused, the Theoretical Attitude figured as the villain of the piece, though without itself being the centre of attention; indeed Heidegger seems happy to gather together in his concern with the Theoretical Attitude a concern also with assertions, propositions, cognition, and so on. Chapter 3 considered some concepts that are seemingly closely tied to the Theoretical Attitude and which often form the starting point for any explanation of Heidegger's early work. A sense of the myopic or misleading character of the Theoretical Attitude is often articulated through the notion that the *Zuhanden* are, in some sense, 'prior' to the *Vorhanden*, the latter being the kind of entity revealed by the Theoretical Attitude—or, rather, the Theoretical Attitude amongst a long list of other 'channels', including the experience of the breakdown of our everyday activities, the making of assertions, the entertaining of propositions, 'just looking', interpretation, and so on. The hope that one might come to understand Heidegger's notion of the Theoretical Attitude and the 'founded' character of 'the propositional' through an invocation of *Vorhandenheit* must then be tempered, I believe, by a recognition of how problematic this notion actually is. A significant number of different proposals seem to be bundled together in association with it, and the relationship between these proposals is less than clear—a lack of clarity that I illustrated in examining the supposed connection between the *Vorhanden* and assertions, and the *Vorhanden* and science. In the latter case, for example, Rouse and Blattner have argued that Heidegger's broader commitments ought to lead him to think that the objects revealed by science are not *vorhanden* but actually *zuhanden* after all. What makes an evaluation of that proposal difficult is the fact that *Zuhandenheit* is itself another loosely specified idea or bundle of ideas.

Chapter 4 went on to look at the most influential attempt to understand Heidegger's notion that the theoretical and the propositional are 'non-primordial' because of their being 'founded' modes of Being-in-the-world—the attempt made by Dreyfus. He proposes that the possession of intentional states such as the entertaining of propositions or theoretical claims represents 'a derivative and intermittent condition' that 'presupposes' a 'background' of 'skills', 'know-how', 'customs', 'habits', and so on. But again I urged caution, arguing that the form of 'founding' that 'the intentional' received on that reading is hard to fathom. I argued, in connection with two of the central arguments invoked in support of the need for such a 'founding' 'background', that it is unclear quite how the 'background' is meant to address the problems that those arguments seem to expose: it is unclear what job the 'background' is meant to do.

So I suggest we start again, as it were, guided by notions that Part I sets out. I will develop what one might call a more 'formal' or 'abstract' notion of the 'founding' of the theoretical/propositional in Being-in-the-world, a notion which is—at least *prima facie*—independent of any 'founding' of 'the propositional' in 'the practical and economic' (BT 83 (57)). Later comments that Heidegger makes clearly show that any more 'pragmatic' notion of 'founding' needs to be 'subordinated', as he himself puts it (EG 121 n. 59), in something like this way:

I attempted in *Being and Time* to provide a preliminary characterization of the *phenomenon of world* by interpreting *the way in which we at first and for the most part move about in our everyday world*. There I took my departure from what lies to hand in the everyday realm, from those things that we use and pursue ... It never occurred to me, however, to try and claim or prove with this interpretation that the essence of man consists in the fact that he knows how to handle knives and forks or uses the tram. (FCM 177)[1]

---

[1] Cf. also EG 121 n. 59 ('The ontological structure of entities in our 'environing world'—insofar as they are discovered as equipment—does, however, have the advantage, in terms of an *initial characterization* of the phenomenon of world, of leading over into an analysis of this phenomenon and of preparing the transcendental problem of world. And this is also the *sole* intent—an intent indicated clearly enough in the structuring and layout of secs 14–24 of *Being and Time*—of the analysis of the environing world, an analysis that as a whole, and considered with regard to the *leading goal*, remains of subordinate significance') and MFL 183 ('One cannot pack transcendence into intuition, in either the theoretical or the aesthetic sense, because it is not even an ontic activity. Even less can it be packed into a practical comportment, be it in an instrumental-utilitarian sense or in any other. The central task in the ontology of *Dasein* is to go back behind those divisions into comportments to find their common root, a task that need not, of course, be easy. Transcendence precedes every possible mode of activity, prior to *noesis* [belief], but also prior to *orexis* [desire]').

Okrent has argued that 'the fact that the later Heidegger thoroughly rejected anything that smacked of a pragmatic interpretation of his early *magnum opus* at most shows that he could not accept such a reading of his work, not that that reading is wrong' (2002: 198). But if we can avoid that conclusion, the principle of charity requires that we do so.

I will begin by identifying in Heidegger's early 'constitutional' reflections a notion that I will suggest we call that of a 'measure', a 'constituting' form of understanding that makes it possible for us to identify entities.[2] This idea, of which BT's 'pre-ontological understanding of Being' (BT 35 (15)) and the Prior Projection Claim are descendents, emerges out of Heidegger's early engagement not only with Husserl's notion of 'constitution' but also with his analysis of truth as the 'fulfilment' of 'empty intentions', and Section 5.2 will examine that engagement. The idea finds expression in several different ways in the intervening years, and Section 5.3 will take as an illustrative example its manifestation in the *Logik* lectures as the idea of a prethematic '*Hinblick*'. Out of those reflections will emerge a skeleton upon which we can arrange some central themes of BT's fundamental ontology, including Being-in-the-world, its critique of scepticism, and its distinctive and controversial views on truth. So interpreted, that ontology invites a number of obvious objections—in particular, that it leads us once again to a form of idealism, 'the foul fiend incarnate' (BPP 167, quoted in Section 2.2). The chapter that follows the present one will provide what one might call a phenomenological examination of some basic descriptive practices which will, in turn, help to provide a concrete sense of what the fundamental ontology's claims might amount to (as the chapters that follow that spell out explicitly) and of how the objections mentioned might be addressed.

5.1 Constitution and measure

Chapter 1 examined the 'constitutive' concern that Heidegger traces in St Paul's reflections on the Last Judgement. Heidegger sees a similar concern at work in St Augustine and, for example, in his question, 'What do I love when I love my God?' (1961: 211, quoted in PRL 130). He sees in

---

[2] In addition to the passages quoted here, the motif of 'measure' recurs again and again in L (e.g. pp. 54, 65, 71, 80, 81, 269, 318, 386, 390), and in many of Heidegger's other early works: cf., e.g., DSTCM 43–4, 63, 75, 79, and 91–2 and PS 18, 150, 192, 198, 312, and 321. It can also be found in his later work: it is, for example, a central focus of PMD. For other studies of Heidegger's work that highlight the role of this motif, while interpreting its role there in rather different ways, cf. Cooper 2002, Beck 2005, Elden 2006, and Crowell 2008.

St Augustine the characteristic to-and-fro of his own 'radical' notion of 'constitution', an attempt to recognize once again the way in which we 'have' or 'comport' ourselves towards an entity—in this case God—with a view also to recognizing once again what kind of entity that is.[3] In St Augustine's question, Heidegger sees a concern that we have forgotten what God is like because we have forgotten what loving God is like; in response to that forgetting, St Augustine attempts to re-cognize how we 'have' God and thereby 'determine the sense of the objecthood of God' (PRL 67).

We see here an early articulation of an idea fundamental to BT: that of an always presupposed 'pre-ontological' understanding of the entities to which one relates.[4] Prior to any question of whether an entity is there before us or is real, we must, first of all, possess a sense of what it is for something to be that entity. To adapt Smith's formulation and draw on Husserlian terms to which we will come soon, 'the meaning content' of our 'empty' intuition 'projects a certain structure in the projected object, and so the object-as-intended is constituted with the projected structure' (Smith, quoted in Section 2.2) In Heidegger, this becomes the claim that '*every intentional relation has within itself a specific understanding of the Being of the entity* to which the intentional comportment as such relates' (BPP 208). Heidegger defends this claim through, for example, a discussion of St Augustine's remarks on another supposedly intentional 'state', that of 'utterly forgetting', that might be thought to have severed its ties with an intended object. First we have Heidegger translating St Augustine:

[W]e have not yet utterly forgotten that which we remember ourselves to have forgotten. That which we have forgotten entirely, therefore, we will never be able so much as to search for. (St Augustine 1961: X, 19, 28, translated and quoted at PRL 140)

Heidegger comments:

Understood relationally: As long as we have still lost something, we still 'have' it. What does '*omnino oblivisci*' [having forgotten entirely] mean? Not at all living in the enactment of the representation, not at all having at one's disposal the direction of

---

[3] A related example is his discussion of 'the happy life': 'What the happy life is... is to be established at the same time, and by way of, the explication of the How of having... What it is: this question leads to the *How* of having it' (PRL 143).

[4] For a yet earlier intimation of such a view, cf. DSTCM 39, discussed in McManus forthcoming-b.

access, to have shut oneself off against it, or having covered oneself up to the point of not seeing that it is still there in certain relational directions. But this one does not grasp! (PRL 140)

Forgetting 'has its *intentional relational sense*' and is no 'radical privation' (PRL 140). What we might imagine when we imagine 'having forgotten entirely' is one's no longer 'living in the enactment of [a] representation'; but this 'state' is *non*-intentional, lacking a 'direction of access', a 'relational direction' to an object of any sort, and as such it does not constitute 'grasp' of anything. Such states are not merely non-committal or uncertain; rather they are, as it were, closed or darkened. It may, of course, be the case that the object of a genuine intentional state

is not itself—in the flesh—present; and yet, it is not nothing, otherwise I could not say anything at all about it. But what, now, really is this 'not nothing'? (PRL 137)

Heidegger confronts again a 'constitutive' question: to understand the Being of this 'not nothing' I must consider how I 'have' it, my mode of 'comportment' to this 'not nothing'.

Such a concern is anticipated in Husserl's notion of 'horizons' within which objects appear and, in particular, in his discussion of truth Heidegger's appreciation and exploration of which the next section will explore. As we will see, this discussion plays an important role in Heidegger's own reflections on truth, and in particular his reflections on the conception of truth as correspondence—*adaequatio intellectus et rei*—a conception he will depict as 'superficial' (PS 10).

5.2 'Empty intending' and truth as 'fulfilment'

The crucial notions in Husserl's discussion of truth are those of the 'fulfilment' [*Erfüllung*] of an 'empty intending' [*Leermeinen*]: very roughly speaking, we 'emptily intend' an object when we, for instance, contemplate its possible existence, but that intention is 'fulfilled' when we recognize that object as standing before us. As Heidegger puts it in his own exposition of these notions in HCT,[5] our 'empty intending' achieves 'intuitive fulfilment

---

[5] Cf. also L 99–115.

up to a certain level' in our 'intuitively envisaging' the intended object, in contrast with which '[p]erception... is a superlative case of intentional fulfilment' (HCT 44).

Among other difficulties that these concepts raise, it is tempting to doubt their usefulness: one might suspect that they provide exotic but ultimately unilluminating ways of saying that images are images and perceptions are perceptions. But in a discussion in PRL, which repeatedly invokes the language of 'empty' and 'fulfilled intentions',[6] Heidegger makes clear an important feature of intentionality that Husserl's descriptions does throw into relief:

> The woman who searched for and found the lost drachma—how could she search for and find it if she did not somehow still have it present to herself? If, while searching for something, different things offer themselves, and I reject each and everything until I 'have' found the 'right' thing I am searching for, then I must 'have' what I am searching for and that according to which I evaluate what I find. (PRL 139)

Despite the fact that the woman searches because a particular object is absent, her search is the search that it is by virtue of the fact that that very object will 'fulfil' it. Using motifs to which we will return, Heidegger proposes that, in such a search, I 'evaluate' each object I encounter by 'measuring it... against that which I know in anticipation [*was ich vorgreifend weiss*]' (PRL 142 n. 62).

As a general condition of recognition, this picture can be generalized so as to present 'consciousness' as such—to borrow from Dahlstrom's discussion—'as a striving that is directed at an accomplishment', as possessed of an 'entelechy' (2001: 60). It can be generalized further still to subsume propositional truth[7]—it too being 'a unity of coincidence of the presumed and the intuited' (HCT 68)—and, crucially—as we will see—for his own distinctive view of truth, Heidegger sees it as presupposed by the very notion of an *adaequatio intellectus et rei*:

> [F]ulfillment means commensuration (*adaequatio*) of what is presumed (*intellectus*) with the intuited subject matter itself (*res*)... [A]*daequatio* refers to this commensuration in the sense of bringing-into-coincidence. (HCT 51)

---

[6] Cf., e.g., PRL 130, 141, and 142.   [7] Cf., e.g., HCT 54, 55, 57, 68, and 72.

Even if, as Heidegger seems to think,[8] Husserl sheds little light on these matters, his contribution is showing us what we have to make sense of. As Tugendhat puts it:

Only because we have the remarkable possibility of meaning something that is nevertheless not 'directly' given to us and because this same thing meant *can* be directly given in turn, does the talk of true and false have any sense. (Tugendhat 1970: 30)[9]

Heidegger turns to the idiom of this discussion in further elaborating St Augustine's 'constitutional' project; he sees Augustine as attempting to answer his question ('What do I love . . . ?') by asking

what gives a 'fulfilling intuition' if he [Augustine] lives in the love of God, what suffices for, or saturates, that which, in the love of God, he intends. (PRL 130).

Hence, in order to recover our sense of the Being of God, for example, what we must explore is our 'empty' intuition of God; by seeing what kind of 'fulfilment' that calls for, what kind of entity 'fulfils' this kind of intuition, we see what kind of entity God is; as Heidegger articulates the question in PRL,

According to what do I recognize and grasp something as God? What gives the fulfilment of meaning: '*sat est*' [it suffices]? (PRL 141)

Heidegger proposes that when seeking an entity 'I "have" it only when I can say: Enough, here it is' and here adds the note quoted above: '[t]hat is, by measuring it at the same time against that which I know in anticipation' (PRL 142). An 'empty' intuition contains, as it were, an understanding of the 'intended' entity; it determines what it is that 'fulfils' it, what 'suffices', and thereby the intuition's 'object' is 'constituted', 'projected', 'anticipated'.

The notion of a 'constituting' 'anticipation' which provides a 'measure' up to which entities may or may not match will be central in what follows. We see it at work not only in BT's discussions of a 'pre-ontological understanding' and of 'projection' but in a range of discussions in Heidegger's lectures, including his discussions of Aristotle—on the '"as" structure' and the 'synthesizing-and-separating' structure which are inherent in asser-

---

[8] Cf. HCT 47 and Heidegger's criticism of Husserl in HCT Secs 10–13.
[9] The translation quoted here is from Dahlstrom 2001: 62.

tion and which 'give objects' (HCT 64)[10]—and of Plato—on the 'productive' or 'disclosive negation' (PS 388, 395) that is the 'non-being' of the *eraton* (PS 384), which we must grasp if an entity is to be able to manifest itself to us, to 'descen[d] out of absence' (PS 448).[11]

The need to fathom the presupposed 'remarkable possibility' of 'having' what I am searching for'—of 'emptily intending' the same thing (be it an object or, as with a proposition, a state of affairs) as may subsequently be 'intuitively given'—seems to be key also to Heidegger's sense of something problematic and 'tacit' in our understanding of truth as correspondence. That phenomenon is 'superficial' because entertaining the possibility of any such correspondence or fit seems to presuppose another form of understanding of the world (that embodied most clearly in our 'emptily intending') which, as such, cannot itself be understood as the appreciation of such a correspondence—a theme to which we will return.

But this Husserlian framework also raises certain familiar idealist worries. To 'search for a drachma' is to 'project' on to the contents of the world a range of possibilities, to use a Wittgensteinian expression, a 'logical space',[12] if a rather simple one, within which the contents of the world can then be placed: drachmas, on the one hand, and non-drachmas, on the other. The con-formist worry—to use Section 2.1's expression—that arises now is: what basis do we have for thinking that in enacting this 'projection' the framework projected has any traction, so to speak, on the world 'outside'? The realist that that section envisages imagines reading this framework off characteristics of that 'outside' world, but then runs into the problem that any such reading involves the use of—and hence presupposes the intelligibility of—such a framework: as Section 2.3 put it, intentional agents must then '*live in*' such 'projections'. But if not through such a reading, how can we make sense of this framework's 'anticipation' of the forms of entity that could populate the world?[13] Can that 'anticipation' be understood without embracing an extravagant idealism? The next section and Section 5.4.4 will

---

[10] Cf. also L 148–9, 153–61, BT 201–2 (158), BPP 182, 198, 209f, EP 47, 51f.
[11] Cf. also DSTCM's discussion of Rickert on 'heterothesis': '[t]he logical beginning, the one and the many' which 'must already be since there isn't any object if there isn't the one and the other' (quoted at DSTCM 46). Cf. also DSTCM 42.
[12] Cf. Wittgenstein 1922: 1.13.
[13] 'Could' because the con-formist 'projection' only presupposes that drachmas' existing is among the world's possibilities, not its actualities.

show that other important discussions of truth in Heidegger's early writings lead to similar conclusions to those reached in the present section, but also to similar worries.

5.3 'Living in the *Hinblick*'

I have suggested that the 'formal' notion of a 'constituting' 'anticipation' which provides a 'measure'—up to which entities may or may not match—represents an important continuous theme that runs through the young Heidegger's work; it emerges out of his appropriation of Husserlian notions of 'constitution' and 'empty intending' and manifests itself in BT in the notion of a pre-ontological understanding of Being. On the road from that first appropriation to that later manifestation, we find its articulation in Heidegger's *Logik* lectures of 1925–26, and I will examine this next.

Heidegger proposes that experience—seeing things as thus and so—presupposes a *vorgängige Hinblick* (L 275, 274):

[E]xperience is always ordered experience [and in] such experience the *Hinblicknahme* is always operative (constitutively and beforehand). (L 285–6)

'*Der Hinblick*' is Heidegger's nominalization of what is in German a prepositional expression. This is a strategy that we encounter repeatedly in his work: in, for example, BT's *das Worumwillen* (the 'for-the-sake-of which') and *das Wo-für* (the 'for-which'), and also in an expression that Heidegger often links with *der Hinblick*, *das Worauf* or *das Woraufhin*, which Macquarrie and Robinson translate in BT as the 'upon-which'. '*Hinblick*' itself both echoes '*Blick*', a look or glance from a physical eye, so to speak, and can be used to mean 'bearing in mind that', 'with reference to' or—to find the echo of *Blick* also in English– 'with regard to', 'with a view to' or 'in the light of'. He goes on to give the following example:

Suppose we have a bunch of spheres of different sizes and made of different kinds of material—and suppose they are to be ordered. The task is to sort them out and group them. But how? The task—'The spheres are to be ordered'—is insufficiently determined because what that job entails has not been stated. Yes, the unordered bunch is to be ordered, but the question is: Ordered with regard to what [*im*

Hinblick worauf]? We adequately determine the task of ordering only when we indicate the with-regard-to-what [*des Hinblicks*]. (L 284)

The idea that Heidegger is trying to articulate seems, once again, to be that of a standard- or theme-setting understanding that must already be in place whenever we make a determinate judgement or indeed have an experience with determinate content:

[W]henever we encounter something that is given with any character of order at all, that thing is encountered within regard to something-in-terms-of-which [*in einem Hinblick auf etwas, von wo aus*] it is, and can be, ordered. (L 284)

To characterize our relationship to such *Hinblicke* and *Worauf*, Heidegger invokes—and does so over and over again[14]—a turn of phrase that echoes Section 2.3's talk of 'living in the categories' and, as we will see, BT sec. 44's claim that *Dasein* 'is "in the truth"': although 'I am not thematically focussed these upon-whichs [*diese Worauf*]'—in that they 'do not appear in the field of everyday concern and observation' where we are instead concerned with the 'thematic', 'specific content' that they allow us to order—'I do live in them' (L 286, 288).[15]

As the following sections will show, this is not merely an observation about 'what it's like' to have a *Hinblick* 'in view' (L 286); it provides a skeleton on which one might hang some central themes of what Heidegger will later call a 'hermeneutics of facticity', and later still a 'fundamental ontology'. There can be no such thing as a subject who 'comes to' or 'arrives at' *Hinblicke*, since the '*Hinblicknahme*' must already be 'operative (constitutively and beforehand)' in any 'ordered experience'; hence, *Dasein* is 'thrown' into, 'lives in', such an understanding. For the same reason, entities cannot be encountered independently of the *Hinblicke* that reveal them,[16] and which also therefore cannot be 'read off' those entities.[17] Indeed, as the next section will explain, one might state that *Dasein* must

---

[14] Cf., e.g., L 146, 147, 151, 183, 192, 209, and 288.

[15] Cf. BT 185 (145)'s parallel remarks about the 'possibilities' that 'understanding' 'projects'.

[16] Talk of 'constitution' is again not far away. 'The *Hinblicknahme* itself is what constitutes every order as such' (L 277) since the *Hinblick* is 'constitutive for the task of ordering' (L 284): without it, no particular task—and hence, also no particular order—can be identified. Cf. also L 281–2, 284f, and 320–1.

[17] Cf. BQP 58–9 and 71, WT 72, DSTCM 140 ('If actual natural reality is to be determinant of the categories of meaning, then I have to *know* beforehand about this reality and its structure') and Heidegger's charge that realism fails to appreciate that 'Being cannot be explained through entities' (BT 251 (207)).

always already live *bei*—'with', 'amidst' or 'amongst'—the entities that their *Hinblicke* reveal. Such a prior familiarity would provide the kind of *vorgängige Hinblick*, the kind of 'anticipation', that seems necessary for the 'remarkable possibility' of truth, of *Dasein* already 'emptily intending' that which it subsequently 're-cognizes'. But once again, can we understand this 'anticipation' without throwing in our lot with 'the foul fiend incarnate'?

Heidegger interweaves his discussion of the *Hinblick* in the *Logik* lectures with a reading of Kant, whose discussion of space and time Heidegger sees as a discussion of *Hinblicke*. In the context of that juxtaposition, our conformist idealist worry emerges in a vivid form. If 'experience is always ordered experience [and in] such experience the *Hinblicknahme* is always operative (constitutively and beforehand)'—indeed '[w]e adequately determine the task of ordering only when we indicate the with-regard-to-what [*des Hinblick*]'—then that *Hinblick* has an *a priori* status with respect to any experience in which it is 'operative'. The con-formist worry that this generates—why think that the order thus 'projected' on to the world corresponds to the metaphysical order of that world?—echoes the worry raised in Section 2.1 about 'the pure concepts of the understanding': how can these concepts embody a 'determination of the content of nature's Being'?

How can these pure concepts of the understanding, as unities constitutive of merely empty actions of understanding, have any relation to objects [*Objekte*], to content-determined objects [*sachhaltig bestimmte Gegenstände*]? (L 333)[18]

Such worries lead Kant to conclude that space and time actually can be neither 'real existences [nor] determinations or relations of things... such as would belong to things even if they were not intuited', but instead 'belong... to the subjective constitution of our mind, apart from which they could not be ascribed to anything whatsoever' (1961: A23/B37–38). But Heidegger believes that there is no inevitability about such conclusions, about space, time, or *Hinblicke* considered more generally, because 'Descartes' position shines through' the underlying con-formist problematic that leads to those conclusions (L 318). Heidegger argues that Kant is led to regard space and time as inherently bound up with the subject, on the grounds that, as that which 'is given first and before anything else', they must belong to the subject, and that

---

[18] Cf. also L 378.

the latter premise represents 'Cartesian dogmatism, which Kant himself took over without any further discussion' (L 278):

> This is the basic thesis of that dogmatism: What is given first, foremost, and prior to anything else—i.e. what is given *a priori*—is the *ego cogito* . . . Kant has correctly and phenomenologically shown in his treatment of space and time . . . that space and time are given prior to any specific spatial or temporal thing . . . But it does not follow that whatever is earlier than something else has to be a *cogitatio*. But Kant in fact draws this conclusion. In directing himself to the phenomena, Kant sees that space and time are something given antecedently as the conditions of the possibility of understanding any manifold at all. But on the basis of Descartes' dogma this means: Because it is *a priori*, what is originally given in this way prior to something else must be subjective, must be a *cogitatio*. (L 278)[19]

Without this 'dogma' there is no reason, Heidegger seems to think, for regarding *Hinblicke* as 'resid[ing] first of all and fundamentally within the subject' (L 318).[20]

But what sense can we make of what now seems to be necessary if there is to be ordering, which is in turn necessary if there is to be experience, namely, a non-subjectivist *a priori*?[21] How can there be a genuine *a priori* that is not bound up, as the Cartesian/Kantian, subjectivist *a priori* is, with a 'content with the character of being prior' and which 'resides first of all and fundamentally within the subject' (L 318)? Crudely put, will not the bearing of this supposed '*a priori*' on the world 'outside' require that it be informed by *a posteriori* insight? For Heidegger, this follows only from 'Cartesian dogmatism'; if we reinterpret the Being of the subject then the insight that Kant construes as *Hinblicke* being 'subjectively given' will also require reinterpretation, and this leads us again to the key notion of Being-in-the-world:

> 'Subjectively given' now means: given with the subject, which now means: given with *Dasein*, and specifically *Dasein* as Being-in-the-world. (L 291)

---

[19] Cf. also HCT 73. In L's discussion, Kant's space and time are presented as, in a sense, preeminent among *Hinblicke*; Section 9.1 will touch on the significance of that within the project Heidegger envisages for BT.

[20] With this line of thought in mind, it is natural that, after an extended examination of Husserlian notions of 'categorical intuition' and 'constitution', HCT goes on to stress Husserl's idea that the *a priori* is not confined to the subjective (HCT 74).

[21] Cf. L 291 on a *Hinblick* which is '"objective" and yet still *a priori*—admittedly "*a priori*" in a sense that is still to be determined, namely, as the "what" of what we are already-with'.

5.4 A skeleton for some themes of the fundamental ontology

The English translations disguise to some degree the presence in BT of the notions that the previous section discusses. So, for example, when we make an assertion we are said 'to be already taking a look directionally at what is to be put forward in the assertion' (BT 199 (157)), or as Stambaugh has it, 'one has a directed viewpoint of what is to be stated'; the expression that the translators are wrestling with here is '*ausgerichtete Hinblicknahme*'.[22] In the same passage we read of 'that with regard to which we set our sights towards the entity' or, with Stambaugh, 'the direction in which beings that have been presented are envisaged': the expression translated here is '*Woraufhin das vorgegebene Seiende anvisiert wird*'. Indeed, there is reason to think that these concepts have a central role to play in BT. It would take a study of its own to document this, but in addition to the passages just quoted above, BT 371 (324) states that '[t]o lay bare the "upon-which" [*das Woraufhin*] of a projection, amounts to disclosing that which make possible [*ermöglicht*] what has been projected', 'that in terms of which something can be conceived in its possibility, as that which it is' (BT 371 (324)). Unsurprisingly then, this notion is closely tied to the very notion of Being, which BT 25–6 (6) identifies with 'that on the basis of which [*woraufhin*] entities are already understood'.[23]

The notions of '*Hinblick*' and '*Woraufhin*' are interwoven in BT with others—such as that of 'fore-sight [*Vorsicht*]', 'fore-having [*Vorhabe*]', and 'fore-conception' [*Vorgriff*]—and embedded within the broader context of a reflection on 'possibility', 'projection' [*Entwurf*], and 'understanding' [*Verstehen*], according to which, 'in the projecting of the understanding, entities are disclosed in their possibility' (BT 192 (151)).[24] Against this background—or 'horizon'—of 'projected' possibilities, entities are said to have 'meaning [*Sinn*]', and to be 'intelligible [*verständlich*]', Heidegger describing 'meaning' as '*the "upon-which"* [*Woraufhin*] *of a projection in terms of which something becomes intelligible as something*' (BT 192, 193 (151)). The

---

[22] Other occurrences include BT 65 (41) and 119 (86). Cf. also HCT's talk of the 'to-which of the regard [*das Worauf des Hinsicht*]' (HCT 67).

[23] Cf. also BT 372 (325) and HCT 306. For related remarks concerning *der Hinblick*, cf. BT 27 (8), 28 (8), and BPP 235 and 238.

[24] Cf. also BT 184f (144f).

present section will suggest that a recognition of the philosophical implications of this discussion, within which the notions of *Hinblicke* and of the *Woraufhin* are embedded, provides a skeleton upon which we may arrange some central and difficult themes from the fundamental ontology (though, so arranged, each will, nonetheless, leave us asking some difficult—if now familiar—questions).

Two concepts I will mention only briefly—'projection' and 'thrownness'—though I will raise a significant issue that the latter raises. Inasmuch as we cannot read off the Being of an entity from the entity itself, our understanding could be said to embody a 'projection' (BT 185 (145)). Such a formulation is far from unproblematic: it may suggest a Humean projectivism (according to which *Dasein* 'spreads itself' on to a body of entities (1975b: 1.3.14.25), 'gilding and staining' them with meanings which have no basis, so to speak, in the entities themselves (1975a: Appendix 1.21)) or a fantastical idealism (according to which the entities are somehow brought into existence by the projecting agent, *Dasein*). But the grounds on which our previous discussion provides a basis for the theme of 'thrownness' itself provides us with reason for finding both of these 'options' untenable.[25] We might believe that we can envisage the subject existing prior to its experiencing entities through *Hinblicke* and, on that basis, imagine that those *Hinblicke* might represent a 'projection' on the part of the subject. But if 'experience is always ordered experience [and in] such experience the *Hinblicknahme* is always operative (constitutively and beforehand)', then the subject who 'precedes' *Hinblicke* is no subject at all.[26] Instead, the subject finds itself 'thrown' into certain *Hinblicke*. At its most fundamental level this understanding cannot be arrived at, at least if this is understood as anything like the subject discerning for itself through some sort of examination of the world about which it will think that that world has certain features. To the impossibility of our reading our understanding of the Being of entities off those entities corresponds the impossibility of such an 'arrival' at our understanding of the Being of entities, at least with respect to the most basic forms of that understanding: so no more can a

---

[25] Bases for *interpretive* doubt abound. Cf., e.g., Heidegger's critical discussions of the notion of interpretation as 'throw[ing] a "signification" over some naked thing which is present-at-hand' and 'stick[ing] a value on it' (BT 190 (150)), and of the notion that 'what is in the first instance just a material Thing, gets stamped as something good' (BT 132 (99)).

[26] Compare BT 249 (206) and BPP 168.

Hinblick be 'read off' the objects it picks out than can the subject that 'projects' that *Hinblick* be seen as thinking that *Hinblick* into existence, so to speak.

Obvious questions that arise here are: How does this understanding come about? How do we come to find ourselves 'living in' these 'projections'? These questions come, of course, in two forms. One can wonder how a particular creature comes to live in such 'projections'; and one can wonder how we as a community—or as a species—came to do so. Here we confront issues that are pressing for philosophers of many stripes: there is reason to think, for example, that Brandom, Davidson, and McDowell are three contemporary exemplars; Bar-On (unpublished) has argued as much, labelling the view to which their ideas appear to commit them 'continuity scepticism'.[27] The worry that Heidegger is committed to such a view arises out of his seemingly sharp distinction between the mode of Being of *Dasein* and that of nature, an analogue of which one of Bar-On's 'continuity sceptics' seems to express in insisting that '[w]e must sharply distinguish natural–scientific intelligibility from the kind of intelligibility something acquires when we situate it in the logical space of reasons' (McDowell 1994: xix). But worries about such continuity arise even for views that one might assume precisely make a place for it, such as the view that thought 'emerges out of practical engagement', a view often ascribed to Heidegger. If that 'engagement' is understood as more than mere reflex action, then its emergence from 'mere nature' is itself a puzzle;[28] but if instead this 'engagement' is understood as mere reflex action, then it becomes mysterious how thought emerges from it; Dreyfus raises a version of this worry when he bemoans the fact that '[p]henomenologists lack a detailed and convincing account of how rationality and language grow out of non-conceptual and non-linguistic coping' (2005: 61);[29] and Heidegger's characterizations of the

---

[27] Davidson, for example, makes the following claims: 'In both the evolution of thought in the history of mankind, and the evolution of thought in an individual, there is a stage at which there is no thought followed by a subsequent stage at which there is thought. To describe the emergence of thought would be to describe the process which leads from the first to the second of these stages. What we lack is a satisfactory vocabulary for describing the intermediate steps.' (1999: 11) Others at whom Bar-On points the finger include Bennett, Chomsky, Grice, and Sellars; Haugeland (2000: 350) would also seem to enthusiastically add himself to the list.

[28] A similar worry arises when one reads that 'holistically integrated functional systems of tool types are articulated independently of and prior to the activity of any given agent' (Okrent 2002: 201).

[29] Cf. also his 2007: 364.

'mental lives'—if we allow ourselves that expression—of children and animals provide reason to think he too senses that there is an important issue here. He talks of the 'being-amidst [*Sein bei*] entities' of children as 'still, so to speak, clouded over, still not cleared up' (EP 126), and of animals as 'poor in world' (FCM 186).[30] But one senses that Heidegger offers neither of these formulations with real confidence.[31]

We will return to these matters again in Part IV. But in the rest of this chapter we will concentrate on Heidegger's notion of 'Being-in-the-world', his critique of scepticism, and his controversial views on truth.

5.4.1 *An abstract case for our 'Being-in-the-world'*

'Being-in-the-world' is a difficult notion. We cannot, for example, rest comfortably with supposedly explanatory gestures such as that we are 'already out there with entities' or 'always already open towards entities', since 'there is still at bottom the supposition that [we were] once closed', 'at some point on the inside' (MFL 167). Such gestures serve to specify what we are not, denying that we fit the Cartesian picture of a 'closed', 'inner' Subject. But Heidegger tells us that the meaning of those very terms, as Section 9.2 will discuss, is 'indeterminate', 'indefinite' (BT 368 (321)); so what can the above denials hope to tell us?[32]

Moreover, many different paths seem to lead Heidegger to our 'Being-in-the-world'. Fathoming just how Heidegger's thinking develops is an obviously difficult task; as, I suspect, with most significant thinkers, his thought seems to advance not in a planned way or along a single linear path but across several fronts and in ways he could not foresee. Being-in-the-world, it seems to me, is so overdetermined that it is tempting to call it a motif rather than a concept, suggesting as the latter term does that it might be tied to a single definition or even a single inspiration.

The young Heidegger's Husserlian concern with 'constitution' focuses on the need to recognize the diversity of Being. But, as Section 2.4 indicated, that recognition also provides grounds for a more general revaluation

---

[30] Related discussions can be found at, e.g., BPP 171, 190–1, 319, and 326.

[31] Though making the case would be a complex matter, I believe that related concerns may underpin the later Heidegger's characterization of 'disclosures of Being' as 'fated' 'happenings', 'gifts', or 'grantings' (cf., e.g., QCT 18, 18–19, 24, 25, 29, 32, 44, and 169 for related passages) and in claims such as that '[i]n poetry the taking of measure occurs' (PMD 221). (cf. also ch. 2 n. 65 and ch. 7 n. 30.)

[32] I return to this question again in Section 7.5, and in a rather different way in my (forthcoming-d).

of the very terms through which that need is initially expressed: 'subject-correlate', 'object-correlate', and 'constitution' itself. Reflection on the diversity of 'original havings' encourages a recognition of their character as diverse 'forms of life' and particular such 'havings'—such as tool-use and the 'environmental experience'—may encourage a recognition of subjectivity as actually a 'worldly' business.

Another strand of thought woven into the overdetermined motif of Being-in-the-world is an obvious echo of a theme that emerged in the discussion of *Hinblicke*: any entity that we encounter and judge to be thus-and-so is encountered within a particular range of possible orderings. So we see the *Logik* lectures' spheres (L 284) as of this size, rather than this or that size, or as made of this material as opposed to this or that material, or as of this colour as opposed to ... This familiar holistic point presents any such encounter as necessarily placing its object within a 'space' of possibilities, and it is important in that—if a case can be made for thinking that we must possess some kind of 'prior disclosure' of objects—then it will also necessarily be a disclosure of them within such a 'space'. But there seems to be something less metaphorical in Heidegger's talk of Being-in-the-world than one finds in such talk of a space (or world) of possibilities. Not only is what we experience in such a space or world, but we ourselves are too. One contribution to that thought we have already glimpsed: the entity that can encounter the *Zuhanden* exposes itself to the world, concerns itself with—and allows how its life fares to be a matter of how events turn out in—the 'world outside'. But there are more 'strands' interwoven here.

First of all, though, we need to approach with care the above talk of our 'being in space'. Heidegger challenges the notion that the world, indeed space itself, is, as it were, first and foremost the space of Cartesian extension, and he goes out of his way to attack a construal of *Dasein's* Being-in-the-world as essentially 'spatial' in that challenged sense:

[O]ne cannot think of [Being-in] as the Being-present-at-hand of some corporeal Thing (such as a human body) 'in' an entity which is present-at-hand. (BT 79 (54))[33]

That does not mean that Heidegger denies that *Dasein* occupies physical space: he declares explicitly that *Dasein* '*can* with some right and within certain limits be *taken* as merely present-at-hand' (BT 82 (55)) and, within

---

[33] Cf. also BT 170 (132).

those 'certain limits', it will then make sense to think of *Dasein* as occupying physical space.[34] But there is a 'but': 'To do this, one must completely disregard or just not see the existential state of Being-in' (BT 82 (55)).[35] So a simple 'spatial' interpretation of Being-in-the-world misses the mark, and Heidegger offers the following alternative vision:

'In' is derived from '*innan*'—'to reside' [*wohnen*], '*habitare*', 'to dwell' [*sich aufhalten*]. '*An*' signifies 'I am accustomed', 'I am familiar', 'I look after something' [*ich bin gewohnt, vertraut mit, ich pflege etwas*].

Regarding this entity, *Dasein*, 'which in each case I myself am [*bin*]',

[t]he expression '*bin*' is connected with '*bei*', and so '*ich bin*' means in its turn 'I reside' or 'dwell amidst' [*ich wohne, halte mich auf bei*] the world, as that which is familiar to me in such and such a way [*als dem so und so Vertrauten*]. (BT 80 (54))

In a clearly related passage in HCT, we read

Being as being-in and 'I am' means dwelling amid [*bei*] . . . and 'in' primarily does not signify anything spatial at all but means primarily *being familiar with* [*vertraut sein mit*]. (HCT 158)

This might seem to press upon us a 'cognitive' rather than a 'spatial' construal of Being-in-the-world. But a careful reading of the above remarks point to something more nuanced, which our discussion of *Hinblicke* also helps elucidate.

Just as our schooling in 'traditional philosophy' may encourage us to construe 'in' as 'spatial containment' (HCT 157), so too it may encourage us to construe 'familiarity' as already-possessed knowledge. But this would be to overlook the connotations of intimacy that '*vertraut*' carries (a word derived from '*trauen*', to trust, sometimes to marry),[36] and also do some disservice to its translation as 'familiar', by overlooking the connotations of family and home that the English word conveys.[37] Does that call for a picture of *Dasein* as first and foremost 'practically engaged' with the world around it? Or through a 'background' of skills? Before leaping to those conclusions (in which Chapter 7 will suggest there is some truth, despite Part II's critical discussion),

---

[34] Cf., e.g., CT 7–8 and BPP 271, 297.   [35] Cf. also BT 419 (368).
[36] Kisiel translates '*vertrauterweise pflegen*' as 'taking care in intimate familiarity' (HCT 158).
[37] In his discussion of authenticity, Heidegger will also talk of *Dasein's* '*Unheimlichkeit*' (cf. BT 233–4 (188–9)), with its connotation of 'not-being-at-home'. Though important, that notion will not concern us here.

let us explore how our discussion of *Hinblicke* itself suggests an understanding of, and a case for the need for, our 'always already' being 'intimate' with—indeed 'amidst'—entities around us.

In the previous section it was noted that we can make no sense of *Hinblicke* being 'read off' objects. as any such 'reading' would require that a *Hinblick* already be 'operative'. But, for related reasons, it also makes no sense to imagine evaluating the 'fit' or 'correspondence' of a *Hinblick* with the objects that are there for us to encounter. To see to the bottom of this 'impossibility', let us first consider how our earlier notion of an 'original having' leads us to parallel conclusions.

Heidegger talks of Being-in-the-world as 'a basic phenomenon' and as 'not resolvable further [*weiter auflösbar*]' (PS 256); this would seem to be a necessary characteristic of 'original havings' also: in viewing them as '*original*' we rule out the possibility that the engagement with entities that such 'havings' embody might be 'resolved' into forms of engagement that other 'havings' embody. Among the implications of that (an implication which will have importance later) is that there is no further or broader perspective or 'having' from or through which to survey the entities revealed by a particular 'original having'. For that same reason, we also cannot see this understanding and engagement as arrived at through some other, 'earlier'[38] understanding, or observation, of those entities: it cannot be seen as having been 'read off' those entities. Recognizing that such an 'arrival' is a myth, one might say—echoing Sections 2.3 and 5.3—that we *live in* such 'havings'. Moreover, we cannot come to see how an 'original having' is applicable to a particular domain of objects, because seeing such a 'fit' would require that we grasp that domain independently of its disclosure through that 'original having', when, *ex hypothesi*, there is no other way of grasping that domain of entities.

Notably, we find here a sense—if a rather abstract one—for the idea of a non-subjectivist *a priori*. A key feature of the modes of understanding and entities in question is that there is no such thing as encountering the entities in question other than through these modes. The latter can be seen as embodying an *a priori* species of understanding in that we can make no

---

[38] In a sense, my later discussion of whether such understanding can be legitimated or questioned on the basis of a 'fit' with what it reveals focuses on problems associated with the notion of a 'later'—reflective—understanding.

sense of the idea of finding out 'more'—through other 'means'—about these entities that might subsequently undermine the understanding embodied in these modes of understanding, or of the idea of learning *about* these entities when one comes to master these modes of understanding: rather, one learns *of* them.

That final formulation suggests an important point that our presentation so far may otherwise disguise. It concerns whether the crucial issue—and the confusion at bottom—set out above is an epistemological one: that we cannot *evaluate* how 'original havings' or *Hinblicke* fit the entities that we grasp through them. Recall Heidegger's example of the ordering of a set of spheres; one *Hinblick* that might be adopted would allow us to order them by size (as opposed to by colour, or material, say). Now imagine the project of evaluating the fit or correspondence of that *Hinblick* with the spheres it is meant to allow us to order. To ask that question we must have a determinate sense of 'how these spheres are'—how, one might say, they are ordered; but upon which *Hinblick* ought we to draw now? The colour-*Hinblick*? The material-*Hinblick*? We surely have no reason to think that the size-*Hinblick* ought to allow one to grasp the spheres as ordered by colour or material. The only seemingly sensible answer is to adopt the size-*Hinblick*; but I say 'seemingly' because we would now seem to be evaluating a possible 'fit' between ordering spheres by size and the spheres ordered by size. The 'issue' we might have imagined under the title, 'the fit or correspondence of a *Hinblick* with the objects that are there for us to encounter', turns out to be one to which we can assign no clear sense. It turns out that when we imagined adopting this 'view-from-sideways-on', we confronted not merely something we could not 'evaluate' or 'measure' (but at which we could only 'wonder', to echo Cooper); rather we had no clear idea of what we wanted, or were trying, to do.[39]

In the collapsing of the notional 'gaps' that we might imagine are crossed when *Dasein* comes to master *Hinblicke* or when *Dasein* comes to appreciate how *Hinblicke* fit the entities revealed, a certain notional 'distance' of *Dasein* from the entities it understands also collapses. As such 'views-from-sideways-on' turn out to make no sense, one might say that, if we 'have' these entities at all, then we 'live in' the relevant *Hinblicke* and 'amongst' or 'amidst' the relevant entities. To echo Section 2.4's remarks on the 'environmental

---

[39] McManus 2006: sec. 3.5 discusses what I take to be parallel concerns.

experience', they are already 'around' us and the 'world' or 'space' which they inhabit is part of the very fabric of the Being of we creatures who intend them. If they are not so present for one then, whatever else one might be, one is not a master of the relevant *Hinblicke* and not intentionally related to the relevant entities: one does not instantiate those particular forms of subjectivity. Section 7.2 will return to this issue; but now I want to turn to Heidegger's well-known view of scepticism. I will sketch a basis for that view which arises out of our earlier discussion, but a basis which also identifies worries that that view then raises.

5.4.2 *Heidegger's critique of scepticism*

In our earlier discussion we can see emerging a basis for a transcendental argument of sorts, according to which things cannot be as bad as we might sceptically imagine: we may worry whether our beliefs correspond to reality, but the possibility of such a correspondence seems to require that we subjects already be familiar, be-at-home, with the entities around us. For that reason, the radical sceptical question cannot be formulated coherently: it 'persists only on the basis of a constant misunderstanding of the mode of Being of the one who raises the question' (HCT 215).[40]

But dispensing with scepticism has an unfortunate habit of coming at the cost of idealism; in order to secure knowledge for ourselves we make a Faustian pact with 'the foul fiend incarnate'. This may be a useful point at which to confront some particularly striking versions of the idealist anxieties that we have recurrently encountered. One such version is the following: it is all very well being led by *a priori* considerations to the conclusion that we must 'live in' 'intimate familiarity [*vertrauterweise*]' (HCT 158) with entities, but how can this be so, since—not to put too fine a point on it—we did not create these entities in the first place?[41] There may seem to be what one might call a worrying *cosiness* to the notion of

---

[40] Cf. also BT 246–7 (202), 249 (205) and HCT 161.
[41] Relatedly, plenty of work would have to be done to show whether—and if so, how—the 'deduction' above (that scepticism cannot be coherently formulated) can help us deal with the kinds of thought experiment that can make scepticism seem unavoidable: for example, what about the 'person' who (in some sense) experiences being taught and (in some sense) coming to learn a method of description (say, to anticipate our later discussion, the use of a measuring rod), but who is actually a brain in a vat? Though the final section of my (forthcoming-b) makes some comments on this, I think this is a very serious concern.

Being-in-the-world, it seeming to undermine not only scepticism but also the notion that human knowledge is finite knowledge, that human understanding did not find itself 'already out there with entities', but instead has had to work its way 'out' and continues to need to do so. Viewing the worry from another angle, how can we account for the kind of 'anticipation' upon which Heidegger insists, this 'prior' 'having of that for which we search', without needing to abandon—in something like the way that Kant does—the notion that what we know through such an 'anticipation' is 'how things are in themselves'?

Crispin Wright articulates a related worry, arguing that the rejection of the notion of a certain 'intermediacy' in our engagement with the world makes a nonsense of what he calls our 'conception of [our] cognitive *locality*': 'the idea of a range of states of affairs and events existing beyond the bounds of [our] own direct awareness' (2004: 52). Through such intermediacy, 'the ultimate justification for one kind of claim ... rests upon defeasible inference from information of another sort' (p. 28), as, to take one particular example, one might suppose one's knowledge of physical objects rests upon one's knowledge of one's own representations. A motivation for rejecting such a 'justificational architecture' is clear enough in that it invites sceptical worries; but

Globally to avoid the [above] justificational architecture ... would be to forgo all conception of oneself as having position in a world extending, perhaps infinitely, beyond one's cognitive horizon. In particular, it would be to surrender all conception of our own specific situation within a broader objective world extending *spatially and temporally* beyond us. (p. 52)[42]

I will postpone a response to these worries until the work of Chapter 6 is done. That will offer a more concrete sense of what might be meant by some of the abstract conclusions that Heidegger reaches, and to which the *a priori* considerations of Sections 5.2, 5.3, and the present section's final subsection lead. It will show how those conclusions might preserve for us a sense of the 'finitude' of our knowing, and might—just might—be true.

---

[42] Such a thought seems to play a role in Tugendhat's insistence that 'talk about truth and untruth ... is only called for because our relation to beings is a specifically mediate one' (1969: 234).

5.4.3 Truth I: The puzzles of BT sec. 44

But there are other puzzles with which Chapter 6 will help us deal. These arise out of Heidegger's remarks on truth. These remarks are controversial and well-known—best known, in fact—from their presentation in sec. 44 of BT, which draws Division One of that book to a close and draws many of its strands of thought together.[43] According to what Heidegger calls the 'traditional conception of truth', the "locus" of truth is assertion (judgement), and 'the essence of truth lies in the "agreement" of the judgement with its object' (BT 257 (214)). Heidegger claims that the 'traditional conception', which finds canonical expression through Aquinas as *adaequatio intellectus et rei*, is, for all its influence, 'by no means... primary' (BT 56 (33)) because 'assertion is grounded in *Dasein*'s... *disclosedness*', which 'embraces the whole of that structure-of-Being which has become explicit in the course of Division One' (BT 269 (226), 264 (221)).

There is a familiar story extractable from BT to which Sections 3.2 and 3.4 alluded, and from which I am hoping to help us keep our distance: it is that our engagement with the world is 'fundamentally practical', assertions emerge only out of processes of 'interpretation' that themselves only come into play when that engagement undergoes a certain kind of 'break-down', and the resultant assertions reveal the *Vorhanden*, the 'present-at-hand'. Each of these claims has a textual basis, and my reading could be seen as assigning particular senses to all three; but I will seek to present an alternative basis for Heidegger's judgement of the 'traditional conception of truth' as 'superficial' (PS 10) to that which such more familiar readings of the above claims suggest—not least because of the significant interpretive and philosophical problems that they raise, and which Sections 3.2 and 3.4 have explained.

Sec. 44 of BT begins its case for thinking the 'traditional conception of truth' 'superficial' by asking '*What else is tacitly posited in this relational totality of the* adaequatio intellectus et rei?'(BT 258 (215)) Indeed '[i]n what way is this relation possible as a relation between *intellectus* and *res*?' (BT 259 (216)) But why think it *im*possible? OET (PM) 282[44] points us towards one familiar philosophical gulf:

---

[43] I can also only address a small part of the large and complex literature that examines sec. 44's claims and some important, recent contributions I will not discuss here are Wrathall 1999, Dreyfus 2001, Carman 2003 and 2007, Cerbone 2005, and W. H. Smith 2007.

[44] 1924's BBA and 1926's OET (PM) clearly constitute earlier drafts of some of BT sec. 44's most difficult passages.

How can there be an agreement between the inside of the soul and the outside of the object?

And BT points us towards another: 'the ontologically unclarified separation of the Real and the ideal'. We do not say that the 'judging as a Real psychical process' is true—that is just 'present-at-hand or not'—but rather that its 'ideal content' is: but '*How are we to take ontologically the relation between an ideal entity and something that is Real and present-at-hand*', in the cases of both 'the Real Thing . . . which is judged about' and 'the Real act of judgement' (BT 259 (216–17))?

At this point, Heidegger turns to a puzzling discussion of 'the phenomenal context of demonstration', where, he insists, 'the relationship of agreement must become visible'. It begins with the 'proposal', if one can call it that, that the assertion, 'The picture on the wall is hanging askew',

> demonstrates itself when the man who makes it, turns round and perceives the picture hanging askew on the wall.

What Heidegger seems to feel the need to insist on is that, prior to perceiving the picture, when the asserter might be said to be 'merely representing' to himself the picture being so, the man is, nonetheless, 'related' not to a representation—'a "picture" of that Real Thing which is on the wall'—but 'rather . . . to the Real picture on the wall': 'What one has in mind is the Real picture, and nothing else' (BT 260 (217)). We are familiar enough with attacks on representationalist theories of mind; but what Heidegger seems to be presenting—in some sense—in their place is unclear. We confront formulations that seem, by turns, truistic and absurd. What is clear is that Heidegger attaches great importance to them; the passage is, for example, awash with italics:

> In carrying out such a demonstration . . . the entity itself which one has in mind shows itself *just as* it is in itself; that is to say, it shows that it, in its selfsameness, is just as *it* gets pointed out in the assertion as being—just as *it* gets uncovered as being . . . The Being-uncovered [*Entdeckt-sein*] of the entity itself—*that entity* in the 'how' of its uncoveredness[—] . . . is confirmed when that which is put forward in the assertion (namely the entity itself) shows itself *as that very same thing*. 'Confirmation' signifies *the entity's showing itself in its selfsameness*. (BT 261 (218))

These remarks can seem trivial, 'proposing' that when you confirm the truth of a claim, the entity itself which one had in mind shows itself to be just as the assertion said it was. But they can also seem absurd. Familiar forms of 'direct realism' propose that 'when we perceive mind-independent physical objects', 'we are directly or immediately aware of them' (Hoffman 2002: 163); Heidegger goes beyond that already-contentious view by asserting that we are 'related' to the 'Real Thing' not only when we perceive it but also when we merely represent it to ourselves. To point to the most obvious objection, what if it turns out that 'the entity which one has in mind' does not exist 'outside'? This worry elicits from Heidegger what might seem to be an evasive backing away from the strong notion that 'the entity which one has in mind' is the '*very same thing*' as that which one finds 'outside':

Even if that about which an assertion is made should turn out not to be, an empty illusion, this in no ways gainsays the intentionality of the structure of assertion but only demonstrates it. For when I judge *about* an appearance I am still related to entities. (BPP 207)

In place of the strong claim, we find talk of the need for the subject of 'an assertion [to] be *somehow* given' (BPP 208, italics added) or 'intended at some point' (L 184), of our needing to grasp the '*type of Being* of the entity about which [one] is speaking' (BPP 211, cf. 314), 'making assertions about X [being] only possible on the basis of *having to do with X*' (MFL 126), 'some access to the entity, that is, the tendency and intention to understand and possess it' (L 183); or we read that the asserter 'must in general live in the comportment of uncovering' (L 183), having 'an intention toward seeing uncovered entities' (PS 443).[45] Consider finally the following picturesque example:

Human *Dasein* can... only make discoveries in the narrow sense, e.g. of an island unknown until now, because it qua *Dasein* already tarries alongside entities, e.g. by sailing the sea. (EP 121)

So one of our tasks will be to determine just to what the requirement envisaged here amounts.

---

[45] Cf. also HCT 31, PS 416–17 and EP 152–3.

But Heidegger has yet more striking claims to make. One I will call the 'Dependency Claim':

'There is' truth only in so far as Dasein is and so long as Dasein is. (BT 269 (226)).

He goes on:

> Newton's laws, the principle of contradiction, any truth whatsoever—these are true only as long as *Dasein* is. Before there was any *Dasein*, there was no truth; nor will there be any after *Dasein* is no more.

Heidegger then seems to temper these shocking claims by saying that, prior to their discovery, Newton's laws were 'not "true"'—now in scare quotes—and also not 'false', and that this does not imply that 'there were no such entities as have been uncovered and pointed out by those laws' (BT 269 (227)). He declares that '*all truth is relative to Dasein's Being*' (BT 270 (227)) but also that this 'does not endanger objectivity [or] objective truth' (EP 155), nor mean that 'the Being-true of "truths" has in any way been diminished' (BT 269 (227)). But where then does that leave us? And how does truth's supposed presupposition of *Dasein's* existence sit with what seems to be a corresponding claim about *Dasein's* existence 'presupposing' truth?

We must 'make' the presupposition of truth because it *is* one that has been 'made' already with the Being of the 'we'. (BT 271 (228))

In one of the section's most evocative formulations, Heidegger tells us that '*Dasein is "in the truth"*' (BT 263 (221)).[46] Striking though that is, Heidegger goes further still when he declares a page later that, in addition, *Dasein* 'is in "untruth"' (BT 264 (222)).

To this catalogue of puzzles we should add one more—one that has received more attention than all of the others mentioned. Heidegger presents *Dasein's* 'disclosedness' as not only 'grounding' the notion of truth as correspondence, but also as itself '"true" in a still more primordial sense' (BT 263 (220)); but, as Tugendhat has famously asked, 'with what right and with what meaning' (1969: 228) does he use that word of this supposedly

---

[46] Cf. also, e.g., PS 16, HCT 52, and BPP 216.

deeper 'uncovering' or 'disclosure'? Is it right that he 'simply gave the word "truth" another meaning' (p. 236)?[47,48]

A proper response to these puzzles must await Chapter 6 and will be spelt out in Chapter 7; but some of the ideas that the present chapter has reviewed should, I hope, have already given us some sense of how we might address them. The proposal that '*Dasein is "in the truth"*' (BT 263 (221)) should at least have a familiar ring, even if its sense and plausibility remain to be settled. The notion of the *Hinblick* is also at work here. Sec. 44 (a) denies that the relation between *intellectus* and *res* could be one of similarity or equality, or be compared to that of a sign and what it indicates ('the road-pointing sign does not agree with the village that it points to' (OET (PM) 281)); but there is one feature of numerical equalities that Heidegger does see in the *adaequatio intellectus et rei*: such numbers 'are equal with regard to the question of "how much?" [*im Hinblick auf das Wieviel*]' (BT 258 (215)). He also asks, '[i]n the *adaequatio*', when 'something gets related',

what is that with regard to which [*im Hinblick worauf*] it agrees?... With regard to what [*Im Hinblick worauf*] do *intellectus* and *res* agree? (BT 258 (215–16))

The 'direct realism' of BT 261 (218) ought not to be so strange to us either, echoing as it does the Husserlian understanding of truth that we have already considered. The *textual* connection is clear enough: at the end of the 'direct realism' passage quoted above, Heidegger refers explicitly to the discussion of truth in Husserl's 6th *Logical Investigation*,[49] and in the corresponding section of OET (PM) (p. 284), Heidegger draws explicitly on notions taken from that discussion. But noting this connection also immediately has some *philosophical* pay-off. For example, we can dispel straightaway some of the mystery of BT 260–1 (217–18) by considering it as a response to what might seem the most natural analysis of 'empty intending',

---

[47] To avoid confusion, I have placed 'truth' in quotation marks here; Tugendhat does not and Macann's translation reproduces this.

[48] In what follows, I will focus on what I take to be the illuminating core set of notions that Heidegger has to offer in his early discussions of truth and not on some of the dubious ways in which he occasionally expresses or defends those notions. For example, he argues that 'what first makes correctness possible must with more original legitimacy be taken as the essence of truth' (OET 142, cf. also BT 263 (220)). Cf. Künne 2003: 106–7 for criticism of this argument and Lafont 2000: ch. 3 for criticism of the '*strong* thesis' that it is meant to support (though I will argue—in response to Tugendhat's criticism—that describing the 'prior disclosure' that 'makes correctness possible' as 'something altogether different' (Lafont 2000: 173) is not quite fair either).

[49] Heidegger continued to refer to the 6th *Investigation* throughout his career; cf. e.g. TB 76–9.

one which understands that feat as one's having a representation of the object that one might then go on to perceive. That passage's response may seem to miss the point of the proposed analysis. Heidegger emphasises that we don't intend—consciously focus on, as it were—any such representation; that's fine, one might respond, as a bit of 'mere phenomenology'; but the point is that we intend the object *through* the representation. But, crucially, how do we do that? If we reply, 'Because it is a representation *of that object*', the next question we face is: what makes that particular object the object *of* that representation? As Husserl asks of imagist versions of the above analysis, '[w]hat... enables us to go beyond the image... and refer to the latter *as* an image of a certain extraconscious object?' (2001: vol. 2, 125) To be the object *of* a particular representation is to be the object intuition of which 'fulfils' that representation and this connection is also presupposed—not explained—when we bring representations into our story.

This points us to the single most important contribution that our earlier discussions have made: we already have a sense of why Heidegger regards the 'traditional conception of truth' as 'superficial'. The discussions of Sections 5.2 and 5.3 have both pointed us to reasons for believing that the possibility of any such correspondence presupposes another form of understanding of the world which cannot itself be understood as the appreciation of such a correspondence. The next section will show another route by which Heidegger reaches the same conclusion; he does so drawing explicitly on the motif of measurement and pointing to a sense in which the propositional and its distinctive kind of truth are 'founded'. But, in a way with which the reader should now be familiar, the section will also lead—as Sections 5.2 and 5.3 did—to idealist anxieties. Chapter 7 will provide a response to these, along with the remaining mysteries of BT sec. 44, building on the analysis set out in the next chapter.

5.4.4 Truth II: Measures and methods of comparison

The motif of measurement runs explicitly through many of Heidegger's discussions of truth. In MFL, he glosses the 'traditional conception of truth' as follows:

Truth was defined as *homoiōsis, adaequatio*, as adequation to [*Angleichung an*] something, as measurement by [*Messung an*] something. (MFL 124)

BBA provides the following intriguing gloss on the problem of the 'gulf' that OET (PM) 282 (quoted in Section 5.4.3) identified:

How is a correspondence of thought with reality supposed to be established if thought is something occurring in the subject, in consciousness, or in the soul? How can I measure [*messen*] this psychic aspect, that is, this aspect of consciousness, against the external world if I have not first recognized this external world as the standard of measurement [*Maßstab*]? (BBA 220)

And in FCM, Heidegger identifies the deeper issue in comparison with which the 'traditional conception of truth' is 'superficial' as follows:

The old received definition of truth: *veritas est adaequatio ad rem*, *homoiosis*, measuring up [*Anmessung*], conformity [*Angleichung*] of thinking to the matter about which it thinks ... is merely a starting point [*Ansatz*] ... It is merely the starting point for the question: in what in general is the possibility of measuring up to [*Anmessung an*] something grounded? (FCM 342)

In the roughly contemporaneous OET, Heidegger proposes the need for a prior 'openness' [*Offenständigkeit*]' to, a prior mastery of, that which we might describe using an assertion, through which the 'assertion is invested with its correctness', is made something that invites comparison with that particular region of reality; only through such an 'openness'

can what is opened up really become the measure [*zum Richtmaß werden*] for the presentative comparison [*vor-stellende Angleichung*]. Open comportment must let itself be assigned this measure [*dieses Maß*]. This means that it must take over a pregiven measure [*eines Vorgabe des Richtmaßes*] for all presenting [*Vorstellen*]. (OET 142)

I would suggest that the early Wittgenstein makes a similar point when he says that a 'method of portrayal must be completely determinate before we can compare reality with [a] proposition ... in order to see whether it is true or false':

The method of comparison [*Vergleichsmethode*] must be given me before I can make the comparison. (1979: 23)

But quite what the issue is here and how it bears on the 'traditional conception of truth' are questions that need to be handled with care.

In PS, Heidegger sketches 'a certain line of thinking' according to which 'a concept of truth, which determines truth as the correspondence of the soul, the subject, with the object, is nonsense':

For I must have already known the matter in question in order to be able to say that it corresponds with the judgement. I must have already known the objective in order to measure the subjective up to it. The truth of 'having already known' is thus presupposed for the truth of knowing. (PS 18)

This passage, which points to a deeper kind of 'truth'—'the truth of "having already known"'—which the 'traditional conception of truth', with its focus on 'the truth of knowing', presupposes, may seem simply to echo the following familiar objection: 'It would be odd, wouldn't it, to test whether the proposition that Toby sighed was true by taking the fact that Toby sighed and seeing whether the proposition fitted it?' (C. J. F. Williams 1976: 76).[50] This objection is less than compelling, because it mistakes the 'traditional conception's' attempted *definition* of truth—a specification of what it is for a proposition to be true—for a *criterion* of truth—a specification of how one might go about determining whether a particular proposition is true.[51]

But Sections 5.2 and 5.3 suggest a different construal of the above passages. For there to be a determinate matter of fact about whether there is a 'correspondence' or 'adequation' of *intellectus* and *rei*, it must be settled which *rei* are relevant to the truth or falsehood of the particular proposition that the *intellectus* is entertaining; there must be, so to speak, a *way* in which that proposition corresponds or fails to correspond to the world. I suggest that Heidegger's point is that, without a method or standard of comparison in place, a question of correspondence is not so much undecidable or unconfirmable as, to echo L 284 (quoted in Section 5.3), 'insufficiently determined'. Setting about trying to settle whether a proposition corresponds to, measures up to, reality presupposes an answer to the prior question '[w]ith regard to what [*im Hinblick worauf*] do *intellectus* and *res* agree?' (BT 258 (215–16), quoted above) Without a *Hinblick* in place, one's predicament is not that of being unable to *tell whether* *intellectus* and *rei* correspond but not having anything to *try* to tell.

---

[50] For a similar criticism of 'copy' theories of cognition, cf. DSTCM 91.
[51] Lafont has argued that Heidegger repeatedly succumbs to just such a confusion, resulting in an 'exceedingly dubious' 'epistemologization of truth' (2000: 155, 149)—a reading which provides encouragement for, for example, verificationist readings of Heidegger such as Okrent 1988. I criticize Lafont's argument in my (forthcoming-a), touch upon some of her other concerns below (cf., e.g., ch. 6 n. 27 and ch. 7 n. 3.)), and—in Section 7.4—discuss another potential misunderstanding that might arise out of the 'method' formulations that passages presented above employ.

Several now familiar negative outcomes emerge again here. The understanding that mastery of these measures embodies cannot be read off the objects or states of affairs they reveal. Instead it must be 'pregiven' for any entity capable of relating intentionally to those objects or states of affairs; and, in 'founding' our grasp of correspondences, it cannot itself rest on the grasp of a correspondence with—an 'adequation to'—objects or states of affairs. But now-familiar worries emerge again also. PS 18's 'truth of "having already known"' clearly raises idealist worries of the sort that we have frequently encountered and that passage actually concludes that this 'truth' 'is non-sensical' (and that the 'traditional conception of truth' which presupposes it 'cannot be maintained'). More fundamentally, the mastery of a *Hinblick* that allows us to 'measure' the world clearly cannot itself come in the form of a grasp of yet more 'truths of knowing', since such questions of correspondence are only 'sufficiently determined' if such *Hinblicke* are already in place.

Idealist worries of a recognizably con-formist character also loom. Echoing Kant's discussion that we considered in Section 2.1, one might ask what it is that renders entities and the minds that contemplate them fit for such an 'adequation', a correspondence. We have already touched upon one account of the 'suitability of *adaequatio intellectus ad rem*' (IPR 139), though one that Kant saw as a 'pious or speculative figment of the imagination' (Kant 1968: 114, quoted above).[52] Heidegger's IPR lectures trace that account in detail in Aquinas' *De Veritate* (1994). According to it, the world is thinkable—is apt to be the subject matter of true or false beliefs—because it was created by a thinker:

[O]nly insofar as a *res* is *qua ordinata ad intellectum divinum* [only insofar as a thing exists as ordained to the divine intellect], can it be a *mensura* [measure] at all for a human *intellectus*. (IPR 130)

In creation, the created thing is 'determined by' 'the *intellectus practicus*', the *intellectus* 'that conceives a plan'; as such, this intellect is 'the measure of the thing' (IPR 129–30). As Kant puts it, 'divine knowledge' provides 'the prototype of the thing' (quoted in Section 2.1 above). Having been made to match such a measure, the thing is itself fit to provide a measure by which a belief about it may itself be measured, a human claim to knowledge

---

[52] Cf. also Kant 1961 B 166–8 for other criticisms.

rendered true or false. Having been made to match God's plan—His vision of how things should be—it is fit to match our plans—our human visions of how things are. In this way, '*[r]es ergo naturalis inter duos intellectus constituta* [a natural thing is thus set up between two intellects]':

> [T]here are proportions of measure as to how *intellectus* and *res* can be respectively *mensurans* [measuring] and *mensuratum* [measured]. The *res* itself is principally related to *two intellectus*. *Secundum intellectum humanum* [according to the human intellect] the *res* is the *mensurans*. Knowledge that grasps something measures itself on the thing to be grasped. Insofar as the same thing is regarded *secundum intellectum divinum* [according to the divine intellect], the *res* is *mensurata* [measured], that is to say, *artificiata* or better *creata, causata* [produced or, better, created, caused]. (IPR 130)

When a human being's belief about a thing is true—that is to say, when that proposition measures up to that object—this is then a '*derivatum*' of a prior truth, the prior measuring up of that object to a 'plan' of God's (IPR 137). As OET later puts it, 'the possibility of truth as human knowledge is grounded in the fact that matter and proposition... are fitted to each other on the basis of the unity of the divine plan of creation': '[b]ecause of agreement with the Creator, there is also agreement [of entities] *among one another*' (OET 139, 139 n. a), human belief and its also-created objects.[53]

This account offers, then, an answer to BT Section 44's question, '[i]n what way is this relation [of 'adequation'] possible as a relation between *intellectus* and *res*?' Many today will view this account as Kant did. But then if that does not provide the answer, how are we to deal with this question? Along with exploring the many other puzzles that this and previous chapters have raised, the following chapter will explore how the significance of this question is transformed in the light of Heidegger's ontology of the intellect as 'Being-in-the-world', by its vision, not of things 'set up between intellects', but of intellect as a being-amongst (*Sein-bei*) things.

---

[53] What prepared the ground for this view was the fact that 'ancient philosophy interprets Being in the horizon of production', the roots of our notion of 'essence' in that of the manufacturer's 'plan' or 'measure [*Richtmaß*], as guide and standard': it is 'as if ancient ontology... were cut to fit the Christian world-view and interpretation of that which *is* as *ens creatum*' (BPP 286, 106, 118).

6

The 'Founding' of Measurement in Understanding without Fit

The previous chapter provided an abstract account which assigns senses to central elements of Heidegger's fundamental ontology, including the notion of 'Being-in-the-world', his critique of scepticism, and his view of the 'traditional conception of truth' as 'superficial'.

But because of the abstract character of that account, and the remarkable paucity—but for the occasional hammer and lectern—of examples in Heidegger's early writings,[1] significant challenges remain. Firstly, we are still in need of a concrete sense of how what Chapter 5 has abstractly argued must be so can be so and of how the puzzles that BT sec. 44 (set out in Section 5.4.3) can be resolved. Secondly, and relatedly, to the extent to which we do have a concrete sense of what Chapter 5 envisages, it would seem to push us towards a species of idealism. Thirdly, Chapter 5 has assigned no clear place to the theme of 'the practical', as we have encountered it in the Primacy of Practice Claim and its special case, the Primacy of Scientific Practice Claim. I have raised doubts about how well understood this theme is, but a theme of some such sort is undeniably present in Heidegger's work; so how might Chapter 5's account accommodate it? Fourthly, Rouse and Blattner's construals of that theme led to their renouncing Heidegger's considered view of the sciences, but it remains to be shown that Chapter 5's account is any better placed to retain that view, for reasons related to the second worry above.

The present chapter attempts to take on these challenges. It focuses less closely on Heidegger's text than do previous and subsequent chapters, and

---

[1] For instance, in search of examples that fit her critical account, Lafont turns to discussion in lectures from 1935/36 (WT).

my concern here is, in a sense, to fill a gap that those texts leave—a gap which, as Part II argued, other readings have filled with proposals that are hard to identify, implausible, or inconsistent with Heidegger's own claims. I attempt to offer here an alternative 'filling'—one which is not only largely consistent with Heidegger's texts, but which also helps resolve many of the puzzles that those texts pose and which previous chapters have identified. The story I offer is also, I will suggest, not without philosophical plausibility. It provides a more concrete demonstration of how the making of assertions might indeed be said to be 'founded' in modes of understanding which provide a 'prior' or 'anticipatory' 'measure' (as the Prior Projection Claim requires), and which, crucially, cannot themselves be seen as 'corresponding' to their 'objects'. It takes as its central examples assertions using which we describe simple characteristics of the physical environment, which I think we might reasonably see as illustrating the 'extreme' form of assertion that the *Logik* lectures identify—'a determining *qua* assertion about what is there, what occurs'—and oppose to, for example, 'assertions in and for a practical function' (L 156 n. 131, quoted in Section 3.2). But, nonetheless, it also demonstrates that the understanding in which such assertions are 'founded' is recognizably 'practical' in form (as the Primacy of Practice Claim requires).[2] My strategy could be seen as one of taking Heidegger's measurement motif (and, in particular, its development in Section 5.4.4) literally, since the forms of 'practical' understanding to which I will draw our attention are those embodied in mastery of practices of measurement; but, in adopting this focus, I follow the prompting of Heidegger's 'activist' proposals about science that Section 3.3 presented: that 'theoretical research is not without a *praxis* of its own' (BT 409 (358)), its results 'made possible' by 'the antecedent, unobjective, founding projection of the constitution of the Being of entities, which stakes out a field' (EP 199). The perspective that emerges is very much in the spirit of Heidegger's considered view of 'scientific knowing', as 'an autonomous way of being involved with' the world, 'solely aimed at entities themselves', and revelatory of 'a new abundance of things' (quoted in Section 3.3).

What will also become apparent is how the practices in question 'constitute'—in the specific sense Section 1.1 spelt out—the objects that they allow us to describe. Moreover, these practices would appear to be instances of

---

[2] Section 6.3.1 will explain the caution manifest in my scare-quoting 'practical' here and elsewhere.

another of Part I's central concepts, that of 'original havings'; and this insight will be important in showing that the account given here does not lead to a form of idealism. Instead, drawing on Section 2.1's sketch of the notion of intelligibility as con-formity, I will attempt to set out a clear sense of just what it might mean to 'reject both realism and idealism', and of how Heidegger's claim to do just that could be true.

To break down this work section by section, Section 6.1 identifies a mode of understanding that Chapter 5 has argued must be there to be found: namely, a mode of understanding onto which we cannot project a correspondence structure. That mode, I propose, is that which is found in paradigmatic cases of the *Zuhanden*. Moreover, in connection with instances of such understanding, con-formist questions—and hence their proposed realist and idealist answers—make no sense. In this way we acquire an initial sense of the significance of the Primacy of Practice Claim and of how one might 'reject realism and idealism'. But what of those modes of understanding through which we recognize the *Vorhanden*? Might con-formist questions have sense here? And what of the claim that those modes of understanding are 'founded' in the *Zuhanden*? Section 6.2 argues that answering the latter question also answers the other two; it proposes that when we reflect on our practices of measurement, we can see how the Primacy of Practice Claims has sense here too, as indeed does the Prior Projection Claim and without that entailing a form of idealism: measurement is made possible by modes of understanding that both are naturally labelled 'practical' and embody in a recognizable way 'projections of the Being' of that which is measured, but in connection with which con-formist questions of intelligibility again make no sense. Section 6.3 will elaborate on this picture in responding to a number of objections that it might seem to invite;[3] and Chapters 7 and 8 will spell out explicitly how this account helps us deal with the difficulties that we have encountered in previous chapters.

But the present chapter has one further aim. It is a concern of mine to question the notion that Heidegger is, in some way, hostile to the sciences;[4] he is, nonetheless, also concerned to reveal a way in which scientific practices can obscure as well as illuminate our world and a 'forgetfulness

---

[3] My (forthcoming-a) considers other potential objections.
[4] Cf., e.g., Philipse's claims that 'Heidegger... calls for a phenomenology that essentially adopts an anti-scientific attitude', and that, for Heidegger, 'science turns out to belong to a special modification of *Dasein* called its falling (*Verfallen*)' (1998: 115, 114).

of Being' in which he suggests the sciences partake.[5] To understand how there can be these two sides to the Heideggerian story and how that story might yet become a plausible one about science as we know it, we must turn once again, I suggest, to his discussion of authenticity.[6] It is also here that we must look if we are to make sense of BT's claim that *Dasein* 'is in "untruth"' (BT 264 (222)).

An important part of what follows is an attempt to undermine the notion of a certain kind of evaluation of our most basic descriptive practices—an evaluation of how well they 'fit' the objects that they reveal. But Section 6.4 will show how my account still leaves room for a critical evaluation of how such descriptive frameworks are used. A certain kind of pernicious emptiness can enter our discourse—an emptiness which I use my earlier discussion of measurement to throw into relief and which, in Section 6.4.3, I suggest is naturally characterized in the terms that Heidegger uses in characterizing inauthenticity. When inauthentic—a condition into which the working scientist is constantly in danger of falling—our words are unintelligible, nonsensical; but, to adapt Wittgenstein's words, 'it is not as it were [their] sense that is senseless' (1967: sec. 500), their saying something that is ill-suited to making claims about the world, something that fails to achieve a 'con-formist' 'fit' with the world's possibilities. Instead, our words descend into an 'indeterminate emptiness' (HCT 269); they become 'idle talk' (BT 211 (167)); and Chapter 9 will draw analogies with such failures in clarifying Heidegger's understanding of philosophical confusion and the metaphilosophical outlook that this understanding suggests.

6.1 Understanding without fit: Manipulating the *Zuhanden*

Chapter 5 showed how Heidegger leads us—from a number of directions—to view as 'superficial' forms of understanding of the world in which we recognize a correspondence or fit between representations of ours and that

---

[5] Cf. CTSH 50, BBA 229, HCT 1–2, PICPR 23–4, and EP 224.

[6] Thus while Dreyfus' notion that Heidegger presents a kind of 'plural realism' (cf. Dreyfus 1991: 262) seems to me to be on the right lines, we will not get a full appreciation of Heidegger's view of scientific knowledge as long as we try, as Dreyfus has until relatively recently (cf. his 2000a and 2000b), to keep Heidegger's discussion of authenticity at arm's length.

world because entertaining the possibility of any such correspondence or fit seems to presuppose another form of understanding of the world which cannot itself be understood as the appreciation of such a correspondence. I will suggest that, in his exploration of the *Zuhanden*, Heidegger reveals that deeper understanding.

Heidegger draws our attention to a number of aspects of our understanding of the *Zuhanden*. For example, when we come to master tools, they acquire a 'transparency' for us; in our 'primordial relationship' to it, the hammer 'withdraws' (BT 99 (69)):

The less we just stare at the hammer-Thing, and the more we seize hold of it and use it, the more primordial does our relationship to it become. (BT 98 (69))

But a further crucial feature of such forms of intelligent action is that they are themselves characterized by reference to the 'objects' that they involve. Hammering, for instance, is an activity that involves . . . hammers; it is an activity that takes place *among* particular objects, a way of using objects that cannot be characterized except by reference to the relevant objects. As a result, there is no sense to be made of the idea of a fit or correspondence between the person's activities and the objects, of the idea that hammering and hammers fit—or might fail to fit—one another. We cannot distinguish 'what the person is doing' from 'what is happening to the objects involved' in a way that will yield two separate elements that might fit—or fail to fit— one another, because 'what the person is doing' is itself a matter of 'what is happening to the objects involved'. This does not imply that we cannot distinguish the craftsman from his tools—'[t]he shoemaker is not the shoe' (BPP 171)—but it does imply that what makes him a craftsman is something to do with those tools: to understand what hammering is is to understand hammers and to understand what hammers are is to understand hammering. The activities of the person are not constituted independently of the relevant objects;[7] and thus, between them, there can be no question of fit or correspondence. As Heidegger puts it, a *zuhanden* object 'can genuinely show itself only in *dealings cut to its own measure* (hammering with a hammer, for example)'; hammering 'appropriates' hammers 'in a way which could not possibly be more suitable' (BT 98 (69), italics added).

---

[7] A similar thought can be found in Olafson 1987: 107 and Blattner 1999: 58: '*Dasein's* abilities-to-be are interdefined with the functional roles served by paraphernalia.'

So we see here a form of understanding of the world which cannot itself be understood as the appreciation of a correspondence—a form to which we were led by the discussion in Sections 5.2, 5.3, and 5.4.4. Moreover, we begin to see why, for Heidegger, the realist/idealist question of fit is confused: it presupposes an ontology of understanding that does not fit that central aspect of our lives that is our involvement with the *Zuhanden*. By concentrating our attention there, Heidegger challenges a shared assumption of the idealists and realists described in Section 2.1: namely, that intelligible thoughts 'con-form' with the world, that we can think about the world because the form of our thinking fits the form of the world. Such a vision suggests itself if we think of intelligent activity as, at its foundation, a matter of bringing into correspondence a thinker and a world, as we might imagine when we fixate on relations of observation and contemplation. But a rather different picture emerges when we focus 'not [on] a bare perceptual cognition, but rather [on] that kind of concern which manipulates things and puts them to use' (BT 95 (67)).

But to have shown that con-formist questions make no sense in connection with the *Zuhanden* is not to have shown that they do not make sense full-stop: might they have sense precisely in connection with observation and contemplation? Chapter 5 provided an abstract argument for thinking that they cannot, that all 'correspondence truths'—including those of observation and contemplation—are 'founded' in a form of understanding that cannot itself be understood as the appreciation of a correspondence. As developed there, that argument also suggested a sense for the following remarks:

> Knowing is nothing but a mode of Being-in-the-world; specifically, it is not even a primary but a founded way of Being-in-the-world, a way which is always possible only on the basis of a non-cognitive comportment. (HCT 164)

If that argument holds, we do not really understand the question of fit that realists and idealists propose to answer: when we reflect on thought, including observation and contemplation, we will always, perhaps unwittingly, rely, at some point, on an understanding of the thinker as already *in* the world about which she thinks, as possessing an understanding of the world which cannot be seen as the appreciation of some kind of correspondence.[8]

---

[8] Remarks of Rouse's suggest a recognition of a similar view (one according to which 'Heidegger's ... questioning [of] the representationalist conception of scientific knowledge ... undercut[s] the questions that realism and anti-realism alike attempt to answer' (1998: sec. 3). His remarks on tool-use as 'not mediated' (1998

But can we give ourselves a concrete sense of how this can be true? One interpretation of the above claim presents perception of the *Vorhanden* as arising only through a break-down in our involvement with the *Zuhanden*. Although the *Zuhanden* will play an important part in what follows, I have indicated above some worries that this particular interpretation raises, and in the rest of this chapter I will offer an alternative. Following the clue of our 'measure' motif, and the promptings of the Prior Projection and Primacy of Scientific Practice Claims, I will suggest that our practices of measurement embody 'projections of the Being' of that which is measured which 'anticipates', and are 'antecedent to', our arrival at any determinate measurements, 'projections' which we master when we acquire certain recognizably 'practical', 'worldly' forms of understanding, and in connection with which conformist questions of fit make no sense.

6.2 The 'founding' of measurement

It makes sense to talk about discovering a particular number of stones because this has implications for what one might say about them—'how many there are'—in a minute's time or when seen from a different angle, or when inspected by other people we would describe as 'competent counters'. Shadows that a group of objects throw, however, do not present the same stable patterning: different people may individuate the shadows differently, and the forms that the shadows take may constantly fluctuate. Since our 'results' lack the robust implications that our enumeration of stones boasts, there is very little point in counting such shadows or, for that matter, the clouds in an overcast sky or the ripples on the surface of a lake. We certainly could come up with *some* figures but the 'results' derived would be unreliable in the sense that there would be virtually nothing that we could do with them: if our assessments of the number of stones before us were as fluid, we could not use those assessments in anything like the way we presently do and to the suggestion that one counts stones one might reply not merely 'Why?' but 'Why bother?' One might propose that such cases show us a particular descriptive framework—here arithmetic—'failing to

---

sec. 1) also seem to be on what are, to me, the right lines; but, as I argued above, I find the way that Rouse articulates the upshot of these insights misleading.

fit'—to con-form to—the world. But an immediate objection to this proposal would be to say that it may well be possible to apply arithmetic in such cases but that it may take some work before we discover how to do it. Of crucial concern here is just what such 'work' and such 'discoveries' look like.

Let us consider an example. Pouring one amount of water into a tank which already contains another amount of water does not yield two amounts of water; but the level of the water increases. Let us suppose that each 'amount' is the contents of a particular cup filled to the brim. Let us further suppose that the cross-section of the tank is uniform from top to bottom, and that there are gradations on the side of the tank, equally spaced all the way from the top to the bottom. We can now predict the number of gradations covered by remembering how many times we poured in cups of water that were full—if pouring in one cup's-worth raises the level one gradation, pouring in another will raise the level up to the second gradation from the bottom—and we can now answer some interesting questions. For example, if we know how many times we poured the contents of the cup into the tank, then we can determine whether the cup was always full to the brim by seeing how many gradations the total amount covers.

By introducing the 'technology' of tanks with uniform cross-sections and equally-spaced gradations, and the practice of using a particular container so as always to add what we come to call a 'standard unit' volume of water, we are now treating water in a way which allows us to apply arithmetical rules to it meaningfully.[9] In this ' *"technischen" Aufbau*'—to echo BT 409 (358) quoted in Section 3.3—we have found a way of treating this domain in a way analogous to that in which we treat other 'countables'; a domain which appeared to resist arithmetically informed description has succumbed.[10]

---

[9] We see similar concerns in an account of the 'founding' of counting presented in DSTCM 71–2: '[I]f counting is possible in actual reality, that is, if number has gained any footing there and any applicability, there is no possibility of that without *homogeneity*. If I view this tree only in its individuality as not having been there before and never recurring, and if I view *any other tree like this*, then a count could never be arrived at, I could only say: the one and the other. But they could only be called "two" if the one and the other were projected, as it were, into a homogeneous medium—a projection in which only the *general determinateness of being-tree* would be retained. This projection into a homogeneous medium means then: Only a certain aspect of objects is looked at *and only that*'.

[10] Whether we are still dealing merely with arithmetic here is obviously questionable, but is not an issue I will worry over here.

In this example we see how particular measurements presuppose an 'interpretation', an 'anticipatory' 'projection of the Being', of the domain measured and also the *kind* of work—the kind of stage-setting, as Wittgenstein might put it[11]—involved in establishing such a 'projection': it is an innovation in the sphere of the *Zuhanden*—what one might call a 'practical' development. The necessary measuring tools—BT 97 (68)'s *Messzeug*—share key characteristics of paradigmatic *zuhanden* objects. For example, our normal relation with these tools and the framework of description that they enact is usually one of unreflective use; the usual 'transparency' to us of such tools shows up in the fact that we need to remind ourselves of their role (as I have attempted to do above), and normally only become aware of their playing that role when their use misfires, when we realise that the cup leaks or that the cross-section of the tank is not quite uniform after all.[12]

But what about the crucial question of 'fit', and its inapplicability in connection with the *Zuhanden*? There is something that merits the label 'understanding' here in that one can apply these measuring tools correctly or incorrectly; but there would be something potentially misleading in calling it an understanding that the world is a particular way. I want to suggest that what we discover when we develop the technology of measuring cups, and so on, is not the way in which liquids have hitherto hidden their 'arithmeticality'. Instead, we have reconceptualized liquids so as to foreground something about them that we can describe in arithmetical ways. We place the entities described within a different 'projection' and allow other features of theirs to become apparent. We do not learn how to measure characteristics that we previously could not measure; instead we come to measure characteristics with which we had previously not engaged.

To use an analogy, imagine a person who did not understand that to measure the height of a person one needs to lay the measuring rod *straight* along the body, as opposed to criss-crossing all the way up. One *could* proceed in that way—perhaps Wittgenstein's famous 'wood-sellers' represent an analogous case (1978: Part I)—but ought one to say that such a person will produce *mistaken* measurements of height, whereas the person who lays the measuring rod straight along the body produces *correct* measurements of

---

[11] Cf. Wittgenstein 1967: sec. 257.
[12] Rouse makes this point and sees it as promoting a 'realist illusion' in which we 'confuse the object as worked on using the instrument with the object as it *really* is apart from its disclosure in practice' (1985: 208). I will question the force of this qualification.

height? In one sense that seems right, but it might mislead, for instance, if one concluded that laying the measuring rod straight along the body must therefore be the *correct* way of measuring height. This formulation sounds like a matter of contingent fact: 'It turns out that this happens to be the correct way of measuring height.' But it is not; laying the measuring rod straight along the body *is* what it is to measure height. To learn how to measure heights by learning to lay the measuring rod straight along the body is not so much a matter of learning *how* to measure heights as how to measure *heights*. It is not that one learns something *about* heights; rather one learns *of* heights.[13] To echo a sentence I used earlier, one might say that the activities of the subject—laying the measuring rod *straight* along the body—are not constituted independently of those of the relevant objects—their characteristic being measured being precisely their *height*. No question of 'fit' between these two kinds of 'activity' on the part of 'subjects' and 'objects' emerges here, because heights too 'show themselves only in dealings cut to their own measure'.[14]

6.3 Objections and clarifications

A useful way to elaborate upon, and clarify, this picture is to consider some of the (no doubt many) objections that it invites; and this section will address three.[15]

6.3.1 'Impure beholding' and the manipulating/seeing distinction

The above picture clashes with another, familiar interpretation of the contribution that the technology of measurement makes. In BT, Heidegger identifies—as 'the foundation of western philosophy' no less—the thesis that '[p]rimordial and genuine truth lies in pure beholding [*reinen*

---

[13] Wittgenstein makes a very similar point: 'What "determining the length" means is not learned by learning what *length* and *determining* are; the meaning of the word "length" is learnt by learning, among other things, what it is to determine length' (1967: 224–5).

[14] Some of the claims I make here echo claims made by Barad (in her 1996). Barad does not connect her work to that of Heidegger, but Rouse has (2000: 351). (Ihde is another reader of Heidegger who has emphasized the role that instrumentation might play in our understanding of science (cf. his 1979 and 1991); but I will not discuss his work here.)

[15] N. 28 will note—but no more than indicate how one might set about meeting—some others.

Anschauung]'.[16] Immediately after the passage from BT 409 (358) that I quoted in Section 3.3, Heidegger articulates the following possible objection to his remarks on the 'praxis' of 'theoretical research'—a natural objection for we philosophers with our professional commitment to the 'remarkable priority of "seeing"' (BT 215 (171)):

> Someone will hold that all manipulation in the sciences is merely in the service of pure observation—the investigative discovery and disclosure of the 'things themselves'. 'Seeing', taken in the widest sense, regulates all 'procedures' and retains its priority. (BT 409–10 (358))

From this perspective, 'manipulative' 'procedures' merely serve to get us into a position from which our powers of 'pure observation' can take in what there is to see; different 'procedures' more or less successfully achieve that objective, but such 'external precautions' (EP 178) are of no significance when it comes to characterizing what it is that we come to see; thought of such 'procedures' can be dispensed with once we are ready to allow 'pure observation'—'pure beholding'—to take over once again.[17]

But if applied to the contribution that the technology of measuring cups, and so on, makes, this picture is misleading. The emergence of such tools is at the same time a reconceptualization of the subject matter: we find a way to apply arithmetic to liquids by introducing a refined sense in which we are dealing with 'volumes' of liquid, and we articulate criteria of identity for such 'volumes' through the invocation of tools such as measuring cups. The 'practical' achievement of mastering this *Messzeug* is not merely learning a means for describing or accessing a certain kind of entity and its properties; it is learning what kind of entities and properties these are. 'Such activity belongs to the sciences [in question]', in that if one wants to understand the entities and the properties that these sciences study, one must master these activities: 'the objects of the relevant sciences demand such activities' (EP 178).[18]

---

[16] Cf. also L 56's remarks on 'the fact that seeing or looking—*theoria*, *intuitus*, intuition—was the primary mode of comprehension for the Greeks' and L 113–26's tracing of the notion that 'knowledge properly speaking is intuition [*Anschauung*]' (L 121) through Augustine, Aquinas, Descartes, Leibniz, Kant, and Hegel.

[17] This vision, which—as I will show—Heidegger gives us reason to reject, is, in essence, that which Rouse ascribes to him. Cf. Chapter 3 n. 60.

[18] This conception of the nature of scientific practice finds echoes elsewhere. Heidegger emphasizes the need to consider sciences not as systems of propositions but 'concretely' and 'as enactment' [*Vollzug*], 'as actual research and collaboration' (PRL 5, 7). 'It is a fool's errand to expect that traditional logic will teach us how to think', he proposes; instead it is 'only through a living and effective connection with the

From this perspective these tools appear to be more than merely contingently linked to the conceptualization that we use when we use those tools. There are, of course, certain dependencies that can be immediately ruled out: clearly the existence of any one particular measuring cup is insignificant, as is the particular standard sizes of measuring cups we use. But it seems plausible to say that an inability to understand how such cups or some analogue thereof need to be used in such contexts would constitute a failure to understand what it is to describe liquids in terms of their volumes: imagine a person who does not worry over how full the measuring cup is; or recall the person who measures people by laying a measuring rod crisscross along their bodies. What we seem to confront here are aspects of our lives which do not fit naturally with a hard distinction between 'manipulation' and 'seeing'; 'the practical' and 'the cognitive' fade into one another. Here, as Heidegger says in the passage quoted in Section 3.3, 'it is by no means patent where the ontological boundary between "theoretical" and "atheoretical" behaviour runs!'[19]

6.3.2 Improvement in methods of measurement

Another way in which one can seemingly revive a question of fit between methods of measurement and what they measure is to point to the manifest fact that methods of measurement are improved upon: is not such improvement the production of an understanding of that which is measured which is, in

---

concrete practice of a given science' that we 'can bring to clarity scientific work': '[t]hinking, and especially scientific thinking, can be learned only by getting involved with the subject matter' (L 15–16). (Cf. also IPR 9.)

[19] There are, of course, ways of measuring lengths that do not involve the use of measuring rods, such as 'measuring atomic distances [by] putting together some complicated equations of electromagnetic theory or quantum physics with some observable quantities' (Chang and Cartwright 2008: 368). But there is reason to believe that the establishment of these 'new' 'alternatives' is still an inherently conservative business, their credentials established—their claims to be methods for measuring *lengths*— by showing that their results tally with the 'old'. In attempting to do so one might discover that such methods fail to measure what they were created to measure; that clearly is a possibility with methods of a certain complexity. My main concern here is to question whether we have a grasp of such a possibility with the kinds of basic practices of measurement upon which I have focused. (Cf. also my (forthcoming-a): sec. 6.) My focus—on basic observations of our physical environment—might perhaps be best characterized as a focus on proto-scientific activities; but the discussion does suggest, I believe, some possible morals for science itself. While the latter, in its full complexity, must raise issues that the former do not, the former represent activities out of which it is reasonable to suppose the latter emerges and upon which it continues to depend. But the cogency of extrapolating from insights into these more basic cases of measurement to claims about the sciences they may 'found' will have to be assessed on a case-by-case basis.

some sense, deeper, more truthful, than that which previous methods provided, a 'more suitable appropriation' of the measured? I cannot provide a comprehensive response to this criticism. But I will argue that some of the cases we are most likely to have in mind here may not constitute the counter-examples that we might initially assume, and that therefore such cases of 'improvement' need to be scrutinized on a case-by-case basis. In this sub-section I will comment on two kinds of 'improvement', and in Section 6.4 in greater detail on a third.

Firstly and briefly, what of technical innovations, such as more powerful microscopes, that allow us to produce finer-grained measurements? Such innovations, I suggest, allow us to learn more about particular lengths, say, but cannot be seen as developing our understanding of length itself. Such innovations might be less misleadingly compared to the introduction of different units of measurement, something which no one, I imagine, is tempted to see as making available measurements that are truer or deeper.

A second (though related) kind of 'improvement' is the replacement by descriptions such as '5 litres as opposed to 4 litres' of descriptions such as 'a lot as opposed to a little'. Have we acquired a more truthful description by switching from the latter to the former? It is difficult to deny that the former is a more *exact* description than the latter, but it remains to be shown that a more exact description is a more truthful description. They may be more precise, but are they any more accurate?[20] I described the introduction of the technology of measuring cups, and so on, as bringing about a reconceptualization of volume. Part of what that means is that a *different* set of truths are made available to us; the measurements produced by the old system are not shown to be false by the introduction of the new system. There is no doubt that there are tasks which can be performed with the new system that cannot be performed with the old system. But the reverse is also true, as Wittgenstein argues in a well-known passage:

> If I tell someone 'Stand roughly there'—may not this explanation work perfectly?...But isn't it an inexact explanation?—Yes; why shouldn't we call it 'inexact'? Only let us understand what 'inexact' means? For it does not mean 'unusable'?...'Inexact' is really a reproach, and 'exact' is praise. And that is to say that what is inexact attains its goal less perfectly than what is more exact. Thus

---

[20] On this distinction, cf., e.g., Chang and Cartwright 2008.

the point here is what we call 'the goal'. Am I inexact when I do not give our distance from the sun to the nearest foot, or tell a joiner the width of a table to the nearest thousandth of an inch? No *single* ideal of exactness has been laid down; we do not know what we should be supposed to imagine under this head—unless you yourself lay down what is to be so called. But you will find it difficult to hit upon such a convention; at least any that satisfies you. (1967: sec. 88)[21]

I have questioned whether we can give substance to the idea of 'fit' between the methods of measurement I have considered and what they measure such that, for example, another method might provide a better fit. Wittgenstein's discussion illustrates, and Section 6.4 will further explore, the difficulty of providing such substance, of turning a 'different kind of fit' into a 'better kind of fit', a more 'suitable appropriation', as BT 98 (69) puts it. Indeed I think it is anything but clear that we have any sense of the possibility that the practices we have considered might be 'refined' or 'corrected', in the sense that there might be 'alternative practices' which would reveal more accurately (and not just more precisely) the very objects of our 'original practices';[22] or that particular findings of theirs, which have been correctly judged to be correctly carried out by the lights of these practices, might turn out to be wrong. In this sense they represent 'original havings'.

6.3.3 'Impure facts' I: Projection, falsification, parochialism, and perspectives

Let us consider a third objection to my Heideggerian account—one which will take us back to the dilemma of Section 2.1. Since what 'pure beholding' would reveal would be 'pure facts', an emphasis on the 'praxis' that underpins 'beholding' and a denial that practices of measurement and the measured 'fit' one another might be expected to cast doubt on the notion of 'pure facts', and my discussion has indeed drawn attention to the role of certain 'imposed' 'projections' or 'frameworks' in our making of some of the most mundane of observations of the objective world around us. Might

---

[21] Can we find such a thought in Heidegger? We certainly see him challenging the notion that the physical sciences provide a relevant model of rigour for all sciences (cf. OHF 56–7, WM 83; on psychology, cf. HCT 15, 118, WDR 157; on history, cf. BT 195 (153), EP 42–4, IPR 74, WM 83, L 8; on biology, cf. n. 36 below) and he claims that the kind of 'relativity of truth' to *Dasein* that he points out 'does not endanger objectivity, but on the contrary makes possible precisely the wealth and *diversity* of objective truth' (EP 155, italics added).

[22] That does not exclude the possibility of circumstances arising in which their use might fall into abeyance, as McManus 2000b, 2003, and (forthcoming-a): sec. 8. discuss.

that discussion then imply that forces of the sort that we would intuitively believe render scientific findings artefactual are actually to be found at work here? Does it indeed imply that engaging in such practices can only ever yield artefacts? Or must we accept instead that such explorations are confined to 'appearances' that are ineliminably informed by our subjective presumptions and renounce the notion that they reveal the world as it is in itself, a world we did not create? Indeed, do we not have to restore an understanding of *Messzeug* and the measured as 'corresponding' or 'failing to correspond' if we are to preserve the 'independence' of the latter?

We may, of course, talk here of 'projections' being 'imposed' on the world, because we can certainly imagine our not using the *Messzeug* they inform and not attending to the particular kinds of facts that their use uncovers. Moreover, Section 6.4 will identify a quite different sense in which the use of particular 'projections' might be said to be an 'imposition' that yields artefactual findings, though not a kind of 'imposition' that provides any comfort for the con-formist. My concern here, however, is to uncover the confusion at the root of the worry set out in the preceding paragraph, and the sense that it evokes of 'imposition', of 'confinement', of something somehow getting between us and how things are.

To begin to see the confusion, let us ask what precisely the problematic 'presumption' might be if, having adopted the technology of measuring cups, and so on, I conclude that there are 5 litres of liquid in the container in front of me. It cannot be that the measuring framework might be disguising the fact that the volume in question is, in fact, 4 litres or 6 litres, because those facts are articulated using precisely the same framework. The problem also cannot be that the volumes are *in litres*. There might well be an explanation of some sort—historical, cultural, biological even (as perhaps in the case of yards and feet)—why certain units are adopted; but such explanations do not presuppose that, so to speak, the subject matter itself demands that those units be adopted. In this sense, the choice of units is recognizably arbitrary.

Two more intuitions that might encourage the problematic 'imposition' thought have already been examined: firstly, the worry of whether *our* way of measuring heights is the correct way, suggesting that it might turn out that heights (not any particular height but heights in general) are not as we supposed them to be; and secondly, the worry that our methods of measurement might yet be 'improved', so that our use of existing methods expresses a presumption that the world reveals itself to those particular methods. I hope that I have, at least, weakened the power of these intuitions to doom those who use methods of measurement to the fate of finding no more than artefacts.

There remains, I suspect, the confused intuition that the use of our descriptive tools 'presumes', for example, that liquids have volumes, full-stop! But what then is the contrasting way of things that this might occlude? That they have temperatures will not do, nor that they have geographical locations or perhaps owners, because none of these characteristics stand in any tension with the possession of a volume.[23] The confused anxiety here would seem to be something like the worry that people might not have heights 'in and of themselves', that liquids might turn out not really to have volumes after all, and instead... Well, we do not know what to say.

There would be a related confusion in construing the account I have offered as inviting a worry that pragmatist accounts often invite, namely, that such scientific or proto-scientific observations are now limited to revealing not how things are in themselves, but merely aspects of those things that are bound up with particular sets of human, and hence local and contingent, interests: 'We want to know the physical properties of these elements, not how we can use them to build bridges or indeed any broader, *mere* know-how'. Although there is something to this construal, we need to consider in more concrete detail what the envisaged 'limitation' of such observations looks like. According to the Heidegger I have presented, the 'local' interests in question are, for example, in the heights and weights of objects, and there is something peculiar in the reaction, 'We want to know the true (? inherent?) properties of these elements, not merely their heights and weights'. The dream of revealing objects not with respect to any such interest but 'in themselves' is precisely a dream, and a confused one at that. To approach objects with these particular interests is not to place between them and ourselves parochial interests; rather, it is to ask of them a determinate question; the (confused and impossible) alternatives are either to ask

---

[23] Cf. also Section 5.4.1's discussion of assessing the size-*Hinblick*. The peaceful coexistence described above also helps explain why the projection that a practice of measurement embodies can be called 'non-objective' (since it does not rule out the possibility of many other kinds of 'projection' articulating a 'wealth and diversity' of other objective truths) without that implying that the projection is 'subjective' (since acknowledging this coexistence in no way 'endangers the objectivity' of the truths that it articulates (cf. EP 155, quoted in n. 273)).

questions that are 'insufficiently determined' (to echo L 284, quoted in Section 5.3), or to ask objects to tell us not only how they are but also which of their aspects we are investigating!

Moreover—and for the same reason that these practices I have discussed merit description as 'original havings'—there may be something misleading in describing these practices as 'local'.[24] Just as Husserl claims (as noted in Section 1.1) that the 'constitutive' structures he identifies as necessary for encountering physical objects are necessary not just for human encounters with such objects but any agent's, any agent we might interpret as intentionally related to lengths will have to display in its activities something akin to 'our' measuring practices.[25] Indeed, since it is not clear that we can make any sense here of '*alternative* perspectives' on these objects, there may be something misleading in describing these practices as themselves embodying 'perspectives', beyond its registering the fact that the objects they reveal form only part of what there is. What we actually seem to see when we follow through on the attempt to 'imagine alternatives' to the practices described are, at best, practices that achieve other ends, revealing *other* objects, and at worst, 'an utter inability to apprehend at all' (L 177), a 'not-having-access' (L 183). But either way, we do not find activities which reveal in a more or less accurate way the same objects as those revealed by the practices to which they are imagined as 'alternatives', better (or worse) attempts to measure the same thing. Hence, one might say that these practices embody a 'view of the world' but not a view of the objects that they reveal.[26]

---

[24] Hence, although I wish to question Rouse's reading of Heidegger's understanding of science as marginalizing 'the practical', I would still maintain that, on the view I ascribe to Heidegger, there is something misleading in the notion of 'the irreducibly local character of scientific knowledge' (Rouse 1987: 111).

[25] These thoughts clearly have echoes in the work of Wittgenstein and, perhaps more obviously, Davidson (cf., e.g., his 1973–74).

[26] For similar reasons, the view presented here would deny the claim that an inability to further 'ground' these practices renders them somehow 'arbitrary'. (Cf. Phillips 1999: chs. 1–4, Haugeland 2000: 76, and my (forthcoming-a).) As perhaps befits the part it plays in an attempt to 'reject both realism and idealism', the view offered here resists assimilation to either of the 'two broad positions' into which Chang and Cartwright 2008 classify philosophical views of measurement: a 'realism' that 'takes measurements as methods of finding out about objective qualities that we can identify independently of measurement', and nominalism that 'treats measurement methods as definitive of the concept', in taking length, for example, to be identified by reference to the methods we use in measuring length. The view offered here might appear to be nominalist, sharing in what Chang and Cartwright call 'the core of nominalism': 'a rejection of the realist question about the correctness of measurement' (p. 367). But it cannot be identified neatly with either of the positions that they suggest can be identified within nominalism. For example, the considerations offered above (cf. n. 19) about the 'conservatism' in our

The Heideggerian notion of 'constitution' may seem to stand in the way of the notion that real knowledge—as distinguished from merely 'perspectival', sham 'knowledge'—arises out of a 'view from nowhere', or belongs to an 'absolute conception'. I think it is indeed a part of that notion that not just anyone can 'intend' just anything. The above discussion highlights that even that which we might imagine as part of an 'absolute conception' of the world and as 'viewed from nowhere' must, all the same, be *seen*, as opposed to bumped into: *some* notion must be in play of what distinguishes a subject as such, a viewer as such, any*one* from any*thing*. The above Heideggerian discussion presents a picture of what it takes to 'intend' some very basic physical properties. But it also has the merit, I think, that if rightly understood it does not cast doubt on the notion that the properties revealed are, so to speak, fully real, and shows that the 'constitutive' practices described need not be seen as 'merely local' or 'merely perspectival'.[27]

No doubt these claims leave many questions unanswered. What I have been challenging are intuitions that suggest that the methods of measurement discussed could 'obscure' or 'fail to fit' the world. I suspect that there is actually no limit to the supply of such intuitions, because I do not think one can delimit in advance the ways in which we may confuse ourselves philosophically.[28] But

development of 'alternative measures' counts against Bridgman's extreme operationalist view that 'there are as many concepts of length as there are different types of operation used for measuring it' (Chang and Cartwright 2008: 368). But I also do not believe we can make much sense of our *choosing* the methods described above as ways of measuring what they measure and hence my view fails to correspond to 'the less extreme nominalist view' '*conventionalism*, according to which we are free to choose by agreement the correct measurement methods for a concept' (p. 368). (This is not to deny that we may, for some reason or other, choose to measure particular properties rather than others.) For reasons indicated above, my view suggests that we succumb to an illusion when we imagine a space of alternatives within which we might imagine ourselves choosing to measure lengths in the way that we do measure them. (Cf. also Lafont 2000: 267 on Heidegger's 'conventionalist interpretation of science'.)

[27] For the same reason, I believe Lafont is mistaken when she argues that Heidegger's postulation of a plurality of 'prior disclosures' entails that 'the universal validity ascribed to truth is an illusion' (Lafont 2000: 61 n. 56). (A worry of this form can also be found in Cassirer (cf. KPM 174), Rentsch 1989: 166, and Friedman 2000: 156.) My (forthcoming-a) develops this response and extends the above discussion of the relevance of the notion of 'perspective', in challenging Lafont's suggestion that Heidegger's views undermine 'the supposition of a single objective world' (2000: 230). I also explore there the possible bearing on her reading of Haugeland's interpretation of Heidegger (cf., e.g., his 2000) and of Williams' reflections on the 'absolute conception' (cf., e.g., his 1978).

[28] For a discussion of other such intuitions, cf. Diamond 2001 and McManus forthcoming-a. I will mention here briefly five other significant worries. First of all, how generally does the above story hold? Are not the practices I have discussed peculiar in their dependence on what one might call 'worldly instruments'? One might begin to respond by noting that, if Wittgenstein is to be believed, a similar story might be told about, for example, our colour language, which might seem one of the most pressing examples of a language apparently without 'worldly' mediation: we imagine that we simply look and see

I also believe there is a sense in which the use of particular descriptive frameworks might well constitute an artefact-generating imposition. This sense, which the notion of con-formism will not help us understand, touches on Heidegger's discussion of authenticity, and will suggest a reading of his remarks about the obscuring power of the sciences—about their 'forgetfulness of Being'—and BT's claim that *Dasein* 'is in "untruth"' (BT 264 (222)). It will also be used in Chapter 8 to suggest a different construal of his reflections on *Vorhandenheit* and assertions, and in Chapter 9's discussion of the nature of philosophical confusion.

---

what colour something is. Wittgenstein, however, claims that such languages rest upon the use of samples and that such obviously 'worldly' samples ought to be 'reckon[ed] ... among the instruments of the language' (1967: sec. 16). Secondly, although my view may have affinities with other views that see an important 'worldly' mediation in our language use—of which, there are now many, including the many varieties of externalism—does it not clash with the externalist thought that 'there is no reason whatever—intuitive or otherwise—to believe that having a word S that means X but not Y depends on being able, in principle, to tell Xs apart from Ys' (Boghossian 1990: 77)? All I will say here is that there are plenty of open questions here and those like Heal who—addressing one of the externalist's favourite kinds of concepts—think that 'our practice of using natural kind terms can exist and have the features that it does only because we have ... generally reliable abilities to re-identify particular specimens [of those kinds]' (Heal 1998: 104). A third important question—which again concerns possible dissociations between the kinds of abilities to which I have alluded and one's being intentionally related to the aspects of objects that those abilities reveal—concerns the person who, having mastered the kinds of technique alluded to, finds themselves paralysed; we cannot surely say of them that they no longer grasp length, volume, etc simply because they can no longer pick the measuring tools up. (Related worries are raised by Strawson (2010)'s 'weather watchers' and Dummett's sentient trees who can 'observe the world [but] engage in no other kind of action' (1987: 201).) All I will say here about this important objection is that, as it stands, it represents not only an objection to my specific proposals here about measurement but to any view that gives an essential role to 'practical skills' in cognition, as well as to the whole Heideggerian notion that '[t]he only way to understand *ready-to-hand* entities is to *handle* them' (Polt 1999: 50). Fourthly, can it really be true that someone who has yet to master the kinds of technique described above really does not *see* objects as, for example, possessed of lengths, does not see them 'ordered' in that way? I suggest that such a person may see objects as short, long and/or shorter, longer or the same length as one another; and that may be necessary if she is to come to master the *Hinblick* that reveals objects that are 1 metre long or 2 metres long, and so on. But there does seem to be a recognizably different engagement with the world embodied in the lives of those who have mastered the latter, as there seems to be in the cases of the person who recognizes large, small, and/or larger, smaller, or equal volumes of liquid, as opposed to 1-litre volumes or 2-litre volumes. (One might argue that masters of the simpler *Hinblick* must recognize what the more complex *Hinblick* reveals, because it is only by virtue of an object's being, for example, 2 metres long that it is longer than objects that are 1 metre long; but that seems less than compelling, because one might also argue the reverse; and either way, for reasons given above, such a dependency does not entail that these *Hinblicke* compete with one another.) Finally, relativity theory might seem to have a bearing on some of the claims I have made on behalf of ordinary measuring practices. This is another serious worry, though also one that I suspect is more complex than it may seem. Issues that would need to be resolved include precisely which ways—if any—our engagement in such ordinary practices commits us to *anti*-relativistic views. (Heidegger touches on the significance of discoveries in modern physics at, e.g., CT 3, PS 80–1, BT 30 (9–10), BPP 237, QCT 23, S&R 169 and 172–3. Cf. also Beck 2002's discussion, mentioned in n. 40 below.)

6.4 'Appropriating' or 'being lived by' one's measures

6.4.1 'Impure facts' II: Artefacts and emptiness

To help identify this sense I will identify a way in which phenomena which we have 'arithmetized' by the construction of a technology of measurement may, all the same, be said to resist arithmetically informed description: these phenomena may sustain enumerations and additions, but only ones that are somehow *empty*, *trivial*. I will then argue that the necessary involvement in our observations of technologies of measurement reveals not that all such observations are artefactual, but rather that some such observations are and others are not, and deciding which are which is sometimes a question that one might describe as one of value, or of self-knowledge. It is a question of the place of those observations within our lives construed more broadly—a question not unrelated, I will suggest, to that of what Heidegger calls 'authenticity'.

Let us take an example: *liberté, égalité, fraternité*. Is this a list of three ideas? The intuition that it is would suggest that we can count this domain too, the domain of ideas. But might that intuition rest merely on the fact that we have three separate *words* before us—a fact that only really 'supports' the claim that we can count words. Let us press that worry further. Does it make sense, for example, to ask how many ideas there are in *Leviathan*, or whether there are more or less in *Das Kapital*? One could certainly *construct* or *force* opinions about such matters, sometimes very easily: for example, if asked the number of ideas in *Leviathan*, it would certainly seem wrong to say 'zero' or 'a billion'. But the arithmetical 'interpretation' of this domain seems simply too *ad hoc* for there to be any substance in these figures that we might generate or in any argument that might arise on their basis. Do we, after all, really have *compelling* criteria for when ideas are distinguishable—criteria by reference to which my saying that there are thirty ideas in *Leviathan* and your saying thirty-one would require that one of us had made an error? What would the relevant criteria of 'error' *be* here? The existence of such criteria—the availability of a 'measuring cup' for ideas—would seem to be a minimum requirement for arithmetic really gaining a foothold and, in our present case, it is not clear what such criteria would be.

Moreover, the problems that we face when trying to analyse a text are precisely those which will hinder the establishment of a 'unit of measure' using which one might start counting and adding here too. Disagreement over the meaning of a text might well be characterized—if rather colourfully—as disagreement over when 'the same idea' has disappeared and then reappeared, or when one has been discarded and 'another' introduced, and so on. Compare one plausible interpretation of the failings of the utilitarian dream of adding together volumes of happiness: in order to apply the proposed calculus, we need to have solved many of just the kind of evaluative puzzles that utilitarianism promised to solve, because that is necessary if we are to establish what an 'equivalent amount' of happiness is and the weighting that such amounts should be given. To give a crude example, is it true that attending a football match generates twice as much happiness as attending an opera, but that the latter—as a 'higher pleasure'[29]—ought to be weighted as twice as worthwhile as the former? In order to establish this descriptive framework, that was meant to eliminate moral disagreement, we seem to need in the background an already established set of agreed judgements of worth.

Such questions and the issues that they raise have, of course, generated a great amount of literature. I merely wish to raise the possibility that the difficulties encountered here—understood within parts of those literatures as those of working out a protocol whereby a computer, say, might analyse a text and working out a plausible and applicable 'felicific calculus'—may indicate cases of a descriptive framework 'failing to fit'. But my suggestion is not that we have finally found the kind of failure that con-formism imagines; rather, such cases should prompt us to think about what we take 'the applicability of a descriptive framework' to be and the precise meaning of one 'fitting' or 'being resisted'.

If 'arithmetic being applicable' just meant 'numbers can be stuck on',[30] then arithmetic can be said to be universally applicable. But are the figures we generate *useful*? Can we do anything sensible with them? If 'arithmetic being applicable' meant *that*, then there *do* seem to be limits on the applicability of arithmetic. In discerning such limits, we need to focus less on whether 'arithmetically compliant' results can be obtained and more on the price that we pay in order to obtain them—how much *construction*,

---

[29] Cf. Mill 2002: ch. 2.
[30] Cf. the remark by S. S. Stevens, quoted in Mitchell 1999: 162: 'Measurement is the business of pinning numbers on things'.

technology, and *triviality* we must import. By ignoring these 'mere' circumstances, including the 'mere' 'practical' implications of these cases of application, we will misunderstand this sense in which arithmetic really does need to *find* application.

From this perspective, the mundane observation that we 'ordinarily' apply arithmetic only where arithmetic can be applied *significantly* has a philosophical importance beyond that of an observation about the 'pragmatics' of applied arithmetic. Indeed, a proper appreciation of this fact casts doubt on there being a clear distinction between 'pragmatic considerations' and something one might call the 'bare applicability' of arithmetic, between the 'usefulness' of arithmetic and its 'useableness'. Two senses of 'sensible' seem to merge here, as, once again, 'it is by no means patent where the ontological boundary between "theoretical" and "atheoretical" behaviour runs!' One might say that one *cannot* count ideas—suggesting something akin to a contradiction—or that one *will not* count ideas—suggesting a mere lack of practical utility. But here, saying whether something has a number is something about which one might well say there is no real fact of the matter: clouds and ideas can be counted, but only through the construction of a highly artificial framework—one which we can use to yield sets of figures, but only figures in which no one really *believes*. One might say of the figures that it supports that they are not 'useful' or even 'use-*able*'; but, ultimately, we simply say that they are not *used*: we do not really understand what it would be to use those figures. They appear instead as patterns produced by what we might call a '*merely* projected' arithmetic—empty patterns lacking a significance of their own which instead merely echo the mode of description that one is, for some reason, *insisting* on using.[31]

6.4.2 A sketch of an example: Methodological fetishism in psychology

Such an insistence threatens to degenerate into a kind of methodological fetishism. Consider what I have called elsewhere 'Pythagorean fetishism'[32]—the tendency to treat enumerable differences as, in themselves, what matters. Examples might include some bureaucratic or technocratic demands

---

[31] Clearly this may have some bearing on the extent of what Wigner 1960 called 'the unreasonable effectiveness of mathematics'.

[32] Cf. McManus 2003, which explores possible political implications, and a number of other possible examples, of such methodological fetishism. Section 6.2 above also draws on this earlier piece's discussion of issues that are raised there in connection with Wittgenstein.

for mathematical measures of 'performance', and some of the phenomena that Marx identifies in his reflections on money and commodity fetishism. In such cases a certain descriptive (here mathematical) model is imposed in order to try to track factors—'health', 'value', and so on—that are not obviously capturable in those terms.

Psychology is perhaps the most vivid case of the advance of a science depending on the development of such measures—a case where the thought and labour involved is most apparent, and where the *Messzeug* regularly come in for explicit criticism. Central to the psychological study of personality, for example, has been the attempt to develop scales upon which personalities may be plotted—extroversion/introversion, neuroticism, schizotypal personality, and so on. A routine worry about such scales and the questionnaires used to measure them is whether the measures produced have 'ecological validity', whether they really say anything about how people are in their lives away from psychologists.[33] This is not a worry over whether they have filled in the form incorrectly: the scores may be factually correct in this sense. Rather, the *significance* of such scores remains moot. Similarly, consider how in describing behaviour—say the attachment of a child to a parent—psychologists take them out of their homes, impose certain tasks on the child and certain behaviours on the parent, train observers extensively, and only then elicit the repeatable observations that they seek. Are then the patterns observed the product of this ' *"technischen" Aufbau'*, the unnatural settings, the contrived tasks and behaviours, and the training of the observers?

My Heideggerian answer is: maybe, maybe not. I have no *a priori* basis to offer on which such a judgement might be made, and making such judgements is not a task reserved for the philosopher: reflection on the validity of measures is one of the engines of development of a science, and is one of the ways in which scientists do good science. Despite the impression some of his work may give, the Heideggerian view I have sketched in no way denies that mathematics and science can indeed embody productive and illuminating 'disclosures' of reality; they only cease to be so when we forget that they are particular disclosures, presupposing particular 'projections' of reality. Key to the obscuring power that Heidegger ascribes to the sciences,

---

[33] Cf., e.g., Kellogg 2002: 20: 'Ecological validity refers to the degree to which laboratory tasks accurately measure cognitive phenomena that occur in real-world, everyday settings'.

I suggest, is the notion that if we allow scientific 'projections' to, as it were, 'take on a life of their own' and treat them as *the* way in which reality discloses itself, then they can indeed constitute a threat to our understanding. To adapt Heidegger's later warning about technology's 'ordering', fetishized modes of description 'drive[] out every other possibility of revealing', 'threaten[ing] to sweep man away... as the supposed single way of revealing' (QCT 27, 32).[34] Echoing a theme (to which we will return) in Heidegger's discussion of the inauthentic, we can indeed be said to be 'lived'[35] under such circumstances by those modes of description, our interest and our acts dictated to by what those modes reveal. We then 'move only within the realm of the measurable' (Z 98), in 'a curious excess of frantic measuring and calculating' (PMD 228) delimited by the particular measures by which we are 'lived'. '[S]cience... includes this possibility of falling, and necessarily so', the possibility of 'get[ting] absorbed in their undertakings', and 'in idle talk' (HCT 301).

The notion that psychology *must* pursue mathematical measures in order to be a 'real', 'exact' science played an important role in the emergence of behaviourist psychology and the previous paragraph's warning chimes with a familiar diagnosis of the perceived failures of that movement. In one sense, behaviourism succeeded in describing human conduct using variables that could be handled mathematically. The sense in which it failed was that the variables it used captured aspects of conduct in which no one was interested: what we could measure quantitatively repeatedly turned out to be nothing more than weakly associated with what we wanted to have measured. This realization took a *long* time to emerge, and its precise significance is still disputed. But such a methodological commitment in the face of insubstantial returns—quantification was achieved, but only with measures of negligible validity and thus at the price of triviality—might, I suggest, be a case of Pythagorean fetishism. The behaviourist psychologist generated figures that were, one might say, perfectly accurate—in that they measured what they measure—but were also useless, meaningless. According to this diagnosis, such a psychologist's commitment to 'disclosing' psychological phenomena

---

[34] Cf. also QCT 27, 32, and 174 ('Nature, in its objectness for modern physical science, is only *one* way in which what presences... reveals itself'), and EP 203: 'the scientific truth is only *one* kind and possibility of making manifest of entities'. To fail to recognize it as such is to 'sublime'—as Phillips (1999: 4) puts it—what is in fact only one particular 'measure'.

[35] Cf. HCT 245, quoted in Section 8.5 below.

by pursuing an 'exact', 'mathematical science' makes him comparable to the man in the joke who searches for his keys not where he dropped them, but under the street light where he 'can see better'.[36]

6.4.3 Emptiness and inauthenticity

How do we make judgements of validity? How successfully a quantifiable measure tracks the important events in the 'life' of the non-quantified factor that interests us cannot itself be mathematically established, unless by other measures of whose validity we are somehow confident.[37] That a measure provides the basis for accurate predictions is often offered as grounds for its validity; but this presupposes that the terms in which we describe the predicted outcomes themselves have ecological validity.

One might say, then, that the scientist, understood as the doer of yet more experiments, is not in a position to evaluate the validity of the terms that he uses. Such a figure experiences what one might indeed call a certain 'forgetfulness of Being', concerned, as he is, with improving his capacity to predict certain events, but untroubled by the question of the significance, the meaning, of those events.[38] A reservation I have about such a picture is, as I have indicated, that it overlooks the reflection on the validity of measures that practising scientists carry out. Nevertheless, such judgements certainly pose a peculiar challenge which cannot be assimilated to yet more experimental testing, which a certain kind of positivism might present as 'what scientists do'. Either way, I will suggest that this challenge bears comparison with that which Heidegger calls the challenge of 'authenticity'.

It is characteristic of the cases we have considered to present precisely in an ambiguous manner. For example, it is not at all obvious that one cannot measure happiness or when one cannot describe human conduct quantitatively and informatively. This, however, is exactly what one ought to

---

[36] Compare Heidegger's scepticism about the possibility of a mathematically exact biology: '[L]iving beings permit a certain mathematical determinability as extended bodies, but the unlimited realization of this possibility would fail in the purpose of determining and understanding the organism as such' (EP 43).

[37] To vary a familiar example, if it was suggested that IQ tests predicted later success or failure at school, one would want to know how similar the tests used to determine that success or failure were to IQ tests. Too similar, and the result becomes 'IQ tests predict later success or failure at tests similar to IQ tests'. Cf. also what Chang has labelled 'the problem of nomic measurement' (cf., e.g., Chang and Cartwright 2008: 369).

[38] There certainly are hints of such a view in Heidegger. (Cf., e.g., BPP 52–4 and QCT 176: 'Physics itself is not a possible object of a physical experiment'.) But Heidegger clearly thinks that those involved in scientific revolutions are reflecting on the sciences' 'basic concepts' (cf., e.g., BT 29–30 (9–10)).

expect: to say of such cases that a favoured descriptive tool—mathematics, say—is struggling to find application is, of course, another way of saying that we are unsure how to describe such cases. Our predicament is one in which our descriptions do not become false but empty, our descriptive vocabulary losing import. One might well say that, in the situations sketched, our words continue to make sense—the sense that they make, so to speak—in that neither they nor the measures involved recoil, as it were, from the reality to which they are applied, exposing themselves as incoherent, contradictory, non-con-forming. Our web of judgements becomes threadbare, purely decorative, but does not tear.[39] Similarly, the language of capitalism can, in one sense, describe everything that can happen in our world, and a bureaucracy may have a description for every element of the heterogeneous life that passes before it. The worry—and the worry about science's power to obscure—is rather that these modes of 'measurement' only measure what they measure. For that to be something we might be failing in failing to note, the failure would seem to be a kind of *self-obscurity*—a misunderstanding not 'of the world' but of what *we* are trying to do: a loss of an overarching sense of where what we are doing fits within the rest of what we are doing. To avoid this fate in our scientific investigations would seem to require that those investigations be guided by some overarching sense of what matters to us about the domain investigated; where that sense is weak, methodological fetishism may arise.

Perhaps a good name for this overarching sense is 'conscience', and for its possession 'authenticity'. For Heidegger, to be inauthentic is, among other things, to be captivated by the existing modes of understanding and action in which one finds oneself. Under this 'dominance of the public way in which things have been interpreted', *Dasein* fails to appropriate these modes for itself, and treats them as given or self-evidently significant; as a result, they are 'decisive even for . . . the basic way in which *Dasein* lets the world "matter" to it [and] determine[] what and how one "sees"' (BT 213 (169–70)). In such a condition, '[w]hat is talked about . . . is meant only in an indeterminate emptiness'; '[w]hile the matter being talked about slips away, what is said as such—the word, the sentence, the dictum—continues to be available' and

---

[39] This is a significant difference between my view and that of Haugeland, for whom 'intransigent discovered impossibilities undermine a disclosure of being' (2000: 73). Cf. Chapter 7 nn. 6 and 12, and for a much more detailed discussion, my (forthcoming-a): sec. 2.

'can be repeated and passed along without proper understanding'; one's talk descends into an empty, 'idle talk' and one's hearing into 'hearing *mere talk as talk*' (HCT 269). One is in the grip of what Heidegger calls 'curiosity'—a concern 'with seeing, not in order to understand what is seen (that is, to come into a Being towards it) but *just* in order to see' (BT 216 (172)); and—to echo a theme from the previous paragraph—we experience 'ambiguity'—in which '[e]verything looks as if it were genuinely understood, genuinely taken hold of, genuinely spoken, though at bottom it is not' (BT 217 (173)). These proposals, it seems to me, capture well the phenomenology of methodological fetishism—the manner in which we unwittingly cling to particular modes of description beyond the point at which our use of those modes does for us what we take it to do.

If so, Heidegger's discussion of inauthenticity may help us understand the virtue, intellectual or otherwise, that we must display in order to avoid intoxication or enchantment by modes of description; it may, for example, suggest that a certain 'historical' self-awareness must inform our scientific work.[40] But such a comparison may also help us recognize inappropriate expectations about authenticity too. For example, Heidegger has been criticized for failing to provide clear criteria by reference to which one might establish whether one is or is not authentic. But the absence of such criteria is to be expected if there is indeed a continuity between inauthenticity and methodological fetishism, since we have seen that we cannot expect equivalent criteria using which we might determine whether we have succumbed to the latter. But for now I must leave these as undeveloped suggestions.[41]

---

[40] This chimes with Beck's fascinating interpretation of Heidegger's remarks on relativity theory as both revolutionary and as a revivifying interpretation of the notion of natural laws as universal, as 'a repetition of the initial scientific projection founding modern mathematical natural science' (Beck 2002: 180). Beck too links such a possibility to the notion of the science's 'authenticity': 'The question of science's possible authenticity or inauthenticity [is] a question of whether science is capable of appropriating once again what is most essential to it, that is to say, the scientific projection of the Being of the beings in question' (pp. 185–6). Cf. also Beck 2005.

[41] In a sense, the above discussion points to 'the contingency of our practices *vis-à-vis* the ... entities to which they afford us access' (Carman 2003: 189). Carman has also drawn on Heidegger's discussion of anxiety in support of a realist reading of the latter's early work, taking that mood to reveal that 'occurrent reality' is 'radically, stubbornly, awesomely independent of us and our abilities, our hopes, our fears, indeed the very conditions of our interpretations of things at large' (p. 195). In line with my sketch of authenticity above, I see anxiety as principally providing a challenge to—or a test of—our claims to *self-knowledge*; but this is another of the many topics that would need to be addressed by a full discussion of the ideas I have here merely sketched.

I will end with one more such suggestion. From the perspective I have offered, con-formism and the competing realisms and idealisms that it inspires collectively constitute a comforting and distracting myth of the real difficulty of talking, acting, and living meaningfully. The latter feat demands of us a kind of self-awareness, a kind of self-disciplined attention to what we do and to its place within our lives as a whole and within the 'lives' of the communities to which we belong. It is such self-awareness that we must achieve if, for example, we are to ensure that our scientific practices illuminate what matters to us rather than embodying an empty, *mere* 'projection' of reality. Con-formism caricatures this responsibility of ours, comfortingly projecting it on to a match or mismatch between the 'form of the world' and the 'form of thoughts'—the latter understood in abstraction from the lives of thinkers who think them. In this way, in our quest to understand the difference between meaningful and meaningless lives and the character of the feat of living the former, we are left chasing a will-o'-the-wisp, looking in the wrong direction for the wrong kind of difference and the wrong kind of feat.

PART IV

7

Being-in-the-World and Truth Revisited

The remaining three chapters will turn our attention back to the detail of Heidegger's texts and, in the light of Chapter 6's reflections, return to some of the issues that earlier chapters raised. I will argue that those reflections shed much light on those issues, though some important puzzles remain. I will begin by re-examining Heidegger's remarks on truth and Being-in-the-world. I combine these topics here because so many of the questions that they raise seem best addressed together.

7.1 The 'soul/external world gulf'

Chapter 6 gives a clear illustration of one way in which subjectivity might require reconceptualization as a form of Being-in-the-world. The observations discussed there are made by a recognizably 'worldly' creature, the 'intending' of such facts a recognizably 'worldly' achievement; such intending is a mode of being-amid the entities described. Similarly, the worry identified in OET (PM) 282 over a certain 'gulf' between 'the soul' and the 'outside' world it intends now comes to look like the result of our succumbing to an illusion generated by a confused ontology. What goes on 'inside of the soul' is recognizably a mode of 'being-among' objects 'outside', such that one cannot characterize the former without invoking the latter. It no longer seems natural to describe these 'subject-' and 'object-correlates' as different 'species' (BT 259 (216)), or to find so perplexing the notion that the former might present the latter 'just as' it is (cf. BT 261 (218)): these activities of ours are 'cut to the measure of' their objects. Aquinas' quasi-idealism attempts to bridge this notional gap, that seems to render the possibility of *adaequatio intellectus ad rem* strange, by proposing that such *rei* are 'set up between intellects'; Heidegger dissolves the gap through his notion that *Dasein* exists *as* a mode of being familiar with or being-amongst [*Sein-bei*] *rei*, the latter understood as the 'with-which' of *Dasein*'s existing (BT 117 (85)). The assertion (that an object is 1 metre long, say) and the state of affairs it describes (the object's being 1 metre long) are not one and the same thing;[1] but to describe someone capable of entertaining the former one must invoke the states of affairs that these assertions describe. Before one envisages the latter, one has no clear conception of the former.

As passages quoted in Section 5.4.1 show, Heidegger goes out of his way to play down a spatial construal of Being-in-the-world; instead here '"in" primarily does not signify anything spatial at all but means primarily *being familiar with*' (HCT 158): '"I reside" or "dwell alongside" the world, as that which is familiar to me in such and such a way' (BT 80 (54)). As the next section will show in further detail, Chapter 6 gives a clear sense to these proposals, along with the proposals that *Dasein* 'lives in' or '*is "in the truth"*'—and indeed 'in untruth'—and that its existence 'presupposes' truth. These proposals also now have some plausibility—a claim I will attempt to support in part by showing how they accommodate a crucial intuition that Section 5.4.2 discussed: that of the 'finitude' of our knowing.

7.2 Finite knowing, 'presupposing truth', 'living in the truth' and 'in untruth'

Chapter 6 presents what is recognizably an analysis of the 'founding' of knowledge, and of the notion of truth as correspondence, in our mastery of descriptive practices.[2] But crucial to the case against thinking that that analysis commits us to a problematic idealism is a demonstration that it makes no sense to evaluate the 'truth' of the descriptive practices themselves, in the sense of assessing a correspondence or fit or a lack of correspondence or fit between them and the objects that they allow us to describe. This might seem also to provide a case *against* this 'prior' 'disclosedness'

---

[1] Cf. BPP 171 ('[t]he shoemaker is not the shoe'), quoted in Section 6.1.
[2] Hence, I share the view of Wrathall (1999) and Carman that Heidegger is not attempting to 'supplant' the traditional conception of truth as correspondence (Carman 2003: 260).

being a form of 'truth'. That is, after all, a natural enough gloss of the very similar conclusion that Wittgenstein reaches when he claims that 'the establishment of a method of measurement is *antecedent* to the correctness or incorrectness of a statement of length' and that, in such an establishment, 'there is not any question at all . . . of some correspondence between what is said and reality' (1978: Part I, sec. 156).

While that is surely and, for my purposes, importantly right, it still seems apt, I think, to label such methods as embodying 'modes of understanding *of the world*', inasmuch as mastery of them is necessary if an individual is to be capable of 'intending' the relevant regions of the world 'outside', whether in true or false assertions. The very same 'antecedence' to which Wittgenstein alludes implies that such mastery cannot be assimilated to the knowledge of any number of facts of the kind that these methods allow us to describe; but only through such mastery, through its providing a framework within which these truths and falsehoods are articulated, are we brought 'face to face with' these particular entities, can they in particular become 'binding' for assertions of ours (BT 270 (227)). We now have a quite clear sense of how the following could be true:

If truth means correspondence, adequation to entities, then this assertion measuring itself on entities is evidently founded on the fact that, in our intercourse with entities, we have already, as it were, come to an understanding with entities; entities not ourselves, with which we in some way have to deal, are disclosed to us. So an assertion can finally be true, be adequate in propositional content to that about which the assertion is made, only because the entity it speaks of is already in some way disclosed. That is, an assertion about X is only true because our dealing with that X has already a certain kind of truth. (MFL 126–7)

But, to move on to Section 5.4.2's worry about the finitude of our knowing, is Heidegger really entitled to his talk here of 'com[ing] to an understanding with . . . entities not ourselves'?

To be told that subjects must already be 'familiar with' the objects around them may rule out certain kinds of dissociation between us and the world; but it also points to others. Firstly, it is built into our understanding of the skills to which Section 6.2 alludes that we understand that (and how) they can be misapplied—that 'mediating' our awareness of the objects that those practices reveal is proper performance of the actions that those practices involve. To have mastered such practices is to know to ensure, for example, that the measuring rod is straight, and straight against the object to be measured, that the object and the rod do not move in the course of the measurement, and so on.

Secondly, this story explains the possibility of simple ignorance: having lost a representationalist 'veil of ideas' one might wonder why the facts do not, as it were, all rush in upon us, making a nonsense of our 'cognitive locality'. But the above perspective makes clear that ascertaining the facts requires that we perform certain actions, and that, without doing so, we remain ignorant.

Thirdly, mastery of these skills and the mastery that that brings of a world that 'extend[s] *spatially and temporally* beyond us' is an *achievement* which we are perfectly capable of imagining human beings failing to make; the notion of Being-in-the-world points to certain *demands* that must be met if subjectivity is to be achieved. Section 6.2 describes certain 'worldly' skills that someone must master if they are to be able to intend particular regions of the world. The notion that without a certain 'intimacy' with 'outer' entities, certain species of subject will not be present before us takes on a darker, less cosy air when we add the clause 'even if a living human body is'. The presence of such a body is not sufficient; nor—to align ourselves with an already long anti-psychologistic tradition[3]—is the presence of 'psychic states' or 'immaterial substance'. We come instead to the painful notion that the human being who cannot master various forms of 'worldly' activity will not achieve certain kinds of subjectivity. This also gives a different nuance to the proposal that we must 'always already' have 'come to an understanding with entities': namely, that until we have, then 'we' are not there. '*Dasein is its disclosedness*' (BT 171 (133)) and 'exists by way of this being-by [*Sein-bei*]-things' (MFL 127); but *humans* do not, inasmuch as some will not achieve the forms of intentionality that characterize *Dasein*. Hence, '*Dasein* is in the truth' does 'not imply a bad relativization of truth to man, but rather the other way around' (EP 155).

It is in this sense, it seems to me, that 'the presupposition of truth' 'has been "made" already with the Being of the "we"' (BT 271 (228), quoted above), the 'we' denoting *Dasein*. But at the same time, there is no inevitability that 'entities not ourselves' will become familiar to us—'us' denoting particular members of the contingently evolved species of animal, *homo sapiens*. As Wrathall has put it:

---

[3] That tradition dates back to Kant's—if not Locke's—reflections on 'immaterial substance', and run up to Wittgenstein's 'de-psychologizing of the psychological' (cf. Cavell 1976: 91), with which Heidegger's view has some similarities. As Heidegger observes at L 88, 'a critique of psychologism' must also be 'a critique of psychology'—that is, a reassessment of what we think 'the psychic' is. (Cf. also IPR 48.)

[T]hat entities are independent of us and our wishes, desires, intentions, and purposes for them, as well as our beliefs about them... means that uncovering an entity—making it something with which we can comport easily and transparently—demands something of us. It requires us to struggle to foster and develop the right skills, the right attitudes, and bodily dispositions for dealing with it. (2005: 347)

By presenting subjectivity as 'always already' 'being-amid' 'entities not ourselves', Heidegger may seem to undermine the notion that ours is a finite kind of knowing. But he does not: his identification of the above 'demands' shows that, and does so without exploding that finitude into an impossible scepticism—a view which acknowledges our 'finitude' at the expense of our 'knowing'.[4]

We also acquire a deeper sense of why Being-in-the-world's 'prior' 'disclosedness' deserves to be called a form of 'truth', despite the fact that we may not be able to make sense of that mastery fitting or failing to fit its 'objects'. What we can make perfectly good sense of is human beings failing to 'come out into the world', so to speak, as competent masters of it and the 'entities not ourselves' that populate it. Austin once remarked that '[i]t takes two to make a truth' (1950: 124); to instantiate Heidegger's deeper, 'prior' 'truth' and 'be at home in the world' is something we human animals must 'struggle to foster and develop'—something which 'demands something of us', and as such, something we may lose or fail to achieve.[5]

A remaining worry could be expressed as follows. What entitles us to think that ensuring that the execution of our descriptive acts matches up to the standards endorsed in our practices also ensures that our judgements are

---

[4] I will take the opportunity here to say a little about *Befindlichkeit*—one of the many themes in Heidegger's fundamental ontology that I have largely ignored. Chapter 6 showed that grasping 'bare' physical properties itself requires a mastery of certain capacities that merit the label 'practical', and it is plausible to suggest that that mastery involves the acquisition of certain forms of motivation: for example, a readiness to look out for, and re-examine, anomalous results, and being moved to act when the measuring cup leaks, for example. Haugeland remarks that, faced with such eventualities, there are many different ways in which the scientist might react. 'but nonchalant indifference is not among them': 'No one who simply didn't give a damn... could be a proper scientist' (2000: 60–1). Heidegger's own remarks specifically about the motivation of scientists do not confirm Haugeland's view: these 'passivist' remarks associate scientific observation with 'tranquility' (BT 177 (138)), the mood of the Aristotelian 'leisurely' scientist. But I have suggested that this 'passivist' strand in Heidegger's thinking is, at best, half the story (and Section 8.2 will offer a particular take on that half); remarks such as Haugeland's capture a significant part of what the other, perhaps more illuminating side to Heidegger's story tells us.

[5] What of the dissociation with 'the world outside' that hallucination involves? Although the above story suggests certain ways in which one might understand such radical dissociations, their very specificity means that I remain tempted by the pessimistic view I expressed in my 1996.

true of a 'broader objective world' (Wright, quoted above)? Could not our practices and what they label 'error' and 'correctness' be out of step with such a world? Some commentators want to argue that Heidegger can make sense of such a notion, and that that entitles him to what they feel is the necessary kind of answer to Tugendhat's question, 'in what manner can we inquire into the truth of th[e] horizon' that our 'prior' 'disclosedness' reveals, 'or is it not rather the case that the question of truth can no longer be applied to the horizon itself?' (1969: 237) For example, there is something obviously right in Blattner's claim that 'the use of the word "witch" in the early modern period' involves 'an outlook on the world' that was 'distorted, misguided, false' (2006: 124, 125).[6] But my sense is that Heidegger's later remark that 'we cannot ask at all about the "correctness" of a projection' (CP 229)[7] accurately reflects his early view too; and the need we feel in the face of Tugendhat's question depends very much upon which kind of 'disclosedness' one has before one's mind. For reasons that Sections 6.2 and 6.3 explain, it is far from clear that we can make sense of our practice of measuring length, for instance, as embodying an 'outlook' that could turn out false in anything like the way that the early modern view of witches has;[8] to reapply or adapt a notion which was important in our earlier discussion, these practices can be seen as embodying 'original havings'. Moreover, if my Heideggerian story above is correct—about the need for forms of understanding that are not constituted by the grasp of correspondences but instead make it possible for us to see thought as corresponding or failing to correspond to reality—then at some point we must run into 'disclosures' that are incapable of being false in the sense of failing to correspond to reality.

It may also be useful here to revisit the McDowellian notion that we should reject as confused any 'view from sideways on'—a notion that we touched upon in Sections 2.3 and 4.3.2. Notions of 'living in the truth' 'in the world' or—as in Section 2.3—'in categories' have an obvious

---

[6] As my discussion of authenticity makes clear, I think Blattner, Haugeland and Smith are right to strive to recover *something* in Heidegger that might have for the 'prior disclosure' the status of falsehood; but what I offer is closer, it seems to me, to Heidegger's actual views. Cf. Chapter 6 nn. 12 and 39 below.

[7] Translation from Lafont 2000: 143.

[8] In quite which sense Blattner wants to suggest that the early modern outlook on witches is false is unclear to me. He says that 'the concept of a witch gets no grip on the world', but also talks of using 'true' and 'false' in 'a philosophically extended way' (2006: 124, 125).

resonance with this notion. But going beyond mere resonance, we now have a sense of how the Heideggerian perspective that they help present connects with what Section 2.3 argued was the best philosophical construal of McDowell's notion: that such 'views' are not a kind of view that is ruled out, but rather articulations of illusions of a point of view from which one might engage in a kind of reflection. Sections 5.2, 5.3, and 5.4.4 set out *a priori* reasons for believing that our fundamental relation to the world cannot be one of adequation or correspondence because, for example, any such relation presupposes the availability and mastery of a standard of measurement, of adequation or correspondence. In line with this *a priori* case, the notion of a con-formity of the practices that Chapter 6 discusses with the objects they allow us to describe has turned out to be a confusion: there is no issue about which one might adopt such a reflective point of view.

I have mentioned already that Being-in-the-world is a motif that we come to from a number of different directions, and the connection with McDowell points clearly to one in particular—and, I think, a central one. A sense in which we must always already 'live' or 'be in the world' lies in the fact that a certain vision of a 'distance' from the 'possibility' of judgement or thought makes no sense, the possibility of our *not* 'being in the world' understood as the possibility of such a 'distance', of a 'view-from-sideways-on'. But our anti-con-formist reflections suggest that that 'possibility' is a myth, as is the 'distance' necessary for that 'possibility' to be, in some sense, contemplated or evaluated. At bottom, our relationship to the world is 'intimate familiarity' (HCT 158) in that we cannot assign sense to the 'distance' we might imagine adopting.

But we should also note, firstly, a point on which Chapter 6 suggests that one of McDowell's elucidations of the rejection of such a 'view' makes too blanket a statement, and secondly, the kind of criticism that Section 6.4 identified to which our use of certain 'disclosures' may be subject, despite the fact that their 'truth' cannot be questioned as the con-formist confusedly imagines. This criticism also provides a sense for the claim that *Dasein* 'is in "untruth"' (BT 264 (222)).

As was quoted in Section 4.3.2, 'modest' theories, 'by design, start in the midst of content' and are unable to 'contribute to [the] task of representing content as an achievement' (McDowell 1987: 105). But, as this section has shown, 'content' is 'an achievement', in that there are demands that a 'candidate' for subjectivity must meet if it is indeed to come to stand 'in the midst of content'.⁹ What remains true, of course, is that the 'achievement' in question is not one of seeing how the descriptive practices that Chapter 6 describes con-form to the objects that they allow us to describe or one that might be captured in an 'immodest' 'spelling out', in terms other than those that the practice deploys, of why those terms are somehow suited to, or fit for, describing—con-forming to—those objects. Chapter 6 might also seem incompatible with my criticism of Dreyfus and some of his readers for claiming that he reveals 'conditions of'—has 'accounted for'—the 'possibility' of meaning and intentionality: the 'demands' mentioned above and the kinds of descriptive practices described might seem to embody precisely such 'conditions'. But again, I think the most illuminating way to describe what we learn when we recognize those 'demands' and the character and significance of those practices is that certain notions of meaning and intentionality, which, when thought through, might seem to pose questions about the 'possibility' of meaning and intentionality, are confused.¹⁰

Finally in this section, Section 6.4 identified a kind of non-con-formist criticism to which our use of particular 'disclosures of Being' can indeed be subject. In asking a determinate question, one adopts a particular *Hinblick*

---

⁹ Whether the above formulations illuminatingly present McDowell's own view is also a significant question, and this has a bearing on remarks that he makes in his exchange with Dreyfus (cf. ch. 4 n. 1) which might seem out of kilter with a stress on 'constitutional practices' making it possible for a subject to be intentionally related to particular features of the world around it. McDowell talks of aspects of experience 'com[ing] to constitute the content of a conceptual capacity' by being 'focused on and made to be the meaning of a linguistic expression' (2007a: 348); becoming such a content requires that the subject 'carve [this aspect] out from the categorically unified but as yet, in this respect, unarticulated experiential content of what it is an aspect'; and McDowell proposes that '[i]t is overwhelmingly natural to cash out this image of carving out an aspect... in terms of annexing a bit of language to it' (p. 347). Dreyfus sees in these proposals the assumption 'that nameability (and so thinkability) is always available in our experience of the world', and a vision according to which 'we just drop a name on an already fully determinate feature implicit in the world' (Dreyfus 2007a: 358). Although McDowell questions other claims that Dreyfus makes in this exchange, he does not challenge these; and his silence might suggest that he believes that 'we are *simply* open to the world of facts' (Dreyfus 2007a: 362, italics added). But he need not assume that there is anything simple about it, nor about 'carving out aspects' or 'dropping names on features'; indeed, that thought would be out of step with many themes in his work, especially his reflections on moral sensibility, on the importance of 'second nature', and Wittgenstein's conception of intentionality as necessarily involving certain practices (cf., e.g., his 1984, 1994, and 1998). These, it seems to me, are broadly in the spirit of the 'constitutional' reflections I have offered, and give us reason to think of 'content' as very much 'an achievement'.

¹⁰ A potentially important topic is how the above discussion might help address the worry that attacks on the 'myth of the given' leave thought to a 'frictionless spinning in the void' (McDowell 1994: 11). The Heideggerian perspective, as elaborated here, promises to undo that impression because it presents thought as a way of being-among objects. But I will leave for another day the question of whether this proposal can be developed.

and directs one's attention to particular aspects of the world, the length of objects, as opposed to their weights, their history, their cost, their sentimental value, and so on. To borrow from EP's discussion of the sciences, any such practice 'stakes out a field', 'fixes on and demarcates' a 'determinate region and never... entities as a whole'. In so doing, Heidegger claims, such a practice 'necessarily ventures into an area of concealment which constantly surrounds it' (EP 212–13). But why 'concealment'? One might cite the fact that such a practice embodies 'only *one* kind and possibility of making manifest of entities' (EP 203). To make a judgement one must adopt a particular *Hinblick*, but in so doing one forfeits the possibility of addressing other aspects of the world.[11] But still, why say that this admittedly partial revelation 'ventures into an area of concealment'?

Another way of expressing the above partiality is to say that these modes of 'measurement' only measure what they measure. Section 6.4 argued that the 'overlooking' of this fact constitutes a kind of *self*-obscurity, and may play a role in Heidegger's notion of inauthenticity. Through such self-forgetfulness, one may 'fall' into particular 'kinds of making manifest' without reflecting on the significance of the particular truths to which one is confining one's attention. Confining one's attention in this way is something which one can either recognize or not, and take responsibility for or not, as, for example, when one decides a business deal on the basis of what it will do to the share price, as opposed to what it will do to the employees, or the environment or... One can either recognize and take responsibility for that choice, or one can pass it on—consciously or unconsciously—to others—concrete or imagined—by engaging in reflection that answers not to the question 'What do I think should be done?' but, for example, 'What would a good servant of the share-holders do?' To claim, as I did in Section 5.3, that the choice of a *Hinblick* cannot be justified by judging the character of the objects one encounters is not then to deny that we might choose a *Hinblick* on other grounds or recognize where we have a certain freedom in what we choose to address. Exploring what such possibilities amount to must be left to another occasion, though Section 9.2 will touch briefly on these matters again.[12]

---

[11] Crowell 2001, Dahlstrom 2001, and Wrathall 2005 make similar points.

[12] I share with Smith (2007) and Haugeland, upon whom he draws (cf. his 2000), the sense that the demand that we be authentic demands that we adopt a certain critical perspective towards what our particular forms of disclosive practices reveal. But I do not share their understanding of authenticity nor

7.3 'Empty intending', 'logical space', and the 'most obvious objection'

Another road that leads to Being-in-the-world is the holistic notion that intending an entity is at the same time the intending of a 'space' within which it can be seen to be so, or so, or so. I suggest that this 'road' may be discussed usefully in connection with a puzzle raised in connection with truth—what Tugendhat calls the 'remarkable possibility' of 'emptily intending' that which can subsequently present itself in a 'fulfilling intuition'.[13]

In roughest outline, one might suggest that our Being-in-the-world is what corresponds in Heidegger's philosophy to Husserl's 'empty intending': a prior 'having to do with' that lacks a correspondence structure and provides the 'space' or 'frame' within which particular entities can present themselves as . . . —an 'absence' out of which entities 'descend' (PS 448, quoted in Section 5.2). Presupposed in any measurement of a length—correct or incorrect—is a general mastery of the practice of measurement. That mastery opens up 'an encircling neighbourhood of manifestness' (EP 137) in which these particular ranges of matters of fact, these particular 'fulfilments' of these 'logical spaces', can show themselves.[14] In this way, prior to making any particular measurement, the master of the measuring

---

of the kind of critical perspective it requires. According to my own understanding, we cannot assign a sense to the notion that a disclosure of the kind I have mentioned might be false as such, but that does not entail that such a disclosure tells one what one *needs* to know, and recognizing that is what calls for authenticity, a kind of self-knowledge. That calls for a kind of 'critical consciousness' (Tugendhat 1969: 238), though not the form that Tugendhat, Haugeland, and Smith envisage. Cf. Chapter 6 nn. 6 and 39 above.

[13] Cf. Section 5.2.

[14] Another of Heidegger's notions to which I have given little direct attention is 'projection'. A worry it raises is that it seems to suggest that 'projecting' is something that *Dasein* does—an 'achievement of subjectivity' (LH 231)—but our 'thrownness' seems to dictate that *Dasein* cannot possibly originate such a 'projection' and instead must 'always already' live within one. Chapter 6 suggests a different way of looking at 'projection': upon mastering the descriptive practices in question, we come to live in a particular 'projection' of the objects to be described—'projection' best understood perhaps in the mathematical sense in which, as Macquarrie and Robinson note (BT 185 (145) n. 1), the German term (*Entwurf*) can also be used. (Cf. also WT 92's discussion of 'mathematical projection'.) We come to look at a particular 'aspect' or 'side' of these objects, as when we consider the front or side 'projection' of a building. Inasmuch as different agents intend different aspects of what is there to be encountered, they might be said to 'throw' a different 'projection' over it; but such 'throwing' is now better understood as something that these agents, so to speak, are rather than do. Our lives express, one might say, different 'projections of the Being of entities'; as an intentional agent, I exist *as* a perspective on things as . . . and, 'as long as [*Dasein*] is, it is projecting' (BT 185 (145)).

rod has mastered a 'prior' *Hinblick*, can 'anticipate', what it is for any object to be of any length. Such 'empty intending' relates to 'fulfilment' in that that mastery is at the same time the capacity to evaluate whether a particular object 'fulfils' particular 'presumptions' of length.[15] If it does not, we recognize it as having a different but still determinate length which our general mastery of the method allows us to recognize—other lengths also 'presumed' in our particular claim as those to which the object will *not* match. Skilled use of the measuring rod therefore presents a standard to which an object can match, and what makes that use the use of a measuring rod is that possibility: its 'empty' but inherently 'fulfillable' 'intending', 'into coincidence' with which objects may be brought. This is the mundane fact behind the 'entelechy'[16] of our 'empty intending', its 'striving' at its 'fulfilment': the general capacity that allows us to see someone as 'intending extended objects' is one and the same as the capacity to evaluate whether objects 'fulfil' particular 'presumptions' of length.[17]

I will now also return to Section 5.4.3's 'most obvious objection' to the 'direct realism' that BT sec. 44 might seem to expound. Possession of the general capacity described is consistent with its master failing to perform certain measurements and, on occasion, not performing measurements correctly. We can distinguish—if not with a particularly fine line—the making of such mistakes from a complete failure to master the practice; the former indeed presupposes the latter general skill. This gives us a way of thinking about the apparent evasiveness that marks Heidegger's response to the 'most obvious objection'. A master of the above practices 'liv[es] *in general* in the behaviour of uncovering', grasping the '*type of Being* of the entity about which [she] is speaking'.[18] On that basis we see the finite and fallible master of such a technique as capable of 'presuming', 'emptily intending' a length that may turn out to have no 'fulfilling', perceived analogue. In that general but occasionally fallible mastery, she 'tarries alongside' such entities, having 'the tendency and intention to grasp and

---

[15] I set aside here worries about, for example, lengths of such magnitude that one is physically incapable of measuring them.
[16] Cf. Dahlstrom 2001: 60, quoted in Section 5.2.
[17] I pass closely, once again, to externalist worries (cf. Chapter 6 n. 28), which I will not discuss here.
[18] These passages are quoted in Section 5.4.3 above; the first set of italics have been added.

have them',[19] even if, on occasion, she fails to do so; whereas the person who lacks such general mastery does not: he messes about with a stick.[20]

Does this give us any entitlement to the strong talk above of 'the entity which one has in mind' being the '*very same thing*' as that which one finds 'outside', or of having to 'have' what I am searching for? What we can say is that the master of the technique in question knows everything there is to know about an object *as an extended object*, every relation of greater or lesser in which it might stand to any other extended object. All he does not know is whether there is such an object; that is the only 'surprise' that the object can yet pose for him, the only thing that the person who has the corresponding 'fulfilling intuition' knows about the object that he does not. So he might be surprised to find out that there is a 50-foot woman, but he will not be surprised by the fact that she is 44 feet taller than his 6-foot friend.

7.4 On the 'real/ideal gulf'

In the opening pages of L sec. 10 (a rich section which anticipates BT 261 (218)'s 'direct realism' and examines Husserl's concepts of 'empty' and 'fulfilled' intentions), Heidegger asks whether the 'seemingly profound question about bridging the gap between the real and the ideal' might be 'only a foolish undertaking' that 'gets the semblance of a justification only from this: you first of all invent these two regions, then you put a gap between them, and then you go looking for the bridge' (L 92).[21] The basis of this 'invention' and the subsequent pursuit of 'a "relation" (oriented to the previous separation) between real thinking and the ideal what-is-thought' lies in a failure to recognize that '[t]hinking is the thinking of what-is-thought, because thinking as mental already and necessarily has the structure of self-directedness-to-something' (L 90, 95). Anticipating McDowell's proposal that 'a thought,

---

[19] Quoted in Section 5.4.3.

[20] My (forthcoming-b): sec. 6 builds on the account that Chapter 6 offers in presenting another understanding of why mastery of such a framework might be seen as mastery of, or as the experiencing of, a kind of truth, an understanding that turns on the fact that a person's successful application of a skill—such as that of measuring—is a condition of ascribing the skill to that person. Here again, I suspect that a central Heideggerian motif is overdetermined.

[21] This brings to mind a remark of Heidegger's made in another connection: '[T]he division is not to be rejected because it can actually be bridged, but because it may not be made at all and is, at its root, ungenuine' (PIE 8).

just as such, is something with which only certain states of affairs would accord' (McDowell 1993: 270),[22] Heidegger insists that

[the mental] is not first of all only real, as it were, within consciousness, and then afterwards, by some kind of mechanism, related to something outside... No— instead the mental is first and only as this very self-directedness; it is "real" as such self-directedness. (L 95–6)

I will tentatively suggest that our discussion above suggests a certain filling out of this abstract diagnosis of the 'real/ideal gulf'.

Section 7.2 has argued that although, as human beings or possessors of 'mere psychical states', we are indeed independent of the 'entities not ourselves' that lie around us, the same is not true of the skilled, educated subject. Such a subject has imposed a certain discipline on herself: she has learnt how to 'measure' her assertions 'on entities' (MFL 127). In her hands, the measuring rod is no longer a mere 'present-at-hand' stick, but something with application to—that 'emptily intends' and can be 'fulfilled' by—the lengths of objects; and whatever 'mere psychical states' she may have previously possessed, we now see her as intentionally related to a domain of objects, as the possesser of 'states' that genuinely merit labels such as 'psychic' and 'mental'. As EP 155 puts it, '[o]nly if *Dasein* as disclosed discovering can comply with entities, can it speak out appropriately [*angemessen*] about them'.

What our skilled subject sees around her are also no longer, as it were, simple particulars, in that, in the 'encircling neighbourhood of manifestness' that her mastery 'projects', objects show themselves as instances of the universal, 'extended object', as occupying particular places within the 'logical space' that 'extended objects in general' inhabit and standing in determinate relations (of greater, lesser, and equal length) to other such objects. By 'ascending' into a mastery of that practice, the subject now intends these objects and that 'space'; a world of such universals, of the ideal, is now open before her. Though the unskilled human being is *merely* 'real', *Dasein* is not.[23]

But what do these remarks really tell us about our problematic 'gulf'? I am not at all confident that they tell us much about the metaphysical

---

[22] Cf. Section 4.2.2's 'diagnosis' of the first regress argument.
[23] Cf. PS 55's proposal that the universal 'belongs to *Dasein* insofar as *Dasein* is disclosive'.

question of how particulars relate to universals; but they may shed some light on the question of the relationship between 'ideal content' and 'the Real act of judgement', though only if we recognize the kind of response that they represent: namely, one (like Section 7.1's treatment of our other 'gulf') which identifies, and calls into question, presuppositions that we make in posing the question.

Consider a related problem that BT (BT 258 (215–16))'s question, how— 'with regard to what'—can we compare *intellectus* and *res*?', might seem to conjure into existence—as indeed might our earlier talk of 'methods for comparing' assertions with the world and OET's of an assertion being 'invested with its correctness'. That question—and such talk—may seem to suggest one can identify an assertion *prior* to its being 'invested with its correctness', prior to the identification of a relevant 'method for comparing'. Of such an 'assertion' one might find oneself wondering, 'How ought it to be compared with reality?'

But this question rests upon a conception of the assertion modelled on the 'master thesis', on 'depicturization': regarding such an assertion, 'it is only by virtue of being interpreted in one of various possible ways that it can impose a sorting of extra-[linguistic] items into those that accord with it and those that do not'.[24] To view the assertion in this way is to view it, to adopt some Wittgensteinian terms, as a sign and not a symbol, as a 'dead' physical mark on paper or sound-wave in the air, as opposed to a sign with a 'significant use' (1922 3.326).[25]

As Section 4.2.2 may have led the reader to expect, Heidegger gives the very same diagnosis. The above 'problem' of 'how to compare *intellectus* and *res*' 'takes the spoken sentence as the point of departure'; it imagines that 'you take up a sentence' 'the same way as you pick up a piece of chalk (thereby uprooting it, wrenching it from its proper place)' (BBA 230). Understood in this way, we find ourselves needing to determine what the 'relationship' ought to be 'between things which are present-at-hand (*intellectus* and *res*)' (BT 267 (225)). And this is indeed a hopeless task, because,

---

[24] I say 'modelled' and adapt this quotation (from McDowell 1993: 270, quoted in Section 4.2.2) because the 'master thesis' is formulated in connection with mental states rather than assertions.

[25] Cf. DSTCM 111, 115: 'The word has no intentional character as a complex of sounds or aggregate of letters... [But] *as soon as one lives in knowledge and its presentation ... the alogical character of linguistic structures disappears*. They reveal themselves to be realities charged with a peculiar function, to be *bearers* of meanings.'

of course, one can use a mere string of signs however one wants.[26] The belief that one *ought* to be able to perform this task lies in the fact that the assertion is something 'in which there still lurks a relational character' (BT 267 (225)). The 'point of departure' is a confused vision of the assertion as a 'present-at-hand' object in which a relation 'lurks'.

The same is true if we imagine needing a method for comparing a 'psychic aspect' or 'aspect of consciousness' with something in 'the external world' (BBA 220, quoted above), such a method allowing 'a coordination relative to other realities [which is] *added to* ... experiences taken as psychic states' (HCT 29, italics added). Though we describe these 'states' or 'aspects' as 'psychic' or 'conscious', what grounds do we have for thinking of them as *intentional*? To experience the 'need' to 'add' to which HCT alludes, we must both deny them this property and surreptitiously allow it to remain, 'lurking'.[27]

I think that the 'explanation' of the 'real/ideal gulf' sketched above works—if it works—in a similar way. It persuades us that, when thinking clearly, the only items we see as 'Real *acts of judgement*' are those we see as occupying a place in certain recognizably intentional practices. To instead be stumped by how a 'Real *act of judgement*' could possibly 'relate to ideal content', one must instead identify such an act with something like a 'present-at-hand' state in the brain of an animal or a Cartesian ego, while at the same time unwittingly considering that state against the background of such a practice: we must have 'uprooted' that judgement, 'wrenching it from its proper place' while also letting that 'place' continue to 'lurk'. This is, of course, the basis of the 'dissolving' reading offered for Dreyfus' first 'regress of rules' argument. We require not so much a third kind of Being to provide a 'bridge' by which propositions, for example, come to have application as a recognition of confusions that leave propositions seemingly requiring such a 'bridge'; we have 'invented' our 'two regions', 'put a gap between them', and 'then gone looking for a bridge'.[28] Such a response does not

---

[26] As Wittgenstein puts it, 'the sign is arbitrary' (1922: 3.22): '[w]e cannot give a sign the wrong sense' (1922: 5.4732).

[27] Here again we see a familiar pattern. Our first step in reflecting on 'what else is tacitly posited' in the correspondence relation is to recognize that it rests upon another relation which determines how *intellectus* and *rei* are to be compared. The next step is to recognize that the latter relation must be 'pregiven' if the 'state' or 'aspect' that one has before one is to merit labels such as 'psychic', 'conscious', 'intentional', indeed 'intellect'.

[28] Regarding the second 'regress', I continue to believe that Heidegger has little to tell us about the '*ceteris paribus*' rules' upon which Dreyfus focuses in that argument; but, in line with the 'dissolving'

answer the question with which we began, but instead attempts to 'dissolve' it. As with our puzzlement by the 'entelechy'—the 'striving'—of 'empty intending', if *intellectus* (subjectivity, intentionality) looks like this—mastery of worldly practices of measurement—rather than like that—present-at-hand 'psychic states'—then the puzzle with which we started (the *need* for a bridge) seems to melt away.

The above gives us some feel, I think, for why Heidegger could have felt in a position to raise issues such as 'the real/ideal gulf' in the course of his discussion of truth, and to feel as if he were saying something in response.[29] But clearly, an *awful* lot more needs to be said—not least because the view expressed might even seem to exacerbate another earlier worry: namely, that Heidegger leads us into a species of 'continuity scepticism'.

This is a significant worry, though Chapter 6 does at least allow us to reframe it. That chapter offers a picture of intentional comportment as mastery of certain descriptive practices—hence the puzzle of its emergence is the puzzle of their emergence. Taking the examples considered there, we can at least see a series of continuous steps that a creature or a species must make in emerging into such comportment. For example, there would seem to be a continuity running from judging objects larger or smaller than others—perhaps through finding that one object will not fit inside another—to singling out a particular object by reference to which others might be so categorized, to its iterated use to further categorize larger objects, and the creation of other objects that match that 'standard' object which other members of a group might use to create comparable observations, and so on. Each such step is no doubt a major conceptual innovation, and the first step mentioned might strike some as the most momentous of all. But we have some sense of how such steps might come to be understood as emerging out of more primitive behaviour; and the very fact that understanding such steps recognizably falls within the remit of child psychologists, anthropologists,

---

reading offered for the claims that such considerations elicit from Dreyfus, Chapter 6 gives a vivid sense of how the notion of a 'view-from-sideways-on' may indeed represent a fantasy. In line with Section 2.3's proposal which our subsequent discussion has substantiated, this is not because we are in some way 'confined' to an 'internal view', *unable*, one might say, to look 'from-sideways-on', but because, in the cases discussed, we have no clear conception of the understanding and its 'objects' which will allow us to consider them as 'corresponding' or 'not corresponding'.

[29] I suspect that a full appreciation of Heidegger's approach to this 'gulf' would also require a full examination of his notion of authenticity, since his analysis of 'idle talk' could be seen as an analysis of how 'the ideal' can indeed leach out of supposedly 'Real acts of judgement'.

and archaeologists suggests that we face a more tractable objective than one might suppose if one were instead to see the challenge as that of explaining how the 'light' of intentionality comes to flicker on in a brain, how 'mere animals' somehow suddenly find themselves 'living in projections', or of how worlds that were previously 'clouded' and 'poor' come to be 'clear' and 'rich'. But, as I have indicated, more needs to be said in response to these issues, in facing which—as Bar-On argues—Heidegger is in rather good company.[30]

7.5 Truth's dependency on *Dasein*

I turn now to the final puzzle that we extracted from BT sec. 44, the Dependency Claim: *'There is' truth only in so far as Dasein is and so long as Dasein is*' (BT 269 (226)). As Section 5.4.3 indicated, there is a lot that Heidegger says the Dependency Claim *does not* mean, and we must also—if we can help it—set aside the following interpretation: no truths are *expressed* or *entertained* without the existence of *Dasein*. That may be true, but it is trivially so. I have argued that Part III's proposals serve to expose as confused questions to which realism and idealism each represent answers; and my conclusion here—to anticipate and confess—will be that I can see no philosophically defensible construal of the Dependency Claim, though we can see why Heidegger may have been drawn to make it.

Heidegger seems to have been aware of the thin ice upon which he treads with the Dependency Claim. He talks of the need to 'clarify the ontological meaning of the kind of talk in which we say that "there is truth"' (BT 257 (214)), to clarify 'what this "there is..." signifies' (L 23):

There are automobiles, Negroes, Abelian functions, Bach's fugues. 'Are there' truths too? Or how could it be otherwise? (L 23)

---

[30] My (forthcoming-a) elaborates on some of these thoughts in response to Lafont's claim that according to Heidegger's view, 'the attempt to conceive the historical changes in our understanding of being as a learning process is just an illusion' (2000: xv). The account I sketch is not one which Heidegger himself developed, and one way of viewing the emergence of his later work is as a process shaped by a growing belief in what might call the 'wonder' or 'mystery' of the emergence of 'disclosures of being'; cf. Chapter 2 n. 26 and Chapter 5 n. 31.

In BT, Heidegger scare-quotes consistently the locution 'Being is', acutely aware of the misleading impression that it gives: namely, that Being is itself an entity.[31] The same caution seems to inform the scare-quoting in BT 269 (226)'s formulation of the Dependency Claim, and suggests an anticipation of Glock's (1997: 100) assessment of the following chain of deductions—a chain which begins with a premise that Heidegger certainly seems[32] to accept:

(i) If there were no people, there would still be mountains.

That implies

(ii) If there were no people, it would still be true that there are mountains.

That seems to imply

(iii) If there were no people, it would still be a truth that there are mountains.

And that seems to imply

(iv) If there were no people, there would still be truths

—a conclusion which Heidegger would not accept, since, to repeat the Dependency Claim, '"[t]here is" truth only in so far as Dasein is and so long as Dasein is' (BT 269 (226)). Glock challenges the move to (iii) and thereby to (iv) in the following way:

These statements are not so much false as misleading, in that they speak of the existence of truths or of there being such-and-such a truth. This suggests that truths are objects which are either created or destroyed at a certain time . . . or exist eternally . . . But truths are not things that can begin to exist, cease to exist, or last for ever. (p. 102)

Heidegger surely should agree with this; so why does he jump into that confused game anyway? The remarks we are worrying over here are a central focus for the large literature on Heidegger's discussion of truth. All I will do here is follow through a line of thought which might have attracted Heidegger and which my interpretation might suggest.

---

[31] Cf. BT 228 (183), BT 255 (212), and LH 238.
[32] Cf., e.g., BT 269 (227) quoted in Section 5.4.3 above.

Chapter 6—especially as elaborated in Section 7.3—might encourage one to think of methods of measuring lengths as creating a 'space' into which objects can then fit, and as determining thereby what it is for it to be true that such objects are what we call 'a particular length'. One might then conclude that

(a) Without the existence of the practice of measuring lengths, there would be no such thing as being of a particular length or truths about the lengths of objects.

Such a practice determines what it is to ask 'How long is this object?' and, if we were to find ourselves without—in some sense—that practice, then that question might seem to be rendered 'insufficiently determined'. The absence of *Dasein* might then be seen as leaving not only no mouth to ask—or mind to entertain—the question of what is true (as the trivial interpretation of the Dependency Claim proposes), but also no determinate question to be asked. Mulhall seems to express a similar thought:

[T]here can be no question of a judgement's corresponding (or failing to correspond) with reality without a prior conceptualisation of that reality, and there can be no such conceptualization of reality without *Dasein*... [A] world without *Dasein* would not simply be a world without beings capable of making true judgements, but a world without the ultimate source of the categories in terms of which true and false judgements must be articulated, and so in which those articulations themselves are non-existent. (Mulhall 1996: 99, 103)[33]

Hence, one might say that

(b) There can be truths of a particular sort only if there is a conceptualization of a corresponding kind or an articulation of judgements of a corresponding kind.

The spirit of Mulhall's account is one with which I am very much in sympathy.[34] But taking either (a) or (b) as an interpretation and defence of the Dependency Claim strikes me as fishy, and in a way bound up—

---

[33] There are some parallels with—and parallel difficulties in—a reading of the Dependency Claim that one might derive from Blattner's reading of BT's seemingly idealist claims concerning Being (cf., e.g., BT 255 (212))—a reading on which I will touch briefly at the end of this section.

[34] Its understanding of the relationship between truth and 'a prior conceptualisation of reality' also bears comparison with Rouse's (1987: 158–65), with which I also broadly agree. The step to the kind of problematic reading of the Dependency Claim that I question would naturally be made in Rouse's case from his remark that '[w]e... sustain the configuration [of equipment, practices and goals] within which things can show themselves [for example] as hammers (or not)' (p. 159, italics added).

predictably—with the talk involved of 'practices', 'conceptualizations', and 'articulations' 'existing' or 'not existing'.[35] The construals of (a) and (b) that are plausible as an interpretation of the Dependency Claim entail that

(c) The existence of the truths in question requires that there actually are creatures engaging in the relevant practices, conceiving of the world in the relevant ways, or articulating the relevant judgements.

What else, one might ask, would it be for there to 'be' such practices, conceptualisations or articulations? But I think there are other construals of (a) and (b) that do not entail (c) and that it is those other construals that make us hear (a) and (b) as plausible, *full stop*. For example,

(a*) For there to be such a thing as truth about length there must be such a thing as the practice of measuring length.

and

(a**) For there to be such a thing as truth about length the practice of measuring length must make sense.

The sense of neither (a*) nor (a**) could be described as transparent. We are perhaps imagining something like the following: it is within the universe's possibilities that such practices exist. But most importantly for our immediate concerns, neither (a*) nor (a**) seem to entail that such practices actually exist, that someone or something actually engages in any such practice, and that seems to be the kind of condition that the Dependency Claim lays down. Neither (a*) nor (a**), for example, seems to allude to a situation which might come about or come to an end, as seems to be required by BT 269 (226)'s talk of 'only as long as *Dasein* is', 'before there was any *Dasein*', and 'after *Dasein* is no more'. So my suspicion is that (a) and (b) turn out either plausible, or as plausible interpretations of the Dependency Claim, but not as both.

Before ending this section I will look at two more attempts to render the Dependency Claim plausible—neither of which, I believe, provides anything like a straightforward defence of that Claim. The second will focus on Heidegger's discussion of temporality. But I will first consider an attempt

---

[35] I have similar reservations about Blattner's talk of 'ontological frameworks' 'being' or 'not being in place'. See below.

that focuses on Chapter 6's depiction of a form of understanding of the world which cannot be seen as a form of correspondence—activities of *Dasein* that 'are not constituted independently of' the objects they reveal—and on the fact that the existence of such forms of understanding may seem to entail claims of 'immediate connectedness', or 'internal relatedness'. The latter expression is one on which several commentators have drawn in interpreting Heidegger,[36] and it does indeed seem to provide a natural way to articulate his concern with the intimate interweaving (in some sense) of 'structures' that he feels philosophy has mistakenly attempted to understand in isolation from one another. To take just one example, he insists that '[t]aken strictly, there is no such thing as *an* equipment' since '[e]quipment—in accordance with its equipmentality—always is *in terms of [aus]* its belonging to other equipment' (BT 97 (68)); these items, we might say, are 'internally related'.[37] Most relevantly to our present concerns, such 'internal relations' may seem to entail *existential* dependencies, of just the sort that the Dependency Claim articulates. How, one might ask, can something exist without that to which it is 'internally related'? If truths and the 'projections' that articulate them are 'internally related', then, one might say, there can be no such truths without such 'projections'.

The notion of 'internal relatedness' may have a significant role to play in explaining Heidegger's thought, and it and related metaphors of 'immediacy' and 'intimacy' are indeed natural choices in articulating some of the claims I have made on his behalf.[38] But these articulations need to be handled with care, as indeed must the notion of 'internal relatedness'.[39] In a passage from MFL upon which we touched earlier, Heidegger recognizes a version of the one of the difficulties I have in mind:

Inasmuch as *Dasein* exists *qua* Being-in-the-world, it is already out there with entities; and even this manner of speaking is still distorted [*schief*][40] since 'already out there' presupposes *Dasein* is at some point on the inside. Even if I say, *Dasein's*

---

[36] Cf., e.g., Guignon 1983: passim, Rouse 1987: 74, Minar 2001: 206, and Mulhall 2005: 40.

[37] Another example might be Heidegger's statement that 'Being-in-the-World...is not pieced together, but is primordially and constantly a whole'. He continues, 'the whole of this structure always comes first' (BT 65 (41)), and we might elaborate upon that by saying that what we take to be its 'constituent elements' are actually 'internally related' to one another.

[38] My (forthcoming-b) discusses Heidegger's appropriation of the Aristotlean notion that our judgement ultimately rests on a form of 'touch', *thigein*: here 'there is no distance' (L 180, 181).

[39] Chapters 4 and 15 of my 2006 discuss at length the difficulties that this notion raises.

[40] Heim's choice of 'imprecise' as a translation of '*schief*' gives this passage a very particular spin that its other possible translations—'crooked', 'oblique', or 'distorted'—do not.

intentional activity is always already open towards entities and for entities, there is still at bottom the supposition that it was once closed. (MFL 167)

To assert, in opposition to a Cartesian vision of the Subject as 'closed' and 'inside', that *Dasein* is 'open' and 'out there' threatens to leave these Cartesian confusions in place, drawing, as it seems to, precisely upon them in saying that *Dasein* is *not* 'closed' and *not* 'on the inside'. Such claims *deny* what they are intended to suggest are *nonsensical* claims, claims whose sense is—as Section 9.2 below will discuss—*indefinite*. At best, such claims—if they indeed merit that label—will draw attention to the confusion here of talk of 'closedness' *and* 'openness', of 'being on the inside' *and* 'being out there'; and such claims—about 'openness' and 'being out there'—ought then also to be cast aside in the end.

Let us review the key moral of Chapter 6 in this light. In that discussion, when we saw that no sense could be made of certain 'structures' as standing to one another in a relation of 'correspondence', we discovered precisely that: that a certain thought we believed we could entertain was no such thing. We might then have reached for talk of an 'intimate' or 'immediate' relation;[41] but, in doing so, we would have been in danger of misrepresenting our realization. It is not that we came to a different and better answer to our original question of how these 'structures' 'relate', this being recognized as a matter of a now-well-understood form of 'intimacy' or 'internal relatedness' in place of a 'distance' or 'external relatedness'; rather, we came to see that our original question was confused: we had at our disposal no clear conception of the 'structures' in question such that we might ask how they 'corresponded' or 'related' to one another. We did not come to see that the questions we were inclined to pose about this 'relationship' ought to be answered through talk of its being one of 'internal relation', but instead came to see that we could assign no clear sense to those questions.

---

[41] My own 2007, which presents an earlier discussion of some of the ideas upon which Chapter 6 draws, does precisely that. At the time of writing it I thought that the difficulties that my 2006 identifies could be held at bay in that particular context; but now I think otherwise. For related reasons, upon which I elaborate above, I am uneasy about Pippin's ascription to Heidegger of what he calls an '"inseparability" thesis about subject and object, concept and intuition, Dasein and world' (2007: 204). This seems to me to be the wrong way to articulate what we learn when we realize that, for Heidegger, the question of 'how our requirements of intelligibility might be said to "fit" what we are independently given' is to be 'rejected, not answered' (2007: 203). But it should be obvious that I think that it is a very important insight that Pippin is close to here, even if I believe he misexpresses it.

We saw that we had '*invented two regions*', 'put a gap between them', and then gone 'looking for a bridge'.

My (2006) argued that, in his *Tractatus*, Wittgenstein used claims about 'internal relations' to draw attention to just such realizations; but in doing so I used this proposal as part of an explanation of why he insists that 'he who understands me finally recognizes [my propositions] as nonsensical, when he has climbed out through them, on them, over them': 'He must so to speak throw away the ladder, after he has climbed up on it' (1922: sec. 6.54). I mentioned at the end of Section 2.5 that Dahlstrom (1994) suggests that Heidegger's own claims might be best understood as part of such a 'ladder', and that would indeed be a way of understanding the manner in which MFL 167's claims, that *Dasein* is 'open' and 'out there', might need—as I put it above—to be cast aside in the end. Such claims would then be best seen, as Section 4.2.2 also briefly considered, as 'reactive' or 'dialectical'; and evidence consistent with such a line of thought includes Heidegger's declarations that philosophical concepts are 'formally indicative' (FCM 293), where 'formal indications' possess a 'peculiar "transitory" character' (PIA 87).[42]

I certainly do not want to rule out the possibility that these ideas might play an important part in understanding Heidegger's metaphilosophical vision—a vision which Chapter 9 will show is anything but straightforward. I also do not discount the possibility that they might make possible a tenable understanding of Heidegger's use of the Dependency Claim. But what I do want to stress here is that the reading of that Claim that they seem to make possible makes it a 'reactive' or 'dialectical' claim. If so, it is one which is ultimately to be 'thrown away'; and that may not be the kind of defence of the claim that we originally believed we were seeking.

Finally in this chapter, might then the difficulties we have encountered in arriving at a plausible reading of the Dependency Claim provide support for the thought that Heidegger's reflections on *time* might be key to understanding his remarks on truth? As Section 9.1 will discuss, those reflections are clearly essential to a comprehensive appreciation of BT; but I also believe that we can arrive at a sense for most of Heidegger's central claims about truth without reference to those reflections. That this should be so is suggested by the fact that in many of the contexts in which Heidegger presents these claims, he cannot

---

[42] Cf. my (forthcoming-d) for a rather different perspective on these notions.

have expected his readers and listeners to have any significant grasp of his views on time. We also must not overestimate how much sense can be made of the Dependency Claim by a reading which does factor in Heidegger's reflections on time, as the most comprehensively developed example shows. In his (1999), Blattner ascribes to Heidegger a species of what he calls 'ontological idealism'—a view which itself rests on a brand of 'temporal idealism'—the claim that 'time would not obtain, if *Dasein* did not exist'—and the notion of 'the Temporality of Being'—according to which 'our understanding of Being makes sense of things in terms of time' (1999: 12, 245). According to 'ontological idealism', 'Being'—'the ontological framework that determines whether something of some specific ontological sort is'—'is not in place' 'when *Dasein* does not exist' and, for that reason, the notions that entities exist or do not exist are 'senseless' (p. 244). A construal of the Dependency Claim might then be that the 'absence' of such a 'framework' would also render 'senseless' the question of whether entities are or are not thus-and-so. But crucially, the views upon which the Claim now rests are still deeply problematic: Blattner himself insists that the 'labyrinthine' arguments (p. 279) in support of 'temporal idealism' fail,[43] and that 'the Temporality of Being' 'is never even developed, with or without support, at all' (p. 261).

Heidegger may, of course, have embraced the Dependency Claim understood in one of the philosophically problematic ways that we have discussed. But, since the picture that Chapter 6 offers seems to make some sense of many of the puzzles we have considered, I am inclined to see that Claim—and its talk of the 'existence' or 'non-existence' of truth—as a confused attempt to articulate what that picture reveals, or, at best, a 'reactive' or 'dialectical' claim. But as I also indicated at the beginning of this section, that such talk might turn out to be problematic is precisely what Heidegger's own remarks suggest, since 'the *problem of truth* is *inextricably linked* with the *question about Being*' (L 171). 'Being and truth "are" equiprimordially' and '[b]eing . . . is something which "there is" only in so far as truth is';[44] but an answer to—indeed even the 'concrete asking' of—the question, 'What does it signify that Being "is"?', become possible for us 'only if the meaning of Being and the full scope of the understanding of Being have in general been clarified'; that clarification is bound up with an attempt to make good on a

---

[43] Cf., e.g., Blattner 1999: 181–4.   [44] Cf. also BT 364 (316).

vision of 'a science *of Being as such*' (BT 272 (230))—a vision which gives to Heidegger's thought the distinctive but short-lived framing that it receives in BT, as Section 9.1 will discuss. But this attempt fails, that clarification belonging to the part of the book that was never published, and was, in all likelihood, never clearly envisaged.[45]

---

[45] Cf. ch. 9 n. 2.

8

Vorhandenheit and *Zuhandenheit* Revisited

Chapter 6 demonstrates what one might naturally call the 'priority of the *Zuhanden* over the *Vorhanden*': the capacity, for example, to make assertions about basic physical characteristics of objects presupposes a mastery of certain practices and certain tools, viz. *Messzeug*. But the present and following sections will try to tease out some of the other contributions that that chapter makes to other concerns that previous chapters have raised.

8.1 *Zuhandenheit* revisited

Reflection on our mastery of the *Zuhanden* was important to Chapter 6's discussion in several ways, but here I will concentrate on three. The first is that that mastery illustrates the form of understanding to which, by several routes, Chapter 5 led us: a form of understanding that cannot itself be seen as an appreciation of a correspondence of thought with the world but which can 'found' the grasp of such correspondences. At the same time—and this is the second point I want to stress—that mastery points us to a shared, and flawed, assumption of the idealists and realists described in Section 2.1: namely, that intelligible thoughts 'con-form' with the world, that we can think about the world because the 'form of our thinking' fits the 'form of the world'.

Chapter 6 drew our attention to a sense in which our descriptive practices presuppose our finding a world to-hand, *zu-handen*, already 'close' (BT 135 (102)). The understanding that a master of such practices possesses is not 'read off' the objects which possess the features that that understanding allows us to describe, and there is no perspective from which one comes to see 'how' that understanding 'works', if by that one means how it con-forms to the world while other 'rival' understandings fail to. But talk of 'closeness' may also mislead, underappreciating the significance of our relationship to the tools in question.[1] As Section 7.2 argued, achieving a certain facility with them is what it is to partake in certain forms of subjectivity. Heidegger's emphasis on *Zuhandenheit* as the mode of Being in which we 'first and foremost' encounter entities brings out vividly that *Dasein* is a mode of Being-amongst, that the entities it thus encounters are not ob-jects, which stand over opposite us—an etymology Heidegger often noted[2]—but the 'with-which' of the life of subjectivity (PICA 115, BT 117 (85)). Similarly, the reason why there is no 'view from sideways on' is not that this is a view we cannot adopt, but that no sense can be assigned to that which one would supposedly see from that 'position'. We have found that we cannot make sense of the 'subject-' and 'object-correlates' in question corresponding— 'con-forming'—to one another, of the 'working' that we might confusedly imagine seeing and understanding were we to enjoy that 'view'.

The third point is that Chapter 6 reinforces the worries that Section 3.4 discussed concerning conclusions like those of Rouse and Blattner. I argued there that the 'pragmatic' reflections in question are hard to specify clearly, and lead to some distinctive difficulties (as Rouse and Blattner both in a way acknowledge in presenting their readings ultimately as critiques of Heidegger). Heidegger himself, moreover, seemed to want to distance himself from such reflections—especially in his retrospective comments.[3] But the particular issue I want to reconsider here, in the light of Chapter 6, is the suggestion that we ought to see the output of activities associated with the *Vorhanden* as actually revealing the *Zuhanden*, that, for example, science 'discovers not the present-at-hand, but new ways ... in which things around us can be ready-to-hand' (Rouse 1985: 203).

The view I presented does not, it seems to me, entail that the entities we judge through our use of *Messzeug* must themselves be *Zuhanden* in any 'thick' sense. To know how to take measurements is to 'know one's way around' rulers as *Messzeug*, and that is a very particular way of 'knowing

---

[1] Talk of 'immediacy' and 'intimacy' may also mislead, as the previous section discussed.
[2] Cf., e.g., DSTCM 39.
[3] I do not discount the possibility that the more 'pragmatic' reflections that Rouse and Blattner, among others, emphasise are present too—indeed Section 9.1 will consider a further thought that might require their presence in BT (cf., in particular, ch. 9 n. 13)—or the possibility, which seems to me highly likely anyway, that many of the themes referred to are overdetermined.

one's way around' the objects to which rulers are applied. But 'knowing one's way around' does not render them too, in any obvious sense, tools, nor need they be *first* understood as tools, equipment, 'use-objects', or 'things that have the character of the "in-order-to"'—to borrow from Section 3.4's list of senses of the *Zuhanden*—an understanding which we then have to 'dim down' or 'prescind from'. We do have a certain facility with these objects: borrowing again from that same list, they 'show themselves . . . in our having-to-do-with-them', and could be said to 'belong to a system of references'. But that facility is no more than our being able to produce those measurements; indeed our mastery of the *Messzeug*—their having been 'disclosed' to us—is no more than our mastery of them for this particular use. That use may make possible all sorts of manipulation and control of the world; but no obvious reason emerged in our discussion to disagree with what seems to be Heidegger's own view (see Section 3.3), that that use is not itself a form of such manipulation and control, a form of '*profitable* use' in any 'thick' sense. Nor is it necessarily tied to the serving of some further *human* purpose; indeed, as Section 6.3.3 argued, the need to master particular measurement practices if one is to intend particular objects and properties does not entail that the measured ought to be thought as tied to 'local interests' in any problematic way.

It seems that virtually every commentator feels the need to invoke 'the practical' at some point in order to explain Heidegger's understanding of the *Vorhanden*, the *Zuhanden*, Being-in-the-world, and so on, though they will also typically row back on that invocation, 'thinning' the relevant notions in the way that Section 3.4 describes to the point where a critic might well suspect that '[t]here's the bit where you say it and the bit where you take it back' (Austin, quoted in Section 3.4). My own reading suggests a reason why we may be so often drawn into this condition, and offers an alternative way of approaching these issues. It seems closest to the truth to say that Heidegger seeks to show us how unclear our philosophical thinking becomes when we allow it to be guided uncritically by these concepts—'the practical' and 'the theoretical'. He is explicitly sceptical about the invocation of notions such as 'the practical',[4] and Sections 6.3.1 and 6.4.1 make vivid why we need to be sceptical too. In the young Heidegger's work, his aim seems to have been very clearly one of revealing the diverse forms that

---

[4] Cf., e.g., PRL 88 and HCT 160.

understanding and Being take, and perhaps his 'later early' work is also best seen as directing our attention to what are actually, to adapt the words of Dahlstrom, 'myriad behaviours that make a mockery of the [theory/practice] distinction' (2001: xxv). Obviously, my own emphasis on the 'practical' character of our mastery of measurement procedures ought also to be treated with care.[5] The further end that this emphasis serves is to raise questions about our understanding and application of the practical/theoretical distinction. Commentators who tell us that Heidegger did not seek simply to prioritize 'the practical' over 'the theoretical' are surely right;[6] and nor did he recommend that we understand the scientist's activity as 'practical' *rather than* 'theoretical'. Rather, we must recognize that, when attempting to describe our activities, 'it is by no means patent where the ontological boundary between "theoretical" and "atheoretical" behaviour runs!'

8.2 *Vorhandenheit* and the Theoretical Attitude revisited

The present sub-section will pick out a number of further morals from Chapter 6's discussion. Extrapolating from those, the remaining sub-sections of the chapter will then suggest and defend a possible way of making sense of how and why Heidegger comes to gather together as he does the many notions that are linked with the *Vorhanden*—a way of bringing some kind of order into Section 3.1's otherwise puzzling list.

Chapter 6 gives us a new perspective on just what might be thought to be confused about the notion that one can 'simply behold'—grasp by 'just looking'—facts such as that 'The object is 1 metre long'; instead, such seeing presupposes mastery of a *Hinblick*, and such mastery includes recognizably 'practical' capacities. A mastery of those tools underpins any substantial discourse about such facts, 'founding' assertions about them, in that without that mastery, such 'claims' can only be empty: an assertion like 'The object is 1 metere long' only communicates something to someone

---

[5] A similar—if more obvious—crudity infects my own talk of 'passivist' and 'activist' themes in Heidegger's reflections on science (cf. Section 3.3).
[6] Cf., e.g., Bernasconi 1989: 143, Dreyfus 1991: 62, and McNeill 1999: 75: 'Heidegger does not want simply to privilege the practical'.

who has mastered a range of abilities away from which talk of the 'entertaining of propositions' is apt to draw our attention.

The chapter also illustrates the way in which we may need to be *reminded* of the role that these skills and tools play, pointing out our use of measuring tools by, for example, pointing out how it may misfire; only then do this use and these tools themselves become 'conspicuous, obtrusive, obstinate' (BT 104 (74)). In its brief sketch of a vision of inauthenticity, Section 6.4 has also indicated how we may 'forget' the choices made in using particular measures, the history within which we stand when we ask the particular questions that we ask. One particularly striking form that this 'forgetting' can take is what I labelled 'pythagorean fetishism': we are vulnerable to thinking that the mathematically articulated facts are *the* facts—that mathematics is the language in which *everything* is ultimately to be described—and to forgetting the 'constituting' 'stage-setting' necessary to 'render' domains mathematically describable, along with the 'constituting' choices that are made when we pay attention to those particular mathematical 'disclosures'.

Clearly, these points also have a bearing on our understanding of the Theoretical Attitude. In particular, we have seen that the mere noting of physical facts does not fit the philosophical template of 'pure beholding': a 'pure beholding' is not the medium through which, or perspective from which, we note even very basic features of the physical world.[7] So why should such a mere noting have had any particular role to play in the vices of the philosophical tradition? What the previous chapter also makes clear is that the 'stage-setting' that creates that perspective and that leads to its application *are* apt to be forgotten, and doing so leaves one vulnerable to the myth of a 'pure beholding'. This is a way of relating to the world which expresses a very particular attitude that calls for us to be methodical and disciplined in a very particular way; but it is also one through which we are apt to overlook that call once the disciplines in question have been acquired. It is a particular 'how', a particular 'manner of experiencing', but one which encourages an '*indifference*' (PRL 9) to that very 'how', that 'manner', which we see in the kinds of 'forgetfulness' singled out above.

---

[7] We now have a clear sense, for example, of why it sounds odd to say, as Käufer does, that '[s]taring at an object we can point out its weight, colour, and other properties' (2003: 85). As Chapter 6, n. 28 argues, this may not even be quite true of judgements of colour.

This view also suggests a truth of sorts what I have labelled the 'passivist' strand in Heidegger's reflections on science. To be in the grip of *Seinsvergessenheit/ Verstehensvergessenheit* is to overlook the very possibility of there being kinds of entity, a multiplicity of 'subject-correlates' and special circumstances in which we reveal, for example, the objects revealed by assertion, theoretical reflection, the doing of natural science, and so on. Talk of the 'origin' (PRL 40) or 'genesis of the theoretical' (ZBP 88), a focus on Aristotelian 'leisure', on 'dimming down' and 'prescinding' throws this 'forgetting' into relief, highlighting that the scientist operates within, and presupposes, a disclosure of the world that is not best understood as itself arising out of the making of observations but is instead an already established form of familiarity with the world. When the scientist comes to make her observations she is 'involved' with the observed entity in a particular way,[8] and one which is not *the* definitive form that our 'involvement with', and understanding of, entities takes. The scientist's mode of activity is one particular form that our living amidst, and understanding, entities takes—a form we might indeed be said to take on 'only in exceptional cases' (IPPW 74).

8.3 *Seinsvergessenheit* and '*Vorhandenheit* in the broadest sense'

So what kind of overarching concern might we see in these reflections that Heidegger tethers around the term, '*Vorhandenheit*'? My proposal is that we may see why Heidegger uses this term in the many (36) ways in which he does if we note a 37th use—one which identifies an overarching concern under which those many uses fall.[9] I do not want to rule out the possibility that Heidegger's reflections around the term *Vorhandenheit* are ultimately a bit of a mess. But they can, at least, be seen as less of a mess than they might otherwise if we see the broad range of uses that Heidegger makes of '*Vorhandenheit*' as guided by a *diagnostic* concept, not as identifying a particular kind of entity (in a

---

[8] This indeed seems to be Heidegger's concern when he attacks 'passivist' claims at BT 409 (357) and 412 (361).
[9] Demonstrating that *all* fall under this broader concern is beyond the ambition of this work. It would require, for example, a discussion of anxiety which only a systematic examination of authenticity would make possible. But I will attempt to show that a core set of those different uses may be understood with reference to this 37th sense.

very confusing and rather loose fashion, as Section 3.1's list might suggest) but helping us track a tendency to confusion in our thinking.

The 37th sense for the term presents the *Vorhanden* as the 'kind' of object one 'sees' when one forgets that any seeing presupposes the mastery and adoption of a particular kind of 'measure'. On this interpretation, what is common to the activities that Heidegger declares reveal the *Vorhanden* is that we are particularly vulnerable to that 'forgetting' when we engage in those activities. We 'fall into' the 'purely beheld', 'the viewed', 'the thematic', by 'forgetting' the *Hinblick*, the measure which may be embodied in a whole way of conducting ourselves in the world.

From this perspective the overarching confusion that Heidegger wants to identify with his use of the term '*Vorhanden*' is not that we take it to be self-evident that entities are *vorhanden* in sense (1), or sense (2), or... In using this term as he does, his concern is what unites such cases: our taking the Being of entities to be self-evident and unproblematic, a non-issue, a non-question. *Vorhandenheit* in the 37th sense is not so much a kind of Being as the pseudo-'kind' of Being that corresponds to that attitude. I place 'kind' in quotes because this 'kind' of Being is that which corresponds to a failure to recognize that there are *kinds* of Being.[10] The *Vorhanden* in this 37th sense—this 'kind'—is then an illusion, not a candidate answer to the 'Question of Being', but rather an expression of our failure to ask that question.

At BT 71 (45), Heidegger talks of '*Vorhandenheit* in the broadest sense', contrasting a *vorhanden* entity as a 'what' as opposed to a 'who'. But in his 1929–30 lectures, *The Fundamental Concepts of Metaphysics*, he identifies a sense of *Vorhandenheit* that is broader still, or that has a different kind of breadth, and that seems to correspond to my 37th sense. The passage from FCM quoted in Section 1.3 continues:

[A]t first and for the most part in the *everydayness* of our *Dasein* we let entities come towards us and present themselves before us in a remarkable undifferentiatedness... [H]ere the entities that surround us are *uniformly manifest* as simply *something present at hand in the broadest sense*. (FCM 275)

These remarks echo ones made in notes from 1918–19 which are explicitly directed at the '"fundamental concepts of metaphysics"':

---

[10] Interestingly, this sense seems rather close to that which Fell, in his important essay on *Vorhandenheit*, identifies with the 'improper sense' of that term, and which he is keen to 'first dispose' of (1992: 71).

[T]his conceptual material has such a neutral, faded content, uncharacterized by the sphere of experience, that it is shown in serious investigation as not at all original—that is to say, as not being a conglomerate of sense-elements that originally arise from a sphere of experience. (PRL 246)

Heidegger declares this generic pseudo-'kind' of Being—this 'all too self-evident phenomenon'—'the deadly enemy of philosophy' (FCM 275), a charge with substance in that it corresponds to what one might call a 'forgetting of the Question of Being', in which 'the meaning of Being in general is held to be something simply self-evident' (BT 441 (389)).[11] Now, one might continue this remark: 'to be specific, we take it to be *vorhanden*', having some one, other or collection of our senses (1)–(36) above in mind. But, with *Vorhandenheit* in FCM's 'broadest sense' in mind, the notion of *Vorhandenheit* corresponds precisely to the *forgetting* of the Question of Being—to this indifference, this holding as self-evident—and not to a particular and well understood form that we hold Being to 'self-evidently take'.

The suggestion is not that we discount senses (1)–(36); rather, we should hear some of them as contributing to an attempt to articulate the above confusion, and others as picking out those activities through which we are most apt to succumb to that confusion. Indeed, the literal sense of the term—which we might call our sense (0), namely, that which is 'before the hand'—captures the general phenomenology of the illusion in question: we 'encounter' entities that lie 'before us' simply waiting to be 'grasped', we being unaware of what else must be in place, what else must lie behind us, so to speak, for this 'grasping' to take place. This vision points to a phenomenological truth in proposals such as that the *Vorhanden* are the 'isolated' or 'de-contextualized' (sense 14), as well as in Inwood's delicious formulation, according to which the *Vorhanden* are 'things that we find neutrally reposing in themselves' (1999: 128). Similarly, in the kind of 'indifference' described above, inasmuch as we recognize a Question about the Being of these entities at all, we would seem to imagine that their Being is delivered over to us in a 'pure beholding' (sense 19). Just as the Being of the entities we encounter then represents no significant issue for us, neither does our *understanding* of those entities: 'what they are' is straightforward and correspondingly we simply 'see' what they are. To 'the priority of the present-at-

---

[11] Cf. also BT 126 (93).

hand in traditional ontology' there corresponds the 'priority' of 'pure intuition' (BT 187 (147)), 'pure beholding' (BT 215 (171))';[12] but the 'purity' of these forms of understanding corresponds to our 'indifference' to the question of their own Being, to our *Verstehensvergessenheit*, our forgetting of the Question of Understanding. To return to a theme of Section 1.1, obscurity about the Being of entities here supports, and is supported by, obscurity about ourselves and our understanding. Our failure to recognize questions here gives rise to the illusion of entities which simply lie 'before us' and are grasped in a 'pure'—that is to say, characterless— 'seeing'. The *Vorhanden* are the 'kind' of entity one encounters when one forgets a deep sense in which entities come in 'kinds', the 'kind' that is apt to be 'revealed' by 'havings' of ours in which we are apt to forget that our engagement with entities comes in the form of a diversity of 'havings'.

8.4 *Vorhandenheit* and assertion revisited

The perspective proposed on *Vorhandenheit* suggests a rather different understanding of the relationship between that notion and assertion—a relationship which Section 3.2 identified as problematic. It is an understanding that is to be seen at work in the 1927 BPP lectures, and perhaps even more vividly in the 1928–29 lecture course, *Einleitung in die Philosophie*. In both cases, the background against which Heidegger discusses this relationship is a discussion of truth. His criticisms of those who would see the 'place' of truth as first and foremost in assertions have a variety of profound ramifications, as Chapters 5 and 7 have explored, and in these lecture courses he emphasises another—namely, that in the grip of such an approach, 'the evenness, the undifferentiatedness of stating and talking about...' obscures the variety of forms of Being:

Is [the] manifestness of entities a universally even and regular one, regardless of the prevailing way of Being of the manifest entities? It appears so, since we can easily establish in the same regular way that there are: stones, trees, dogs, cars, 'passers by' (human beings). We can do this about everything, because it is manifest in the same way; after all, we can talk directly, make true assertions about it, in the same way.

---

[12] Cf. Chapter 3 n. 23.

The equal and regular possibility of an assertion about all occurring entities is also the evidence for an equal and regular form of the manifestness, unconcealment, truth of entities. (EP 82)

But Heidegger urges caution:

Perhaps... it is... precisely the evenness, the undifferentiatedness of stating and talking about... which gives rise to the appearance that the truth about entities is similarly indifferent to their own character, that the unconcealment of entities is not determined in its way of happening by the prevailing kind of Being of entities... [T]he assertion suggests to us not only a specific idea of truth, but also that all entities which can be spoken about are, as it were, of the same kind. (EP 82–3)

This critical perspective on assertions retains, for example, BT's metaphor of 'levelling down', but the form of *Vorhandenheit* with which Heidegger associates the assertion here is that picked out by our 37th sense, the undifferentied and 'self-evident' 'kind' that corresponds to an 'indifference' on our part:

Precisely because we do not at first and for the most part never heed the variety of entities, we must pursue it, since the essence of truth should not be determined by the orientation towards the assertion and its indifference, towards its levelled and levelling character. (EP 83)

I propose that for a deeper appreciation of Heidegger's early work as a whole, we are better off seeing the problematic relationship between assertions and *Vorhandenheit* not as an intrinsic tendency in assertions to 'reveal' objects of Nature, the 'de-contextualised', mere *thats* or the like—notions which, as Section 3.2 argued, seem to turn out implausible, unclear or trivial—but as the association with assertions of the danger of an obscuring of the diverse forms of Being that characterize the entities which those assertions describe. We may misconstrue the subjects of assertions as homogenous in their Being—coming to see them all as 'of the same kind'—if our thought is guided by the 'universally even and regular' impression that assertions in general create. As the BPP lectures put it, despite the variety of kinds of Being that the entities that assertions describe instantiate, this variety does not 'protrude... in the linguistic form' (BPP 212).[13]

The problem identified is not a problem with assertions as such. To genuinely *hear* an assertion is to hear more than an empty sentence; rather it

---

[13] Cf. also, e.g., BT 89 (61–2) and 209 (166).

is to hear what is being said, to grasp the entities described in their Being and how they are said to happen to be. An 'orientation towards the assertion and its indifference', on the other hand, seems to leave us—to make what seems a natural connection —with the inauthentic's 'idle talk'. Such talk represents a *decaying* of understanding, a descent of talk away from the offering and evaluation of determinate claims about how things are and towards the mere trading of sentences the meaning of which has become indeterminate:

> What characterizes this rote saying is that in being circulated the validity of what has been said becomes calcified and simultaneously gets disengaged from the very thing about which it is said. The more rote saying dominates, the more the world is covered over. It is in this way that *Dasein* has the tendency to cover over the world and, along with this, itself. (WDR 164-65)

But this, we should note, is a feature not of saying as such but of 'rote saying'—a condition in which we 'forget' the 'animating' understanding that gives assertions meaning.

This tying of assertion into our 37th sense of the *Vorhanden* comes in the form of an argument for thinking that the making of assertions is an activity in which we are apt—though not doomed—to forget the Questions of Being and of Understanding. The proposal that the *Vorhanden* is an illusory 'kind' may seem very close to Rouse's that 'there is no genuine phenomenon corresponding to presence-at-hand' (1985: 200); but I would attach to those words are rather different sense. I believe, and believe that Heidegger believed, that we are apt to succumb to a particular illusion when we allow our reflections, our philosophy, to be oriented around experiences we have when we engage in natural science, assertion, and so on. But the fact that those activities are apt to lead us to succumb to belief in a certain illusory 'kind' of entity does not entail that what those activities reveal *when we are not so confused* are illusions, or, for that matter, ought to be assimilated to the kinds of things and facts that other kinds of activities of ours reveal, for instance, by assimilating them to the *Zuhanden*.

What metaphysical categories ought we then to use in characterizing what assertions and natural science reveal? An answer that I believe my discussion allows us to retain is that assertions reveal states of affairs, physics reveals the physical properties of things, chemistry reveals the chemical properties of things, and so on. (Relatedly, as I will propose in a moment, we should see assertions about the *Zuhanden* as revealing functional properties and assertions about *Dasein* as revealing (roughly speaking) intentional properties.) This may strike some as a metaphysically lavish pluralism, and others as an explanatorily uninteresting quietism. On the former charge, it is not clear that metaphysical parsimony should be pursued at all costs;[14] and on the latter, though my view may indeed undermine some explanatory ambitions that commentators have ascribed to Heidegger—and which, for example, the Primacy of Practice Claim might be thought to express—it offers much in their place. The Heidegger I have presented provides us with a picture of the 'constitution' of the objects of assertions as presupposing our mastery of 'worldly' skills—a picture that provides a reading of the above Claim and the Prior Projection Claim, with its vision of a non-subjectivist *a priori*. That reading is, I think, more plausible than its rivals, and has the philosophical pay-off of undermining con-formist worries.

We are also now in a position to revisit the notion that assertions reveal *only* the *Vorhanden*. As we have seen, this claim is problematic in all sorts of ways. Not only does it give rise to problems such as Dahlstrom's 'paradox of thematization'; it also clashes with Heidegger's own comments on assertion (such as those from L 156 n. 131 and BT 201 (158), quoted in Section 3.2) and, on many of the understandings of *Vorhandenheit* that Section 3.1 identified, it is simply very implausible. It would entail, for example, that we cannot make assertions about the *Zuhanden* or about *Dasein*. Also, we have yet to see a reason for thinking such assertions impossible. For example, one might follow up some of the connections identified in Chapter 3 and argue that assertions only reveal 'the decontextualised': that might appear to be a reason why assertions of the sort mentioned are impossible. But we have seen that there is reason to think that our basic descriptions of physical entities are of 'contextualised entities' too, in that they are necessarily placed within a logical space and are revealed by distinctive practices. If one wants to argue that that renders them *zuhanden*—as Rouse and Blattner might—then it must be acknowledged that they are so only in one of Section 3.4's very thin senses—senses (11) and (12) perhaps—and that one seems to be running

---

[14] The view sketched also might be seen as echoing, for example, the 'plural realism' that Dreyfus (1991: 262) sees in Heidegger, though not the 'multiple realism' that Dreyfus and Spinosa (1999) defend. (For worries regarding the coherence of the latter, cf. Carman 2003: 186–90, and regarding its relevance to Heidegger, McManus (forthcoming-a): sec. 2.) Cf. Section 9.1 for a brief sketch—and McManus (unpublished) for a more detailed examination—of a rather different problem that there being a multiplicity of kinds of Being poses.

counter now to Heidegger's own expressed views on the possibility of such descriptions.[15]

So why, then, does Heidegger tie assertions into the cluster of concepts associated with the *Vorhanden*? From the perspective I have offered here, the philosophical worry that a focus on assertions raises is not that it confines one's attention to, say, the natural scientific world, but rather that it distracts you from the 'measure' that any assertion presupposes, from the forms of understanding that make it possible for us to 'intend' the subject-matter of such assertions.[16] The 'undifferentiatedness of stating and talking about...' distracts from what it takes, so to speak, to be able to make or grasp assertions, the character of, and variety of forms taken by, this presupposed understanding.[17] With our attention directed away from the worldly forms of understanding that 'found' assertions, and captured instead by the 'neutral' and 'faded' philosophy of mind of 'indifferent', 'pure beholding', we are also now just one step away from con-formist worries, and hence two steps from the unappealing choice between an unworkable realism and a fanciful idealism.

8.5 Inauthenticity and the 'double meaning' of the 'Theoretical Attitude'

This final sub-section will show that the above reflections echo an interesting early discussion of Heidegger's of the Theoretical Attitude. I will also go on to develop a little further the connection with authenticity proposed.

---

[15] Having been committed to the notion that assertions reveal the *Vorhanden*, one might feel the need to ask now, 'OK, so what is it that assertions distinctively do?' Heidegger's answer would be, I suspect, the kind of answer that he gives on several occasions: an assertion is '*a pointing-out which gives something a definite character and which communicates*' (BT 199 (156)). Cf. also, e.g., BPP 209f.

[16] My (forthcoming-c) builds on this notion in responding to a problem to which Section 1.2's reflections might seem to give rise: they might seem to cast doubt on the very possibility of having beliefs about God or religious phenomena such as the Last Judgement—a possibility I explore by comparing Heidegger's outlook with strikingly similar reflections one finds in Wittgenstein, who has been accused of maintaining that 'Christian practice is everything and Christian belief, belief that involves doctrines, is nothing' (Nielsen 2005: 116). I suggest there instead that we see Heidegger—as Diamond argues we should see Wittgenstein—as revealing to us 'the genuine complicatedness of the concept of belief' (Diamond 2005: 112). In particular, he is pointing to the rootedness of our understanding of the 'objects' of such beliefs in a 'prior' 'concernful understanding' (BT 201 (158), quoted above), in a relationship to God of worship and love.

[17] To substantiate one more connection in Section 3.1's list, we come to see in the subject matter of assertions the 'neutral' and 'faded' ontology of substances, properties, and relations—categories themselves derived from the 'surface grammar' of assertions, from referring expressions, predicates, and relational-expressions.

In PRL, Heidegger identifies a concept that he will connect intimately with that of the Theoretical Attitude: 'the attitudinal determination and regulation of objects' (PRL 12–13). This is a tendency to focus on the 'content' of our experience, and not upon the 'the manner, the *how*'—or as he also puts it, 'the *relational* sense'—'of the experiencing' (PRL 9). We read:

> 'Attitude' [*Einstellung*] is a relation to objects in which the conduct [*Verhalten*] is absorbed in the *material complex*. I direct myself only to the *matter*, I focus away from *myself* toward the *matter*. With this 'attitude' the *living* relation to the object of knowledge has 'ceased' ['*eingestellt*'] (in the sense of 'it will cease', for instance, as one says, 'The struggle has ceased').

There is a certain ambiguity here of which Heidegger is aware. I may 'focus away from *myself* toward the *matter*'; but is not 'direct[ing] myself only to the *matter*' a '*living* relation to the object of knowledge'? In which case, why say such a relation has 'ceased'? Heidegger goes on:

> We have then a double meaning in the word 'attitude': first an attitude toward a realm of matter, secondly a ceasing of the entire human relation to the material complex. (PRL 33)

What concerns Heidegger here is still less than clear. In particular, when he says that a particular philosopher's thinking is governed by 'the attitudinal determination and regulation of objects', then—according to the first meaning of 'attitude'—she is depicted as adopting a particular 'attitude toward' the 'realm of matter' upon which she is reflecting. But what, then, of the second meaning? How can one's thinking be governed by such a thing, by a ceasing of all such relations to things?

One possibility is that greater stress needs to be heard on the words 'human' and '*living*': that is to say, that this particular 'attitude towards' or 'directing to' is, in some way, neither 'human' nor '*living*': perhaps these are forms of 'directing' from which interest, purpose, or the like have been eliminated. If that is the correct reading, then we now need a reason from Heidegger for thinking that there is something problematic in such a form of 'directing'. Plenty of commentators seem to believe that they have found such a reason, and we have examined some themes from the work of some of these in Section 3.4.

But another possibility is that when we succumb to the 'attitudinal' we do not understand ourselves. On this view I 'focus away from *myself* toward the *matter*', and fail to *recognize* the 'human', '*living* relation' in which I stand to the objects I intend. The previous interpretation makes of the 'attitudinal' a particular 'how'—though not a 'human' or '*living*' one. The interpretation being considered now makes of the 'attitudinal' a forgetting or ignoring of the philosophical importance of the 'how'—a *Verstehensvergessenheit*. Here we see an echo of one of the possible equivocations in the idea of the Theoretical Attitude described at the beginning of Chapter 3: is 'the attitudinal' itself one particular attitude, or a philosophical confusion that fails to recognize that our relations to the world 'express', as it were, attitudes, and a variety of attitudes at that? The latter echoes Heidegger's characterization in PRL 9 of a tendency of 'factical life experience' to 'put[] all its weight on its *content*'. In this '*indifference* with regard to the manner of experiencing', on which Section 1.1 touched, different 'hows' are registered at best in perceived differences among the 'whats':

[T]he *how* of factical experience at most merges into its *content*. (PRL 9)

I become conscious of the diversity of experiences only in the experienced content. (PRL 12)

For a diversity of 'hows' we substitute a diversity of 'whats'; when we should recognize different 'subject-correlates', we see instead different 'kinds of object'. Ironically, however, this also serves to play down that diversity. By presenting engagement with those 'kinds of object' implicitly as a single, unexamined—even characterless—'subject-correlate', we also play down or disguise the diversity of those 'objects', presenting them as all falling under a single over-arching type, a 'thingly-ness in the broadest sense' (PIE 110, quoted in Section 2.5). The *Zuhanden* are seen as 'naked' 'present-at-hand' 'things' over which a 'signification' is 'thrown'—a 'value' 'stuck on' (BT 190 (150), quoted above)—while *Dasein* becomes a *res cogitans*—a thinking thing—and God becomes 'simply a special object' (PRL 149, quoted above).

Into the discussion of this tendency of thought Heidegger weaves talk of a 'theoretical attitude', as he refers to 'the attitudinally theoretical' (PRL 41) and 'the theoretical attitudinal relation' (PRL 42). I suggest that we keep the above 'double meaning' in mind in our thinking about the Theoretical Attitude too: might Heidegger's concern with the Theoretical Attitude, on the one hand, sometimes be with a particular attitude and, on the other, sometimes with a confused indifference to the issue of there being a diversity of attitudes, through which we come to treat our relation to that which we intend as a 'pure'—characterless—'seeing'? Chapter 1 gave us some indication of what the Theoretical Attitude meant to the young Heidegger', and gives some support to the above thought. The 'speculators and chatterboxes' described there might be labelled as having 'adopted the Theoretical Attitude towards God'. But is their problem best understood as their having adopted an attitude that reveals God only partially, or that interprets him in inappropriate ontological categories? Arguably, their fundamental problem is a lack of self-knowledge: they *believe* that they *love* God, but they prepare for the Last Judgement as if they did not. That preparation befits an expectation of the return of an all-powerful and all-knowing being that will bring joy to those who have acted as that being thinks they should have acted, and inflict suffering on those it thinks have not. They may *talk* of their 'expecting righteous judgement' just as St Paul does. But behind the 'equal and regular form' of such assertions—the 'levelled and levelling' impression that such talk presents—they are not living the life in which an anticipation of *righteous* judgement exists. The 'object-correlate' of the search for portents is a coming threat to one's 'peace and security'; the 'subject-correlate' of righteous judgement is 'faithful, loving, serving expectation in sadness and joy'; but an 'orientation towards the assertion and its indifference' hides precisely that. It hides the different lives that endow those assertions with their different senses and which 'constitute' the different 'objects' that those assertions concern.

As was indicated above, Heidegger's discussion of St Paul clearly anticipates themes from the later discussion of authenticity, and I will end this chapter by sketching a further possible connection between the latter, the Theoretical Attitude as I have presented it here, and '*Vorhandenheit*' in the 37th and 'broadest sense'. 'Inauthenticity' is one of a number of labels—others including 'ruinance [*Ruinanz*]' (PIA 98),[18] 'decadence' [*Verfall*] (HCT 129), and 'falling'—which Heidegger applies to a kind of life in which *Dasein* 'is lived by...the world which concerns it in this or that way' (HCT 245).[19] One way to understand this claim is as stating that while we all live our lives in line with the meanings that those lives attach to the entities that we find around us,

---

[18] '*Die Ruinanz*' is Heidegger's Germanization of the Latin *ruere*, meaning 'to fall'.
[19] For one of Heidegger's earliest invocations of this notion of 'being lived', cf. PRL 170. What follows is very much a particular construal of what Heidegger might mean by 'inauthenticity', and not one which I will attempt to defend textually here.

the inauthentic do so in a manner which overlooks the possibility that different lives could be led. They treat the meaning of the entities which they encounter as something that one simply *sees*, but where what they 'see' is simply the meaning that those entities possess within the particular activities in which the inauthentic happen to be engaged. In this state, our attention is focused away from the lives we are leading, the lives which determine the sense that attaches to our words, and the ways in which we deal with the world around us. In this 'tranquilized' condition (BT 298 (253)), the possibility that those lives—and those senses and those ways of dealing—might be something for which we need to take responsibility, is lost from sight. One is simply doing what one does, saying what one says (BT 164 (126–7)), and dealing with entities as they 'self-evidently' are, in that the possibility that we might deal with those entities otherwise, in a life lived otherwise, is an unrecognized issue. Their meaning is instead fixed by this forgotten 'how', as we are 'absorbed' in, or 'fall into' that life and the understanding of entities it dictates (BT 230 (185–6)).[20]

We here return to an idea first broached in Section 1.1: that of the obscuring of a Question of Being symbiotically tied to a self-obscurity—a tendency of *Dasein's*, 'to cover over the world and, along with this, itself' (WDR 165, quoted above). We also now have a sense of what lies behind Heidegger's declaration that philosophy is 'counter-ruinant [*gegenruinant*]' (PIA 121). We can actually identify a triangle of relations:

- Inauthenticity is that state in which we treat the Being of entities as self-evident, as '*vorhanden* in the broadest sense';[21]
- *Vorhandenheit* in this sense is 'the deadly enemy of philosophy' (FCM 275, quoted above); and
- philosophy as 'counter-ruinant' seeks to free us from inauthenticity.

---

[20] One does so also irrespective of whether the life being followed is coherent, which suggests a further sense in which the 'talk' of such individuals might be seen as 'idle'—a sense we can bring out by considering how the above thoughts might be extended to take in our 'speculators and chatterboxes'. Their self-obscurity is simultaneously a lack of clarity about just what event it is that they are preparing for—righteous judgement, or a challenge to their 'peace and security'—and a thoughtless assumption that what they are doing to prepare for this 'Last Judgement'—looking for portents of when it will occur—is *the* way one prepares for this 'Last Judgement'. In this condition they may assert that they love God—and if 'oriented towards the assertion', or subject to a 'theorizing, dogma-promoting influence' (PRL 238, quoted above), one might then see them as indistinguishable from St Paul himself—but what substance their talk of 'love' has is moot. Cf. ch. 9 n. 19 below.

[21] At BT 250 (206), Heidegger declares that the 'diversion' of 'the primary understanding of Being' to 'Being as *Vorhandenheit*' is 'motivated' by '*Dasein's* falling'.

Our tendency to forget the 'how' exists symbiotically with a tendency to indifference about the Being of the 'what' and philosophy seeks to combat both. The tendency to think of Being as *Vorhandenheit* in our 37th and 'broadest sense'—failing to recognize how our thoughts are informed by a particular understanding of the Being of entities and, in this way, treating their Being as self-evident—corresponds to a failure of our *self*-understanding too, to a forgotten Question of Understanding. What philosophy must be in order to combat such forgetting is the topic of the final chapter.

9

Metaphilosophical Issues and Further Questions

The previous chapters give us a sense of why Heidegger regarded the correspondence conception of truth as 'superficial', and claimed that assertion 'has not a primary cognitive function but only a secondary one' (BPP 210): assertions are 'founded' in forms of understanding which cannot themselves be seen as the grasp of a correspondence between thought and world. Philosophy's characteristic focus upon assertions obscures this, and also obscures the forms that that 'founding' understanding takes and with it the diverse modes of Being that the subject matter of assertions instantiates. We come to see the 'objects' of assertion as all 'of the same kind', because their ontological diversity does not 'protrude' in the 'equal', 'regular', 'undifferentiated', 'linguistic form' of those assertions. This suggests an understanding of why Heidegger repeatedly depicts assertions as 'secondary' in the activity of the philosopher too. Section 2.5 documented this depiction and examined one possible construal of it: that offered by Dahlstrom's 'paradox of thematization'. In the light of the intervening discussion that construal no longer seems viable, but the basis of another has emerged.

In the light of the preceding chapters' discussion of assertions and *Vorhandenheit*, it is no longer clear that Heidegger really does face the problem that Dahlstrom identifies. But a more general problem, of which Dahlstrom's is perhaps a particular instance, may seem to arise out of my invocation in preceding chapters of the idea of an 'original having': the problem is that it may be impossible to articulate differences between such 'havings'. Section 9.1 will explain how this problem arises, and suggest—though no more than suggest—that solving this problem may have been one of the principal objectives of the project within which Heidegger reinterpreted his early work in the period around the publication of BT—

the period of, among other texts, HCT, L, BPP, and BT itself. (I will refer to this project as 'the "Being and Time" project'.) Van Buren claims that Heidegger's thought was 'tamed under the influence of the transcendental thought of Husserl and Kant', leading to 'the plodding scientific treatise called *Sein und Zeit*, an aberration in Heidegger's own eyes' (1994: 136). While I think this claim misses much, what is true is that BT represents what one might call a 'conservative' attempt to 'save' a certain 'appearance'—the appearance that philosophy's work is to produce a 'science of Being'. Such a 'theoretical conceptual interpretation of Being, of Being's structure and its possibilities' (BPP 11) promises to map out the many species that fall under the genus, 'Being in general', thereby articulating differences between the 'objects' of different 'original havings'.[1] But this is a metaphilosophical vision he rejects at the beginning and end of the 1920s; and, of course, he never brought the 'Being and Time' project to completion.[2] So what of the problem that project was to have solved?

I will argue that it need not be solved *if* one is willing to embrace a rather different picture of philosophical insight—one which finds expression in Heidegger's texts but which was occluded in the immediate BT period by the alternative response alluded to above. That period led to his writing what—with justification—is described as his 'magnum opus'; but we also should not overlook just how short that period was and the other metaphilosophical visions with which it vied in the turbulent years of reflection and self-reinterpretation that the 1920s were for Heidegger. In particular, Section 9.2 will stress a vision to be found there that echoes themes that have run throughout this book, and which might be summed up in the notion that we are apt to 'forget'—and need to be 'reminded of'—the 'measures' using which we think about, and describe, our world. A consideration of the nature of such forgetting also suggests a novel and non-mysterious understanding of why Heidegger was so often drawn to

---

[1] Cf. also BPP 322.
[2] Some claim that other works of Heidegger's in combination with the published BT 'add up to' the larger—and therefore completed—project (cf., e.g., the translator's introduction to BPP, p. xvii). I very much doubt this. For example, Heidegger reported in 1941 that, through conversations with Jaspers in December 1926 and January 1927, 'it became clear to me that the elaboration of th[e] all important Division (I, 3) drafted up to that point had to be incomprehensible' (translation quoted from Kisiel 1993: 486); the same letter continues: 'Of course, at the time I thought that in the course of the year everything could be said more clearly. That was a delusion.' So Heidegger's opinion in 1941 suggests that nothing he had written since BT—BPP included—quite added up to that missing Division.

depict philosophical propositions as 'superficial', or as playing a 'secondary' role in the pursuit of philosophical insight.

The issues broached in this chapter are large, and, as Section 9.3 will indicate, there are reasons to wonder whether they can be resolved with any finality. But reflecting on them suggests ways of beginning to think about some of the most difficult topics in Heidegger's early work, including the role of time in BT, Heidegger's notion of authenticity, and some of his most obscure metaphilosophical proposals.

9.1 'Original havings' and the 'Being and Time' project

As Section 2.5 explained, Dahlstrom argues that Heidegger faces a serious problem in articulating the ontological diversity that, he believes, philosophy has characteristically overlooked. Theoretical assertions that would distinguish *Dasein* or the ready-to-hand, for example, from the present-at-hand must misfire: the very fact that the former are subjects of a theoretical assertion means that they must be present-at-hand after all. But much has changed since Section 2.5: in particular, we have come to doubt whether Heidegger himself subscribed to the key premise that theoretical assertions reveal only the present-at-hand. Nevertheless, a version of Dahlstrom's worry may seem to arise out of the notion that I have depicted as providing the best way of understanding Heidegger's 'disclosures of Being'. I have suggested that such 'disclosures', which underpin truth as correspondence and cannot themselves be evaluated as corresponding or failing to correspond to what they reveal, are best understood as representing 'original havings'. The problem that this notion may seem to raise is: how does one distinguish 'original havings'? From what point of view can one see the difference between these points of view?

'Original havings' are distinctive modes of intentionality through which distinct kinds of entities come 'into view', so to speak; entities 'visible' through one such 'having' will not be 'visible' through others, and vice versa. But if one grasps x if and only if one adopts 'original having' $x\star$, and grasps y if and only if one adopts 'original having' $y\star$, then from what perspective—through which 'having'—can one grasp *the difference between x* and y? x is 'invisible' to any 'having' other than $x\star$, as is y to any 'having' other than $y\star$. Dahlstrom's 'paradox of thematization' could be seen as an instance of this more general problem: if the *Vorhanden* are only revealed to theoretical propositions, and theoretical propositions only reveal the *Vorhanden*, then from what 'perspective'—through which 'having'—might one identify the difference between the *Vorhanden* and entities with other modes of Being?

There are a number of ways in which one might react to this puzzle, one of which I will sketch in Section 9.2. But the 'Being and Time' project might be seen as articulating another.[3] That puzzle asks of us: against which 'horizon' do we distinguish entities that instantiate different modes of Being? Another way to formulate this question is: when contrasting, for example, *Dasein*, the present-at-hand and the ready-at-hand, *as what* are we contrasting them? Thus formulated, this question raises a worry about the integrity of the notion of 'Being': is there indeed a notion of 'Being in general', a genus, 'Being', of which *Dasein*, presence-at-hand and readiness-at-hand might be seen as species? Given 'th[e] radical distinction of ways of Being in general', such as that 'between the constitution of *Dasein's* Being and that of nature', 'can there still be found any single unifying concept of Being in general that would justify calling these different ways of Being ways of *Being*?' (BPP 176) One of the objectives of the project that Heidegger set out for BT—but did not complete—was to demonstrate that there is.[4]

Heidegger claimed that the completed 'Being and Time' project would show that it is '[w]ithin the horizon of time [that] the projection of a meaning of Being in general can be accomplished' (BT 278 (235)). The notion that time has a certain philosophical fundamentality is not a peculiarity of the Heidegger of the immediate BT period; but a certain speculative interpretation of that fundamentality, one which is informed by a reading of

---

[3] McManus (unpublished) develops in greater detail the picture of the 'Being and Time' project that this section presents.

[4] In the discussion that follows I set aside some central elements of the 'official' metaphilosophy of BT—in particular, its notions of 'hermeneutics' and 'interpretation'. I do so because both are problematic in ways that make them ill-suited to deal with the issues I have raised, not because I assume they are unimportant full-stop. Blattner 2007, for example, has argued that they give rise to what is, in essence, a version of Dahlstrom's 'paradox of thematization': interpretation is among those activities which Heidegger seems to tell us reveal the *Vorhanden* (cf., e.g., BT 89 (61–2)) and, as such, it seems ill-suited to the job of articulating the diverse forms that Being takes. I have argued that the meaning of Heidegger's association of particular activities with the *Vorhanden* is more problematic than might at first appear; but that merely reinforces the worry that the notions in question cannot be invoked as offering unproblematic answers to the questions under discussion.

Kant in particular, is. A reading of the *Logik* lectures of 1925–26, for example, shows how Heidegger was struck by intimations in the first *Critique* that, while every act of judgement places the object of that judgement within a 'pre-viewed' range, or 'horizon', of possibilities, time constitutes, as it were, the horizon of all horizons, the *Hinblick* of all *Hinblicke*, the *Hinblick par excellence*. Despite the 'originality' of such 'projections of Being', time can be seen as 'the condition of the possibility of all projecting', as 'in some sense already concomitantly unveiled in all factual projection' (BPP 307). The metaphilosophical significance of this proposal lies in its apparent identification of an 'horizon' against which different kinds of Being might be distinguished as such, the diverse 'modes of Being' united by their being 'the object of Temporal interpretation' (BPP 291, 322). In this way, Heidegger hoped to show that time '*enabl[es] the thematic interpretation of Being* and *of its articulation* and *manifold ways*'; in doing so, it would 'make[] ontology possible' (BPP 228).

We will see in a moment that there is reason to doubt whether the need that this project attempts to meet is real; I also believe that—not unrelatedly—there is reason to question how deeply embedded in Heidegger's early philosophy this project really is and, hence, also the power of this project to illuminate the ideas at the heart of that philosophy. One can find for many of the ideas expressed in BT a conspicuously longer 'paper-trail' in Heidegger's thought of the 1920s than for the 'frame' within which they are set in BT,[5] a frame whose influence on Heidegger's thinking is also relatively short-lived. The bulk of BT seems to have been written by April of 1926;[6] but van Buren

---

[5] Examination of the early 1920s material asks us to reassess our sense of what in BT is well-worked-out and what isn't. There is a temptation to think that (i) Division One is well-worked out, (ii) Division Two less so, and (iii) Division Three and (iv) Part Two hardly at all. While (iii) seems to be true (cf. n. 2 above), and the existence of HCT and, to a degree, L encourages (i), the themes examined in Division Two are at least as long-standing in Heidegger's thought as those of Division One: indeed some of the apparently most tractable of Division One's concepts (e.g. *Befindlichkeit, Verstehen*) are of much more recent provenance than those upon which Division Two focuses (e.g. falling, *das Man*). (It may also be no coincidence that these late additions are ones which invite depiction as standing in an architectonic that corresponds and contrasts with one in Kant—i.e. *Befindlichkeit* is to Sensibility as *Verstehen* is to Understanding, and so on). Regarding (iv), the notion of a 'historical destruction' is also an old one for Heidegger, arguably dating back to a desire to break through the later layer of 'Hellenism' that 'distorted and buried' 'original' Christian experience (GP 205, translation quoted from van Buren 1994: 146.), as illustrated perhaps in Section 1.2. But the envisaged content and intent of the 'historical destruction' must surely have changed over the course of the 1920s.

[6] Cf. Kisiel's collection in Appendix C of his 1993 of documentary evidence available concerning the drafting of BT.

has argued that Heidegger underwent a 'turn to Kant' as late as towards the end of 1925; Kisiel too talks of Heidegger during the final drafting of BT as 'suddenly enthusiastic over Kant' (1993: 489).[7] The rather sudden emergence of the BT 'frame' is matched by a similarly rapid abandonment. Even in 1926, Heidegger was describing BT as '[o]n the whole ... for me a work of transition',[8] and only a year after it was published Heidegger's confidence in its overarching project seems to have waned:

> [T]he question of the extent to which one might conceive of *Dasein* as temporality in a universal-ontological way...is a question which I myself am not able to decide, one which is still completely unclear to me. (MFL 210)[9]

This would seem to entail that the need that the 'Being and Time' project set out to meet remains unmet. But is it clear that it *needs* to be met? Inwood, for example, argues that '[i]t is ... not obvious that we need to elucidate Being in general to understand the differences between various modes of Being, between rocks, tools, *Dasein*, time and world' (1997: 104). Heidegger would object that without such an elucidation we cannot distinguish these 'modes of Being' *as modes of Being* or make sense of ontology as a 'science of Being as such'. But I believe that Inwood is right to question whether the kind of phenomenological work Heidegger does has to issue in claims of that form. I also believe that Heidegger shared those doubts.

What the work of—among others—van Buren, Crowell, Dahlstrom, Kisiel, and Sheehan shows is that BT is not the expression of a static, complete, and unified perspective, but instead is just one of the attempts that Heidegger made to impose a framing on his thought as it evolved in rapid and complex ways throughout the 1920s.[10] Despite the impression that BT may strive to give, Heidegger's early thinking about the nature of

---

[7] We get a flavour of this in Heidegger's letter of 12 December 1925 to Jaspers in which he writes: 'the nicest thing is that I am beginning *actually to like Kant*' (quoted in Van Buren 1994: 364).

[8] Letter to Jaspers 4 May 1926 (BH 378).

[9] Käufer offers a similar chronology: 'Heidegger develops much of the practice-oriented existential analytic quite early, and has most of it in place in the 1923 [OHF] lectures. Here, and again in the 1925 [HCT] lectures he notices that care has temporal underpinning, and becomes interested in originary notions of time. Trying to make sense of this leads him to analyze the notion of time underlying the deduction and the schematism of the first *Critique*' (2003: 86). But the claim that world and intelligibility are each 'an aspect of time is a thesis that [by 1929/30s FCM lectures] Heidegger no longer maintains' (p. 90).

[10] Van Buren talks of 'the reproductive chain of differing/deferring drafts of the nonbook about the *Sache* of "Being and Time" that [Heidegger] went on reinscribing in many different ways' (1994: 367).

philosophy is very much torn, and, for example, he seems to have switched sides on more than one occasion on the issue of whether philosophy ought to be seen as a science, holding that it was not at both the beginning and end of the decade in which BT was written.[11] Both Kisiel and van Buren seem to see the 'Kantian turn' as an unproductive one for Heidegger. Of that I am not so sure, and I remain open to the possibility that something new and interesting emerges here, there being good though not ultimately compelling reasons behind this 'turn', beyond a new-found and ill-judged 'liking' or 'enthusiasm' for Kant.[12] But I do believe that there is a distinguishable core of ideas that explain much of Heidegger's fundamental ontology—ideas which are not best understood within the 'belated' self-reinterpretation that BT embodies and which are not essentially bound up with the (doomed) 'Being and Time' project.[13] Among these ideas are metaphilo-

[11] Cf., e.g., PIE 130, PRL ch. 4, FCM sec. 7, HCT 25 on the 'covert naturalism' of describing phenomenology as a theory, and, for discussion, Dahlstrom 2001: 208–9 and 392–3. The young Heidegger's talk of philosophy as a 'pre-', 'supra-' or simply 'non-theoretical science' further muddies these waters. Cf. IPPW 81, PRL 9, 35, and Kisiel 1993: 47, 59, and ch. 1 passim, and van Buren 1994: 246–7.

[12] Käufer presents the 'Being and Time' project as devoted to answering the—to use my expression—'con-formist' question that I quote in ch. 2 n. 6 above: 'Heidegger's view in *Being and Time*' is 'that both the forms of judgement and their possible objects derive from a common ancestor' and '[t]he common ancestor is what he calls "originary temporality"' (Käufer 2003: 79). (Cf. also Friedman 2000: 2's discussion of the need for a 'common root'.) The account I have offered suggests instead that Heidegger's reflections around the Prior Projection and Primacy of Practice Claims—taking in what Käufer calls Heidegger's 'practice-oriented existential analytic' (p. 86)—already represent a solution to—or rather a dissolution of—that con-formist worry and what I take to support that claim is the fact that Heidegger's anti-conformist notions of Being-in-the-world and of a 'prior' 'disclosure' that 'founds' truth as correspondence pre-date and outlast the 'Being and Time' project. But clearly, much more needs to be said: for example, an attempt to secure a certain generality for the applicability of that dissolution may be a distinctive aim of the latter project.

[13] Given that there are certain themes in BT that only make sense within its Kantian-temporal framing, some proposals that I have criticized earlier might step forward now and claim a distinctive interpretive power. For example, it is in the immediate BT period that Heidegger seems to stress the notion that scientific knowledge emerges out of the break-down of, or through a 'change-over' or a 'prescinding from', our 'thickly'- construed practical affairs. Rouse and Blattner stress this theme, and it may be that this connection serves a particular purpose within the 'Being and Time' project, such as imposing a certain kind of ordering relationship on the disclosure of the *Zuhanden* and the *Vorhanden*—one which might be extended to include *Dasein's* self-disclosure too, by virtue of the fact that the hierarchy of 'references [*Verweisungen*]' that determine the Being of the *Zuhanden* 'terminates' in *Dasein's* own possibilities (cf., e.g., BT 116–17 (84)). The apparent attempt to 'found' forms of understanding ultimately in a single, temporal, ur-understanding may also play some part in the emergence and similarly rapid vanishing in the BT period of striking transcendentalist motifs and a readiness to sound idealist notes, including those mentioned in Section 2.2 and—perhaps—the Dependency Claim too. (The notion that securing the unity of the subject and of the world it confronts plays a crucial role in motivating transcendental idealism is, of course, a familiar one in the literature on Kant and, recently, Wittgenstein (cf., e.g., on the latter, the recent debate between Moore (1997, 2003, and forthcoming)

sophical ideas that that project's attempt to rehabilitate a 'science of Being' occludes.

9.2 Recalling the measure

> [O]ne only possesses the truth in a genuine sense when one has made it one's own. (CA 499)

According to the perspective sketched in the preceding section, a desire to show that philosophy is, in fact, a science—ontology expressing itself in a set of distinctive propositions—enjoyed an ascendancy, but a relatively short-lived one, in Heidegger's thinking in the period in which BT was written. There he talks of his fundamental ontology as something like an ontology of ontology:

> The question of Being aims ... at ascertaining the *a priori* conditions not only for the possibility of the sciences which examine entities as entities of such and such a type, and, in so doing, already operate with an understanding of Being, but also for the possibility of those ontologies themselves which are prior to the ontical sciences and which provide their foundations. (BT 31 (11))

It is precisely this aspect of BT that Heidegger singles out for criticism in retrospective remarks made in 1949. There he condemns the book's 'inappropriate' 'suggestion' that 'recalling the truth of Being' is 'still a kind of ontology'; in this way, the book's thinking 'blocks and obscures its own path' and, with it, 'the transition from representational thinking to a thinking that recalls' (IWM 288–9).

The motif of 'recollection' and a certain doubt about the philosophical significance of what one might call 'representational thinking' are central to the alternative metaphilosophical perspective that I wish to sketch here. Let us begin by returning to, and reinterpreting, the worries about philosophy's supposedly propositional form that Dahlstrom's 'paradox of thematization' threw into relief. Section 8.4 showed that, for Heidegger, a certain fixation on assertions can draw attention away from the understanding that gives

---

and Sullivan (1996, 2002, and 2003).) Nevertheless, I retain my doubts about whether these notions, here identified as perhaps inspired by the 'Being and Time' project, can be defended philosophically and about whether they help us recognize Heidegger's best thoughts.

those assertions their 'life'—such assertions descending into a kind of 'idle talk'. If philosophy is a 'counter-ruinant' (PIA 121) struggle against that descent, then there is a sense in which seeing assertions—or theoretical claims or 'representational thinking'—as vehicles of philosophical understanding is to misunderstand philosophical misunderstanding. When philosophically confused, we fail to bring to bear in our reflections the understanding of entities that we actually possess: we assimilate the diverse modes of Being of the entities we encounter and the diverse modes of understanding through which we grasp them, by being uncritically 'orient[ed] towards the assertion and its indifference, towards its levelled and levelling character' (EP 83, quoted above). In allowing our thought to be guided by these 'undifferentiated' 'linguistic forms', we succumb to 'a peculiar self-satisfaction at adhering to what is idly spoken of' (PS 136), an 'adhere[nce] to what is said' in which we lose 'an original relation to the beings of which [we are] speaking' (PS 18) and our reflective talk descends into an 'indeterminate emptiness' (HCT 269). Such confusion is a matter of how we *take* assertions, our failing to see behind them—or in them—the 'lives' that give them meaning. This is a condition from which we will not be freed by hearing yet more assertions equally 'lifelessly' taken;[14] and in restoring what one might call an 'authentic' *relation to* our assertions—to our 'representational thinking'—what we are seeking to restore is not itself something that takes a propositional form.

From this perspective, Dahlstrom is right to think that there is a kind of mismatch between Heidegger's concerns and the idea that philosophical insight might be embodied in a set of assertions, a 'science of Being' even; and, in a sense, he is right to think of that mismatch as arising out of a connection between assertions and *Vorhandenheit*. But the relevant notion of *Vorhandenheit* is Section 8.3's 37th sense: on that understanding, the 'subject-correlate' of the *Vorhanden* is *Seinsvergessenheit*, to which corresponds a kind of *Verstehensvergessenheit*, our overlooking of the particular 'measures' which our encounters with entities presuppose. If that is the root confusion that we need to address, then it is true that '[i]t is of the essence of phenomenological investigations that they ... must in each case be rehearsed and *repeated* anew'; we cannot 'simply pull out results' because 'the whole thrust of the

---

[14] My (forthcoming-d) explores the need emerging here for a form of writing that will resist such 'lifeless' taking. Cf. n. 25 below.

work serves to implicate the reader' (HCT 26); engaging in such work would not be acquiring a mastery of 'objects of learning' but 'interpretation of our own situation' (PIA 38, 32). From this perspective, when 'the ontological' is problematic it is by virtue of our succumbing to a kind of *self*-obscurity, failing to, in some sense, 'make our own' the understanding that we have. Indeed if one endorses the notion that we have a pre-ontological understanding of Being—that 'Being is never alien but always familiar, "ours"' (MFL 147)—then that would have to be the case; and from this point of view, it is entirely natural that the motif of 'forgetting' and 'recollection' should appear again and again in the early Heidegger as it does, most obviously in the notion of *Seinsvergessenheit*.

Our broader discussion in this book tallies well with these admittedly rather hazily sketched metaphilosophical notions. A phenomenon we have come upon repeatedly is what one might call a 'forgetting' of 'the measures' that we bring to bear—a forgetting singled out by the 37th sense of the *Vorhanden*. We have encountered this 'forgetting', for example, in Heidegger's discussion of how we 'have' the divine, and his critique of scepticism and of the correspondence theory of truth. In Pythagorean fetishism, we also saw a 'forgetting' of 'measures' as a possibility within science, corresponding to a certain 'forgetfulness of Being' there also. In both the philosophical and scientific cases, an initial, already possessed understanding and concern is 'forgotten', as is the interpretive work and choices behind coming to think of the 'objects' of that understanding in the terms that that understanding and concern dictate. By recollecting—re-cognizing—the latter we come also to re-cognize the former.

In our scientific cases we operated with certain measures made possible by certain 'technical setups' and which make possible the tracking of certain aspects of that which is studied; there is nothing wrong with this 'narrowing' of focus as long as those measures are recognized as such: one might say that they reveal what they reveal. But problems arise when they are not recognized, and neither is the need to evaluate what they do, and can, reveal by reference to what we think needs—overall—to be revealed. Similarly, in our philosophizing we end up using as 'measures' what are actually simplifying analogies, for example, thinking of 'consciousness [as] similar to a box, where the ego is inside and reality is outside' (WDR 163). In one sense, there is nothing wrong with that use as long as these analogies are recognized as such: they reveal what they reveal. But problems arise when neither they nor the need to subject them to evaluation is recognized. In both cases, such scrutiny calls for a certain 'destruction' or 'deconstruction' of the 'measures' that we have 'fallen' into using and a certain 'repetition' or 'recollection' of how we 'originally' 'have' the objects in question. Against that background, the interpretive work and choices behind using the 'measures' we use is thrown into relief, as is our failure to attend to, or 'make our own', the understanding we already possess. Without that scrutiny we may remain in the grip of a certain fetishism, captivated—'distracted'—by certain modes of description that are only loosely associated with one's broader understanding and one's broader aims in seeking to understand.

In this condition those modes of description take on a life of their own, but with the consequence that our claims about the matters in hand descend into 'idle talk', into a kind of 'indeterminate emptiness'. We saw how scientific measures may become 'empty', and it is a repeated charge on Heidegger's part that in our philosophical confusion the concepts we use have become 'indeterminate'.[15] He speaks of 'the ontological indifference in which Descartes and his successors took' the Subject (HCT 216), and of the '*isolated* subject' upon which Kant reflects as 'ontologically quite indefinite' (BT 368 (321)), made 'visible' by a 'neglect' (HCT 222). To echo PRL 246 quoted in Section 8.3, such concepts have 'a neutral, faded content', 'not at all original' and 'uncharacterized by', by virtue of not 'originally aris[ing] from', 'a sphere of experience' (PRL 246).[16] Dissociated as our thoughts then are from the 'original' pre-ontological understanding from which these 'faded' 'concepts' are derived, our fundamental difficulty is that we do not understand what we are saying; confusions have taken over the terms we use: our talk is confusedly informed by an inconsistent set of crude—'neutral', 'faded'—metaphors or models.[17]

So what kind of philosophy might help us recognize that kind of confusion? I think that it is possible that Heidegger may have interpreted phenomenology as targeting such confusions, the 'return to the things themselves' being an attempt to make us aware of the influence of metaphors and models in our thinking and of the amount of active interpretive

---

[15] Cf. e.g., HCT 154, 166, 197, 216, 222–3, BT 46 (24–5), 84 (57), 96 (68), 108 (78), 249 (205), 251 (208), 339 (293), 382 (333), 441 (389), BPP 175–6, EP 114 and 118–19.

[16] Cf. also PIE's discussion of 'the fading of meaningfulness' (pp. 26–7, 141).

[17] Compare the difficulty discussed in Chapters 6–7 of not being misled by the terms 'practical' and 'cognitive'.

work—unrecognized because embedded in the philosophical tradition in which we are 'brought up'—that is needed in order to impose them. Such a 'return' might expose the kind of indeterminacy in our thought that allows us, for example, to vacillate between an understanding of an 'external world' as the 'outside' of the subject and as itself a (very large) object which we may or may not find 'in' such an 'outside',[18] between thinking of 'consciousness [as] similar to a box, where the ego is inside and reality is outside' but also of the 'contents' of that box as inherently 'about' what lies 'outside', and, as Sections 4.2.2 and 7.4 have described, between thinking of assertions as 'spoken sentence[s]' that 'you take up' 'the same way as you pick up a piece of chalk' (BBA 230), but also as something 'in which there still lurks a relational character' (BT 267 (225)).[19] In this way we see that 'so-called fundamental concepts, e.g., "representation" ... are unclear', 'indistinct', with 'different meanings run[ning] confusedly through one another' (PIE 23–4).[20]

Such thinking is marked by 'faded' assimilations—world as an object, consciousness as a box, assertion as a sentence—and by a certain indeterminacy—flipping, for example, from world as an object, to world as the 'outside' of the Subject, and back again. As such, this thinking represents a 'forgetting' of the understanding that we already have; it requires that we 'let entities come towards us and present themselves before us in a remarkable undifferentiatedness' (FCM 275, quoted above) and to recognize this

---

[18] Cf. Minar 2001: 209 and Mulhall 2005: 97.

[19] We see something similar in Section 1.2's 'speculators and chatterboxes'. They too vacillate between seeing their God as an object of love and as an object of fear, a potential obstacle to their 'peace and security'. Their thinking is informed by a crude model of what righteousness is—effectively, 'the obeying of God's orders'—but also by a lurking sense that this coming judgement is righteous and the judge someone they should love. Behind the 'levelled and levelling' appearance that their claims to 'love God' create is a life that endows that talk with an 'indeterminate emptiness', a life that makes it hard to see what is meant by their talk of 'love', if anything at all. Cf. ch. 8 n. 20.

[20] I have argued elsewhere (McManus 2006 sec. 14.3–14.7) that the formulation of the first 'regress' argument rests ultimately on an equivocation over what we mean when we talk of 'representations'—in essence the equivocation that HCT 42–3 (discussed in Section 4.2.2) identifies. From that point of view, our problem arises ultimately not out of an incorrect ontological theory of representation but out of a lack of clarity about what we are thinking about, switching unwittingly back and forth between thoughts about two different things in the course of our reflections around the single word, 'representation'. When we succumb to such illusions, our fundamental difficulty is that we don't understand what we are saying; confusions have taken over the terms we use: our talk of 'inside' and 'outside', 'transcendence' and 'embeddedness', 'engagement', and 'disengagement' is confusedly informed by inconsistent and simplistic metaphors or models. For reasons touched on in Sections 4.2.2 and 7.5, this may entail that 'positive' invocations of 'transcendence', 'engagement', 'openness', and so on, be themselves ultimately 'thrown away'.

'ontological indifference' (HCT 216)—the 'indefinite' character of what we are thinking—would be to recognize the crudity of the terms and habits of thought into which we unwittingly slide when we come to reflect.

This way of thinking also opens up a new way of understanding the difficulty with which Section 9.1 began, by inviting us to consider what failing to recognize the 'originality' of a 'having' is like. In the arguments offered in this book for believing particular 'havings' are 'original', an essential step has been demonstrating the limited illumination provided by the very metaphor of 'perspective' or a 'point of view'. What those arguments have tried to do is demonstrate that in some cases where we may have been tempted to envisage 'other points of view on a particular matter', these 'other points of view' were nothing of the sort, failing to intend 'the same matter' after all. We saw that in Heidegger's argument for believing that 'the speculators and chatterboxes', with their concern with the 'objective determination' of *when* the Last Judgment would come, lack a 'fundamental comportment to *God*'; in adopting their 'perspective', they relate themselves to some event of great moment for their 'peace and security' perhaps, but not to righteous judgement. There was a similar outcome when we considered 'alternative practices for measuring lengths': such 'alternatives' either turned out to be essentially consistent with '*our* practice' (as the confusion leads us to call it) or to intend either something else altogether or nothing at all. In Heidegger's critique of the first regress of rules argument, he attacks the 'infrastructure' within which that regress arises in a striking way; he says that it represents a theory 'without phenomenology' (HCT 43, quoted in Section 4.2.2). In the cases just alluded to, the 'originality' of these 'havings' lies in our inability to make good on our talk of 'other points of view', of 'rival havings'.[21] Recognition of this 'originality' requires not a (perhaps incoherent) attempt to articulate 'differences' between the entities that these 'havings' reveal; rather we need to recognize that imagined 'alternative perspectives' on the 'objects' of such 'havings' 'lack phenomenology'.[22] Such talk seemed to have sense but only as long as we considered its

---

[21] Relatedly, we do not prove that the 'having' and that which is had are 'internally related' but instead realise that we can make no sense of their 'successfully corresponding' to one another (a particular 'external relation') because we can make no sense of other 'havings' intending but failing to correspond to that which is had.

[22] My 2006: ch. 6 develops in connection with the early Wittgenstein a related understanding of 'ontological types' and the 'differences' between them.

'content' in an 'indeterminate' or 'indefinite' way; these 'neutral, faded' 'possibilities' represent so much empty 'idle talk' given the illusion of content by our 'neglect', our 'ontological indifference'.

The outlook I have sketched here suggests that the real sin that Heidegger wants to expose in our philosophical confusion is our allowing our thought and talk to descend into indeterminacy, a failure to subject our thought and talk to the discipline that our 'pre-ontological understanding' would otherwise impose. Given that we already possess an understanding of Being, there is perhaps a naturalness to the conclusion that clarity about 'the Being of entities' might ultimately be one and the same achievement as clarity about the identity of one's own thoughts and the meaning of one's own words, and that achieving clarity about the latter is a matter of a kind of self-knowledge. The distinguishing feature of the enlightened philosopher, the form that 'ontological understanding' takes, would then not be the possession of the right theory or body of doctrine but a form of attention that she pays to what she says and does. Indeed one is reminded of Heidegger's vision of the work done by 'the essential teachings of St Paul'; these 'are and remain entwined with the *How*, with life; they are not concerned with a specifically theoretical teaching', with 'theoretical instruction'; instead his letters are a 'call', an attempt to provoke his readers into actually appropriating what they already know, into keeping this 'unceasingly... alive in the enactment of life' (PRL 83, 76, 94).

The best way to understand such a form of thinking, that seeks to restore our attention to our words and deeds, is perhaps as a form of reminding; and the concern it expresses—that we not descend into a form of reflective thought that is merely a 'construction detached from life' (DSTCMC 68, quoted in Section 1.2)—can be seen as a recurrent moment in philosophical thinking, one which one might trace back to the Aristotelian demand that we 'save' or 'return to the appearances'—*tithenai ta phainomena* (*Nicomachean Ethics*, Book VII, 1, 1145b3).[23] In BT, Heidegger talks of a 'genuine philosophical empiricism' (BT 72 (50) n. x); that 'empiricism' calls not for

---

[23] It barely needs saying but Wittgenstein can be seen as responding to that 'call' too, for instance, in his own call that we 'look and see' (1967: sec. 66). (For a discussion of this connection, cf. Palmer 2004 and my (forthcoming-d).) A certain rediscovered sympathy with Aristotle is also a feature of many of Wittgenstein's most interesting followers, such as Anscombe, Hacker, Lovibond, and McDowell; and there are, I believe, some fascinating and intimate connections to be drawn between the work of the latter two in particular and some central Heideggerian themes, as Chapter 4 begins to show.

we philosophers to adopt something like the methods of empirical science but for us to resist the temptation to philosophize—as Nussbaum characterizes Aristotle's original call—as if we were 'strangers to . . . the life we live, the language we use' (2001: 260).[24] It is just such a demand that seems to motivate Heidegger's concern with the diversity of 'subject-correlates' and 'original havings', a diversity hidden behind 'the assertion and its indifference'.[25]

9.3 Philosophy's 'subject-correlate' revisited

What I have offered in this book is a reading of themes that run up to, through, and beyond BT. I take that reading to shed light on BT; but the question of its fit with the 'official' 'Being and Time' project is complex, as, of course, is the question of the fit between that project and Heidegger's actual texts, since he failed to bring that project, and the metaphilosophical ambition it serves, to fruition. My own book attempts to identify longer-term pressures on Heidegger's thought—pressures with which that project represents one attempted reckoning. Identifying those pressures may perform some of the groundwork necessary for a full exploration of the detail of, and difficulties facing, that particular reckoning. But I hope that the ideas presented here are also of interest in their own right.

This concluding chapter has considered some of the further—and, in particular, metaphilosophical—questions that those ideas raise and has ques-

---

[24] Nussbaum's argument builds on Owen's in his '*Tithenai ta phainomena*' (reprinted as ch. 13 of Owen 1986).

[25] My forthcoming work—d explores some lines along which the account sketched might be developed. It considers, in particular, the kind of writing that might be envisaged as responding appropriately to the kind of philosophical 'forgetting' discussed. In one sense, Heidegger clearly does express himself propositionally; but what kind of work are his propositions meant to do and what kind of response do they seek to elicit from us? In addressing these questions, I examine Wittgenstein's own call for a recollective 'looking and seeing' (cf. n. 23 above), a call based at least in part on an awareness of the confusing power of 'the uniform appearance of words' (1967: sec. 11), and Heidegger's discussion of Platonic dialectic, in which he examines, and extols the virtues of a 'demythologized' version (PS 231) of, the most famous metaphilosophical invocation of 'recollection', Plato's reflections on '*anamnesis*'. I go on to explore connections between that discussion and Heidegger's notion of 'formal indication', of which commentators who see Heideggerian philosophical insights as, in some sense, 'non-propositional' have made much (cf., e.g., Kisiel 1993 and Dahlstrom 2001). But neither here nor there do I meet the most important need that the above vision reveals: namely, that for a thorough examination of Heidegger's concept of 'authenticity'. I hope to remedy this in future work.

tioned the authority of BT's metaphilosophical vision—its claim to be the best guide in 'framing' Heidegger's thought. In 1953–54, Heidegger spoke of BT as 'never [having] more than follow[ed] a faint trail' (OWL 41) and, even in the year of its publication, he declared that 'all ontological interpretations are more like a groping about than an inquiry clear in its method' (BPP 322). That they should be so already becomes clear if we 'unpack', so to speak, BT's plea for a reawakening of our understanding of the 'Question of Being'. In attempting such a reawakening, we cannot but grope, since the meaning of the question—let alone its answer—is, after all, hidden from us:

> [N]ot only [does] the question of Being [lack] an *answer*, but ... the question itself is obscure and without direction. So if it is to be revived, this means that we must first work out an adequate way of *formulating* it. (BT 24 (4))

Our confusion then is deep: if 'we must reawaken an understanding of the meaning of this question' 'of the meaning of Being' (BT 19 (1)), then we lack not only an answer to the question but also a proper understanding of what the question is; we do not understand the kind of question it is that we would be asking were we to ask about the kind of thing that Being is: '[t]he questioning is itself as it were still indefinite' (HCT 144).[26] Being may be 'the basic theme of philosophy' (BT 62 (38)); but if we have forgotten the meaning of the question of the meaning of Being, then that meaning is unavailable to us, as is that 'basic theme': in this condition, we lack any straightforward appreciation of what the business of philosophy is.[27]

The previous section cannot claim to have provided such an appreciation either. It highlights particular themes in Heidegger's metaphilosophical reflections, themes that belong to the complex process of self-reinterpretation that

---

[26] Heidegger declares that his postulated 'historical *Destruktion*' is needed for us to be able to 'demonstrate what it means to talk about "restating" this question [*"Wiederholung" dieser Frage*]' of Being (BT 49 (26)); but since that was not completed, we lack such a demonstration.

[27] Is it then any wonder that the character of the project as set out in the introduction to BT is so very schematic, its explanation of 'phenomenology' abstract in the extreme, and that Heidegger talks of the 'provisional' character of his 'findings' and of the possibility of an 'even more primordial ... horizon' (BT 49 (26))? A further indication of the turmoil behind the settled façade that BT presents is that the notion of 'formal indication', which has been the focus for some of the most radical proposals concerning how Heidegger's metaphilosophy might be understood (cf. n. 25 above), is to be found there—though, as Dahlstrom notes, 'without [Heidegger] explaining it' (Dahlstrom 2001: 242 n. 23, where he also identifies a number of the relevant passages). In a 1927 letter to Löwith Heidegger states regarding BT that '[f]ormal indication ... is still for me there even though I do not talk about [it]' (quoted in Kisiel 1993: 19).

his work in the 1920s contains.[28] The emergence of these deep metaphilosophical questions reflects the fact that, as a form of understanding of which we might need to be reminded, philosophy can be expected to be among its own 'objects': a sufficiently radical philosophical investigation will raise the question of what a philosophical investigation is and what form of 'understanding' such an investigation seeks. In the case of the *Zuhanden*, our understanding takes, at least in some sense, a *practical* form: an appreciation of how to use a tool, for example, is not the capacity to provide an abstract description of that use but the capacity to pick the tool up and work with it. So what *kind* of understanding do we philosophers seek? What is the 'subject-correlate' of that into which philosophical insight is insight? As we deepen our understanding of understanding, our understanding of what it is to understand understanding can be expected to change; among the entities whose Being we will understand more clearly when we have reawoken the Question of Being is the philosopher; that reawakening reawakens the Question of the Being of Questioning, the philosopher's questioning included;[29] and philosophical progress may require us to rethink the *kind* of question that philosophy—when it understands itself—asks.

The thought that the nature of philosophy is itself a philosophical question is one which Heidegger takes very seriously:

[A] philologist is not interested in the 'essence' of philology. But... [p]hilosophy's constant effort to determine its own concept belongs to its authentic motive. (PRL 6-7)

---

[28] In the light of that flux, one might wonder, for example, how incompatible the metaphilosophical visions that the previous two sections present really are. These visions may express different assessments of the significance of philosophical propositions and of the pursuit of a 'science of Being'; but there is no obvious tension between the motif of recollection and the pursuit of systematicity, for example. The previous section articulated its vision against the background of the quite general picture that Chapters 5–8 developed of what it takes to make assertions about the world around us and—to raise questions I will not attempt to settle here—might that vision and its motifs play a part in BT's attempted 'recollection' of the ultimate 'measure' or *Hinblick*? Could the objective that BT pursued in attempting to construct 'a science of Being' be achieved, in some sense, by 'assembling reminders' (Wittgenstein 1967: sec. 127)? It was, after all, '*its own path*' that Heidegger later claimed BT 'block[ed]' when it 'obscure[ed]' 'the transition ... to a thinking that recalls' (IWM 288–89, quoted above).

[29] So, for instance, in setting about '[t]he task of "describing" the world phenomenologically', 'essential ontological clarifications will be needed' just in order to 'determine adequately what *form* [such a description] shall take' (BT 92 (64), emphasis added). For example, if '[o]ne tries to Interpret the world in terms of the Being of those entities which are present-at-hand within-the-world', then one does not just emerge with a misunderstanding of the world; rather 'the phenomenon of worldhood ... gets *passed over*' (BT 93 (65)). (Cf. also HCT 185.) For similar reasons, '[t]he right way of presenting [*Dasein*] is so far from self-evident that to determine what form it shall take is itself an essential part of the ontological analytic of this entity' (BT 69 (43)).

In the light of Heidegger's reflections on 'constitution' and his efforts to reawaken the Question of Understanding, the 'subject-correlate' of 'philosophical truth' must be up for grabs; 'the question about the how of philosophical experience' (PIE 131)—of what philosophical insight is and of what it is to 'have' it—must be seen as open. Just as our investigation of Being is simultaneously an investigation of philosophy—'[t]o raise the question of the meaning of Being does not mean anything else than to elaborate the questioning involved in philosophy in general' (PS 310)[30]— and our investigation of Being an investigation of *Dasein*—since *Dasein* is the entity that 'understands Being' (BT 32 (12))—so too (to complete another triangle of relations) is our investigation of *Dasein* an investigation of philosophy: 'We are already in philosophy because philosophy is in us and belongs to us ourselves... insofar as we exist as human beings' (EP 3). Our pursuing philosophical research—into Being and 'the understanding of Being'—is then simultaneously 'learn[ing]... what real philosophical research looks like' (BBA 231), and one might declare a solution to the problem of metaphilosophy 'the most proper and highest result of philosophy itself' (BPP 4). But it may be closer to the truth to say that the problem of setting a frame around one's work as a philosopher—of saying what it is one is doing—is the last problem that a philosopher might solve.

---

[30] Cf. also PS 444.

Appendix: Heidegger's Critique of Husserl

The character of Heidegger's break with Husserl is a topic of intense debate. Some argue that many of the ideas that Heidegger presented as distinctively his own were Husserl's, and there is certainly some basis for this claim. Husserl talks of a certain 'self-forgetfulness [*Selbstvergessenheit*]' in our tendency to take as fundamental in our philosophizing the perspective of the observing natural scientist, 'whereby' we also 'proceed[] illegitimately to absolutize its world, i.e., nature' (Husserl 1989: 193);[1] more generally, oblivion to a Question of Understanding corresponds to one to a Question of Being in that

Perception and *object* are concepts that cohere most intimately together, which mutually assign sense to one another, and which widen and narrow this sense conjointly. (2001, vol. 2: 277)

Heidegger certainly acknowledged that these thoughts had roots in Husserl, but he saw himself as having grasped their true depth—Husserl remaining in the grip of certain Cartesian assumptions and of the Theoretical Attitude.[2] However, there is reason to question the justice of both of these charges.

As the above discussion shows, quite what the Theoretical Attitude is is a difficult question, and so is that of its relationship to Cartesianism. But one might understand the above charges in the following way: the entities whose Being is revealed through the Husserlian *epoché* are, one might suppose, those which offer themselves up when we step back from our ordinary interactions with the world and 'merely contemplate' or 'merely observe' the contents of that world. But do *all* entities reveal themselves to the subject who adopts such a Theoretical Attitude? Might subjectivity take more forms than that embodied in the adoption of that Attitude and might other 'attitudes' that the subject might adopt reveal other entities? If so, the *epoché* might seem to build distorting presumptions into the 'results' we arrive at when we employ that form of reflection. Turning to the charge of Cartesianism, the *epoché*'s bracketing of the existence of entities which lie beyond consciousness (in some sense) certainly invites comparison with the Cartesian sceptical hypothesis that an external world might not exist; and inasmuch as the essential mode of activity of the Cartesian subject is that of observing or contemplating, and the Cartesian object, on

---

[1] Cf. Dahlstrom 2001: 163.
[2] Cf., e.g., HCT sec. 10–13, WDR 162, BPP 201, MFL 124–5, 133, 134, 150, and EP 141–2.

the other hand, exists as the extended material object revealed by the mathematical sciences, there may seem to be a natural affinity between Cartesianism and the Theoretical Attitude.

Heidegger often distances himself from Husserl by implicating the latter in the above set of presumptions. Remarks of Husserl's that do suggest a 'kinship with Descartes' (HCT 101) include Husserl's remarks on consciousness not 'being touched' by a possible 'annihilation' of 'the world of physical things' (1982: 110) and his claim that, '[i]nsofar as their respective senses are concerned, a veritable abyss yawns between consciousness and reality' (1982: 111, quoted in HCT 114). But how representative are the remarks quoted above? Is Husserl's *epoché* a fundamentally Cartesian mode of thought? And is he really in the grip of the Theoretical Attitude?

I will only give an indication here of the evidence that might be cited in Husserl's defence. Husserl may have had interests that directed him primarily to questions concerning the theoretical,[3] but he also explicitly characterises phenomenology as, in part, revealing 'the pretheoretical';[4] in work unpublished at the time but to which Heidegger had access, Husserl reflects on the character of 'the theoretical attitude [*theoretische Einstellung*]' and on the particular conditions under which we experience the world as 'on hand [*vorhanden*]' (Husserl 1989: 5 and 196).[5] There is also reason to doubt whether the *epoché* essentially involves a 'stepping back' from the world, as opposed to an examination of only one of its aspects. If one's interest lies in 'pure consciousness'—that is to say, consciousness not of any particular object or manifest in any particular creature or species of creature—then that would itself render irrelevant particular natural facts about the world, about the particular objects and particular conscious agents that happen to be found there: an exploration of these 'essential' structures—which Husserl calls an 'eidetic' exploration—can have no interest in such facts which it is, one might then argue, best to 'bracket'.[6]

To be fair to both of these philosophers, Heidegger does acknowledge some of the responses that might be made on Husserl's behalf and which we have sketched;[7] and there are also more subtle strands of thought in Heidegger's tracing of Cartesianism in Husserl: for example, he traces it in Husserl's effort to establish an indubitable basis for science.[8] But I will not attempt to take this interpretive

---

[3] Cf., e.g., Bernet et al. 1993: xii and Moran 2000a: 51 and 60–1.
[4] Cf., e.g., Husserl 1974: 373.
[5] Cf. HCT 121 and Moran 2000a: 61–2.
[6] Cf. Bernet et al. 1993 ch. 2, Crowell 2001 chs 3 and 9, and Hall 1982.
[7] Cf., e.g. HCT 91, 99.
[8] Cf. especially HCT 107 and 120, and IPR Part One ch. 2. Cf. also Crowell 2001: 197, Dahlstrom 2001: 118–19 and 124–5, and Sokolowski 1970, on Husserl's interest in 'subjectivity' as 'a region of experience where a presuppositionless science can be grounded', 'unmarred by the possibility of error or doubt' (pp. 125, 131).

controversy further here. Its difficulty surely lies—at least in part—in that of distinguishing between further generalizing earlier insights and identifying fundamental limitations in such insights. Haugeland notes that 'Husserl...had already generalized theoretical knowledge to intentionality, which includes other cognitive attitudes besides knowing, such as those characteristic of action and perception' (2000: 45). One might then see Heidegger as merely extending this Husserlian programme by further generalizing it. But one might also claim that such generalizations point to shortcomings of the programme as a whole: for instance, revealing modes of 'consciousness' that suggest there is something misleading precisely in the supposedly generalized notion of 'consciousness'. But I will leave these matters for another day.

Abbreviations

Below are the abbreviations used in referring to works by Heidegger. In the text, they are, followed by page numbers except where indicated.

BBA	'Being-there and Being-true according to Aristotle', trans. B. Hansford-Bowles, in BH. [1924]
BH	Kisiel and Sheehan (eds.) *Becoming Heidegger*, Evanston, Illinois: Northwestern University Press, 2007.
BPP	*The Basic Problems of Phenomenology*, trans. A. Hofstadter, Indianapolis: Indiana University Press, 1982. [1927]
BQP	*Basic Questions of Philosophy*, trans. R.Rojcewicz and André Schuwer, Indianapolis: Indiana University Press, 1994. [1937–38]
BT	*Being and Time*. Trans. J. Macquarrie and E. Robinson, Oxford: Blackwell, 1962. [1927]
BW	*Basic Writings*, ed. D. F. Krell, revised edition, New York: Harper Collins, 1993.
CA	'Contributions to *Das Akademiker*, 1910–1913', trans. J. Protevi, *Graduate Faculty Philosophy Journal* 14–15 (1991): 486–519.
CP	*Contributions to Philosophy*, trans. P. Emad and K. Maly, Indianapolis: Indiana University Press, 1999. [1936–38]
CT	*The Concept of Time*, trans. W. McNeill, Oxford: Blackwell, 1992. [1924]
CTSH	'The Concept of Time in the Science of History', trans. T. Sheehan, in BH. [1916]
DSTCM	*Duns Scotus' Theory of the Categories and of Meaning*, trans. H. Robbins, Ph.D. dissertation, De Paul University, Chicago, Illinois, 1973. [1915–16]
DSTCMC	'Conclusion of *Duns Scotus' Theory of the Categories and of Meaning*', trans. R, M, Stewart and J. van Buren, in S, pp. 61–8. [1916]
EG	'On the Essence of Ground', trans. W. McNeill in P. [1929]
EP	*Einleitung in die Philosophie*, Frankfurt am Main: Vittorio Klostermann, 1996. [1928–29]
FCM	*The Fundamental Concepts of Metaphysics*, trans. W. McNeill and N. Walker, Indianapolis: Indiana University Press, 1995. [1929–30]

GA	This abbreviation, followed by a volume number, is used on occasion to identify particular volumes of the *Gesamtausgabe*, Frankfurt am Main: Vittorio Klostermann.
GP	*Grundprobleme der Phänomenologie (1919/20)*, Frankfurt am Main: Vittorio Klostermann, 1993.
HCT	*History of the Concept of Time*, trans. T. Kisiel, Indianapolis: Indiana University Press, 1985. [1925]
HJC	*The Heidegger-Jaspers Correspondence (1920–1963)*, ed. W. Biemel and H. Saner, trans. G. E. Aylesworth, New York: Humanity Books, 2003.
HPS	*Hegel's Phenomenology of Spirit*, trans. P. Emad and K. Maly, Indianapolis: Indiana University Press, 1994. [1930–31]
IPPW	'The Idea of Philosophy and the Problem of Worldview', trans. T. Sadler, in M. Heidegger, *Towards the Definition of Philosophy*, London: Athlone Press, 2000, pp. 1–99. [1919]
IPR	*Introduction to Phenomenological Research*, trans. D. O. Dahlstrom, Indianapolis: Indiana University Press, 2005. [1923–24]
IWM	'Introduction to "What is Metaphysics?"', trans. W. Kaufmann, in P, pp. 277–90. [1949]
KJPW	'Comments on Karl Jaspers' *Psychology of Worldviews*', trans. J. van Buren, in P, pp. 1–38. [1919–21]
L	*Logik: Die Frage nach der Wahrheit*, Frankfurt am Main: Vittorio Klostermann, 1976 [1925–26]
LH	'Letter on Humanism', trans. F. A. Capuzzi, in BW. [1947]
MFL	*The Metaphysical Foundations of Logic*, trans. M. Heim, Indianapolis: Indiana University Press, 1992. [1928]
NUAS	'On the Nature of the University and Academic Study', trans. T. Sadler, in M. Heidegger, *Towards the Definition of Philosophy*, London: Athlone Press, 2000, pp. 173–81. [1919]
OHF	*Ontology—The Hermeneutics of Facticity*, trans. J. van Buren, Indianapolis: Indiana University Press, 1999. [1923]
OET	'On the Essence of Truth', trans. J. Sallis, in P, pp. 136–54. [1930]
OET (PM)	'On the Essence of Truth (Pentecost Monday, 1926)', trans. T. Kisiel, in BH.
OWL	*On the Way to Language*, trans. P. D. Hertz, San Francisco: Harper and Row.

P	*Pathmarks*, ed. W. McNeill, Cambridge: Cambridge University Press, 1998.
PIA	*Phenomenological Interpretations of Aristotle*, trans. R. Rojcewicz, Indianapolis: Indiana University Press, 2001. [1921–22]
PICA	'Phenomenological Interpretations in Connection with Aristotle: An Indication of the Hermeneutical Situation', trans. J. van Buren, in S, pp. 111–45. [1922]
PICPR	*Phenomenological Interpretation of Kant's* Critique of Pure Reason, trans. P. Emad and K. Maly, Indianapolis: Indiana University Press, 1997. [1927–28]
PIE	*Phenomenology of Intuition and Expression*, trans. T. Colony, London: Contiuum Press, 2010. [1920]
PMD	'...Poetically Man Dwells...', in *Poetry, Language, Thought*, trans. A. Hofstadter, New york: Harper and Row, 1971.
PRL	*The Phenomenology of Religious Life*, trans. M. Fritsch and J. A. Gosetti-Ferencei, Indianapolis: Indiana University Press, 2004. [1918–21]
PRMP	'The Problem of Reality in Modern Philosophy', trans. P. J. Bossert and J. van Buren, in S, pp. 39–48. [1912]
PS	*Plato's* Sophist, trans. R. Rojcewicz and André Schuwer, Indianapolis: Indiana University Press, 1997. [1924–25]
PT	'Phenomenology and Theology', trans. J. G. Hart and J. C. Maraldo, in P, pp. 39–62. [1927].
QCT	*The Question Concerning Technology and Other Essays*, trans. W. Lovitt, New York: Harper Torchbooks, 1977. [1938–55]
S	*Supplements*, ed. J. van Buren, Albany, NY: State University of New York Press, 2002.
TB	*On Time and Being*, trans. J. Stambaugh, New York: Harper Torchbooks, 1972. [1962–64]
WDR	'Wilhelm Dilthey's Research and the Struggle for a Historical Worldview', trans. C. Bambach, in S, pp. 147–76. [1925]
WM	'What is Metaphysics?', in P, pp. 82–96. [1929]
WT	*What is a Thing?*, trans. W. B. Barton and V. Deutsch, Lanham: University Press of America, 1967. [1935–36]
Z	*Zollikon Seminars*, ed. M. Boss, trans. F. Mayr and R. Askay, Evanston, Illinois: Northwestern University Press, 2001. [1947–72]

Bibliography

St Anselm (1926) *Proslogium*, trans. S. N. Deane, Chicago: Open Court.
St Thomas Aquinas (1994) *Truth*, Indianapolis: Hackett Publishing Company.
Aristotle, (1984) *The Complete Works of Aristotle, the Revised Oxford Translation*. ed. J. Barnes, Princeton, NJ: Princeton University Press.
St Augustine (1961) *Confessions*, trans. R. S. Pine-Coffin, Harmondsworth: Penguin.
Austin, J. L. (1962) *Sense and Sensibilia*, ed. G. J. Warnock, Oxford: Clarendon Press.
Barad, K. (1996) 'Meeting the Universe Halfway: Realism and Social Constructivism without Contradiction', in L. H. Nelson and J. Nelson (eds), *Feminism, Science and the Philosophy of Science*, Dordrecht: Reidel.
Bar-On, D. (unpublished) 'Expression, Action and Meaning', paper given at the conference, 'Self and Others in Wittgenstein and Contemporary Analytic Philosophy', University of Southampton, 26 March 2010.
Beck, A. (2002) 'Heidegger and Science: Nature, Objectivity and the Present-at-hand'. PhD dissertation, Middlesex University.
——(2005), 'Heidegger and Relativity Theory: Crisis, Authenticity and Repetition', *Angelaki* 10: 163–79.
Bernasconi, R. (1989) 'Heidegger's Destruction of *Phronesis*', *Southern Journal of Philosophy* 28 supp.: 127–47.
Bernet, R., Kern, I., and Marbach, E. (1993) *An Introduction to Husserlian Phenomenology*, Evanston, IL: Northwestern University Press.
Blattner, W. D. (1994) (1995) 'Decontextualisation, Standardisation, and Dewey Science', *Man and World* 28: 321–39.
——(1999) *Heidegger's Temporal Idealism*, Cambridge: Cambridge University Press.
——(2006) *Heidegger's 'Being and Time'*, London: Continuum.
——(2007) 'Ontology, the *A Priori*, and the Primacy of Practice', in S. Crowell and J. Malpas (eds), *Transcendental Heidegger*, Stanford, CA: Stanford University Press.
Boghossian, P. (1990) 'Naturalizing Content', in G. Rey and B. Loewer (ed.) *Meaning in Mind: Essays for Jerry Fodor*, Oxford: Blackwell.
Brandom, R. (1994) *Making It Explicit*, Cambridge, MA: Harvard University Press.
Carman, T. (2003) *Heidegger's Analytic*, Cambridge: Cambridge University Press.
——(2007) 'Heidegger on Correspondence and Correctness', *Graduate Faculty Philosophy Journal* 28: 103–16.
Cavell, S. (1976) *Must We Mean What We Say*, Cambridge: Cambridge University Press.

—— (1979) *The Claim of Reason*, Oxford: Oxford University Press.
Cerbone, D. R. (2005) 'Realism and Truth', in H. L. Dreyfus and M. A. Wrathall (eds), *A Companion to Heidegger*, Oxford: Blackwell.
Chang, H. and Cartwright, N. (2008) 'Measurement', in S. Psillos and M. Curd (eds), *The Routledge Companion to Philosophy of Science*, London: Routledge, pp. 367–75.
Christiansen, C. B. (1997) 'Heidegger's Representationalism', *The Review of Metaphysics* 51: 77–103.
—— (1998) 'Getting Heidegger off the West Coast', *Inquiry* 41: 65–87.
Cooper, D. E. (1997) 'Wittgenstein, Heidegger and Humility', *Philosophy* 72: 105–23.
—— (2002) *The Measure of Things: Humanism, Humility, and Mystery*, Oxford: Oxford University Press.
Craig, E. J. (1996) *The Mind of God and the Works of Man*, Oxford: Oxford University Press.
Crowe, B. D. (2006) *Heidegger's Religious Origins*, Bloomington: Indiana University Press.
Crowell, S. (2001) *Husserl, Heidegger and the Space of Meaning*, Evanston, IL: Northwestern University Press.
—— (2008) 'Measure-Taking: Meaning and Normativity in Heidegger's Philosophy', *Continental Philosophy Review* 41: 261–76.
—— and Malpas J. (eds) (2007) *Transcendental Heidegger*, Stanford, CA: Stanford University Press.
Dahlstrom, D. O. (1994) 'Heidegger's Method: Philosophical Concepts as Formal Indications', *Review of Metaphysics* 47: 775–95.
—— (2001) *Heidegger's Concept of Truth*, Cambridge: Cambridge University Press.
Davidson, D. (1973–74) 'On the Very Idea of a Conceptual Scheme', *Proceedings and Addresses of the American Philosophical Association* 67: 5–20, reprinted in his *Inquiries into Truth and Interpretation*, Oxford: Oxford University Press, 1984.
—— (1999) 'The Emergence of Thought', *Erkenntnis* 51: 7–17.
Davies, P. S. (2000) 'The Nature of Natural Norms: Why Selected Functions are Systematic Capacity Functions', *Noûs* 34: 85–107.
Diamond, C. (2001) 'How Long is the Standard Metre in Paris?', in T. G. McCarthy and S. C. Stidd (eds), *Wittgenstein in America*, Oxford: Oxford University Press.
—— (2005) 'Wittgenstein on Religious Belief: The Gulfs Between Us', in D. Z. Phillips (ed.) *Religion and Wittgenstein's Legacy*, Aldershot: Ashgate.
Dreyfus, H. L. (1980) 'Holism and Hermeneutics', *Review of Metaphysics* 34: 3–23.
—— (ed.) (1982) *Husserl, Intentionality and Cognitive Science*, Cambridge, MA: MIT Press.

Dreyfus, H. L. (1991) *Being-in-the-World*, Cambridge, MA: MIT Press.
——(1993) 'Heidegger's Critique of the Husserl/Searle Account of Intentionality', *Social Research* 60: 17–38.
——(1997) *What Computers Still Can't Do*, Cambridge, MA: MIT Press.
——(1999) 'The Primacy of Phenomenology over Logical Analysis', *Philosophical Topics* 27: 3–24.
——(2000a) 'Could Anything be More Intelligible than Everyday Intelligibility? Reinterpreting Division I of *Being and Time* in the light of Division II", in J. E. Faulconer and M. A. Wrathall (eds), *Appropriating Heidegger*, Cambridge: Cambridge University Press.
——(2000b) 'A Merleau-Pontyian Critique of Husserl's and Searle's Representationalist Accounts of Action', *Proceedings of the Aristotelian Society* 100: 287–302.
——(2000c) 'Responses', in M. A. Wrathall and J. Malpas (eds), *Heidegger, Coping and Cognitive Science*, Cambridge, MA: MIT Press.
——(2001) 'Introduction I: Todes' Account of Nonconceptual Perceptual Knowledge and its Relation to Thought', in S. Todes, *Body and World*, Cambridge, MA: MIT Press.
——(2005) 'Overcoming the Myth of the Mental: How Philosophers Can Profit from the Phenomenology of Everyday Expertise', *Proceedings and Addresses of the American Philosophical Association* 79: 47–65.
——(2007a) 'The Return of the Myth of the Mental', *Inquiry* 50: 352–65.
——(2007b) 'Response to McDowell', *Inquiry* 50: 371–7.
——and Dreyfus, S. E. (1986) *Mind over Machine*, New York: Free Press.
——and Spinosa, C. (1999) 'Coping with Things-in-themselves: A Practice-Based Phenomenological Argument for Realism', *Inquiry* 42: 49–78.
——and Wrathall, M. A. (eds) (2005) *A Companion to Heidegger*, Oxford: Blackwell.
Dummett, M. (1987) 'Can Analytic Philosophy be Systematic and Ought it to be?', in K. Baynes, J. Bohman, and T. McCarthy (eds), *After Philosophy: End or Transformation?*, Cambridge, MA: MIT Press.
Elden, S. (2006) *Speaking Against Number: Heidegger, Language and the Politics of Calculation*, Edinburgh: Edinburgh University Press.
Fell, J. P. (1992) 'The Familiar and the Strange: On the Limits of Praxis in the Early Heidegger', in H. L. Dreyfus and H. Hall (eds), *Heidegger: A Critical Reader*, Oxford: Blackwell.
Fodor, J. (1994) 'Fodor, Jerry A.', in S. Guttenplan (ed.), *A Companion to the Philosophy of Mind*, Oxford: Blackwell.
Frege, G. (1894) 'Review of E. G. Husserl, *Philosophie der Arithmetik* I', in his *Collected Papers on Mathematics, Logic, and Philosophy*, ed. B. McGuinness, trans. M. Black *et al.*, Oxford: Blackwell, 1984.

Friedman, M. (2000) *A Parting of the Ways: Carnap, Cassirer, and Heidegger*, Peru, IL: Open Court Publishing Company.
Gardner, S. (1999) *Kant and the* Critique of Pure Reason, London: Routledge.
Gelven, M. (1989) *A Commentary on Heidegger's* Being and Time, revised edn, Dekalb, IL: Northern Illinois University Press.
Glock, H. J. (1997) 'Truth without People?', *Philosophy* 72: 85–104.
Goldfarb, W. (1983) 'I Want You to Bring Me a Slab: Remarks on the Opening Sections of the *Philosophical Investigations*', *Synthese* 56: 265–82.
——(1997) 'Wittgenstein on Fixity of Meaning', in W. W. Tait (ed.), *Early Analytic Philosophy*, Chicago: Open Court.
Gorner, P. (2007) *Heidegger's* Being and Time, Cambridge: Cambridge University Press.
Guignon, C. B. (1983) *Heidegger and the Problem of Knowledge*, Indianapolis, Hackett Publishing Company.
Hall, H. (1982) 'Was Husserl a Realist or an Idealist?', in H. L. Dreyfus (ed.), *Husserl, Intentionality and Cognitive Science*, Cambridge, MA: MIT Press.
Haugeland, J. (2000) 'Truth and Finitude: Heidegger's Transcendental Existentialism', in M. A. Wrathall and J. Malpas (eds), *Heidegger, Authenticity and Modernity*, Cambridge, MA: MIT Press.
——(2005) 'Reading Brandom reading Heidegger', *European Journal of Philosophy* 13: 421–28.
Heal, J. (1998) 'Externalism and Memory', *Proceedings of the Aristotelian Society* 72 Supp.: 95–109.
——(2004) 'What are Psychological Concepts for?', in D. McManus (ed.), *Wittgenstein and Scepticism*, London: Routledge
Hoffman, P. (2002) 'Direct Realism, Intentionality, and the Objective Being of Ideas', *Pacific Philosophical Quarterly* 83: 163–79.
Hume, D. (1975a) *Enquiries concerning Human Understanding and Concerning the Principles of Morals*, ed. L. A. Selby-Bigge, 3rd edn, revised by P. H. Nidditch, Oxford: Clarendon Press.
——(1975b) *A Treatise of Human Nature*, ed. L. A. Selby-Bigge, 2nd edn, revised by P. H. Nidditch, Oxford: Clarendon Press.
Husserl, E. (1917) 'Husserl's Inaugural Lecture at Freiburg im Breisgau', in *Husserl: Shorter Work*, ed. P. McCormick and F. A. Elliston, Indiana: University of Notre Dame Press, 1981.
——(1974) *Formale und Transzendentale Logik*, ed. P. Janssen, Hague Nijhoff.
——(1982) *Ideas Pertaining to a Pure Phenomenology and to a Phenomenological Philosophy*, First Book, trans. F. Kersten, The Hague: Martinus Nijhoff.

Husserl, E. (1989) *Ideas Pertaining to a Pure Phenomenology and to a Phenomenological Philosophy*, Second Book, trans. F. Kersten, The Hague: Martinus Nijhoff.
——(2001) *Logical Investigations*, two vols, London: Routledge.
Ihde, D. (1979) *Technics and Praxis*, Dordrecht: Reidel.
——(1991) *Instrumental Realism*, Indianapolis: Indiana University Press.
Inwood, M. (1999) *A Heidegger Dictionary*, Oxford: Blackwell.
Kant, I. (1961) *Critique of Pure Reason*, trans. N. Kemp Smith, London: Macmillan.
——(1968) *Kant: Selected Pre-Critical Writings and Correspondence with Beck*, trans. G. B. Kerferd and D. E. Walford, Manchester: Manchester University Press.
Käufer, S. (2002) 'Systematicity and Temporality in Being and Time', *Journal of the British Society for Phenomenology* 33: 167–87.
——(2003) 'Schemata, Hammers, and Time: Heidegger's Two Derivations of Judgment', *Topoi* 22: 79–91.
Kellogg, R. T. (2002) *Cognitive Psychology*, London: Sage.
Kisiel, T. (1993) *The Genesis of Heidegger's* Being and Time, Berkeley, CA: University of California Press.
Kripke, S. A. (1982) *Wittgenstein on Rules and Private Language*, Oxford: Blackwell.
Külpe, O. (1897) *Introduction to Philosophy*, trans. W. B. Pillsbury and E. B. Titchener, London: George Allen and Unwin.
Künne, W. (2003) *Conceptions of Truth*, Oxford: Oxford University Press.
Lafont, C. (2000) *Heidegger, Language, and World-Disclosure*, trans. G. Harman, Cambridge: Cambridge University Press.
——(2002) 'Replies', *Inquiry* 45: 229–48.
McDowell, J. (1981) 'Non-Cognitivism and Rule-Following', reprinted in his (1998).
——(1984) 'Wittgenstein on Following a Rule', reprinted in his (1998).
——(1987) 'In Defence of Modesty', reprinted in his (1998).
——(1993) 'Meaning and Intentionality in Wittgenstein's Later Philosophy', reprinted in his (1998).
——(1994) *Mind and World*, Cambridge, MA: Harvard University Press.
——(1997) 'Another Plea for Modesty', reprinted in his (1998).
——(1998) *Mind, Value and Reality*, Cambridge, MA: Harvard University Press.
——(2007a) 'What Myth?', *Inquiry* 50: 338–51, reprinted in his (2009).
——(2007b) 'Response to Dreyfus', *Inquiry* 50: 366–70, reprinted in his (2009).
——(2009) *The Engaged Intellect*, Cambridge, MA: Harvard University Press.
McGrath, S. J. (2006) *The Early Heidegger and Medieval Philosophy*, Washington, DC: The Catholic University of America Press.

McManus D. (2000a) 'Boghossian, Miller and Lewis on Dispositional Theories of Meaning', *Mind and Language* 15: 393–9.

——(2000b) 'Freedom, Grammar and the Given: *Mind and World* and Wittgenstein', *Journal of the British Society for Phenomenology* 31: 248–63.

——(2003) 'Wittgenstein, Fetishism, and Nonsense in Practice', in C. J. Heyes (ed.), *The Grammar of Politics: Wittgenstein and Political Philosophy*, Ithaca, NY: Cornell University Press, pp. 63–81.

——(ed.) (2004) *Wittgenstein and Scepticism*, London: Routledge.

——(2005) 'Review of D. Charles and W. Child (eds), *Wittgensteinian Themes*, A. Crary and R. Read (eds), *The New Wittgenstein* and T. G. McCarthy and S. C. Stidd (eds), *Wittgenstein in America*', *Mind* 114: 129–37.

——(2006) *The Enchantment of Words: Wittgenstein's 'Tractatus Logico-Philosophicus'*, Oxford: Oxford University Press.

——(2007) 'Heidegger, Measurement and the "Intelligibility" of Science', *European Journal of Philosophy* 15: 82–105.

——(2008) 'Rules, Regression and the 'Background': Dreyfus, Heidegger and McDowell', *European Journal of Philosophy* 16: 432–58.

——(forthcoming-a) 'Heidegger and the Supposition of a Single, Objective World', *European Journal of Philosophy* 21.

——(forthcoming-b) 'Heidegger on Scepticism, Truth and Falsehood', in M. A. Wrathall (ed.), *The Cambridge Companion to 'Being and Time'*, Cambridge: Cambridge University Press.

——(forthcoming-c) 'Heidegger, Wittgenstein and St Paul on the Last Judgement: On the Roots and Significance of the "Theoretical Attitude"', *British Journal for the History of Philosophy*.

——(forthcoming-d) 'The Provocation to Look and See: Appropriation, Recollection and Formal Indication', in S. Reynolds, D. Egan, and A. Wendland (eds), *Wittgenstein and Heidegger*, London: Routledge.

——(unpublished) 'Ontological Pluralism and the *Being and Time* Project'

McNeill, W. (1999) *The Glance of the Eye: Heidegger, Aristotle, and the Ends of Theory*, Albany, NY: State University of New York Press.

Mill, J. S. (2002) *Utilitarianism*, Indianapolis/Cambridge: Hackett.

Miller, A. (1997) 'Boghossian on Reductive Dispositionalism About Content: The Case Strengthened', *Mind and Language* 12: 1–10.

——(1998) *Philosophy of Language*, London: UCL Press.

——(2003) 'Objective Content', *Proceedings of the Aristotelian Society* 77 Supp.: 73–90.

Minar, E. (2001) 'Heidegger's Response to Skepticism in *Being and Time*', in J. Floyd and S. Shieh (eds), *Future Pasts*, Oxford: Oxford University Press.

Mitchell, J. (1999) *Measurement in Psychology*, Cambridge: Cambridge Unviersity Press.

Moore, A. W. (1997) *Points of View*, Oxford: Oxford University Press.

—— (2003) 'Ineffability and Nonsense', *Proceedings of the Aristotelian Society* 77 Supp.: 169–93.

—— (2012) *The Evolution of Modern Metaphysics: Making Sense of Things*, Cambridge: Cambridge University Press.

—— (forthcoming) 'Was the Author of the *Tractatus* a Transcendental Idealist?', in M. Potter and P. M. Sullivan (eds), *The Tractatus and its History*, Oxford: Oxford University Press.

Moran, D. (2000a) 'Heidegger's Critique of Husserl's and Brentano's Accounts of Intentionality', *Inquiry* 43: 39–66.

—— (2000b) *Introduction to Phenomenology*, London: Routledge.

Mulhall, S. (1996) *Heidegger and* Being and Time, 1st edn, London: Routledge.

—— (2005) *Heidegger and* Being and Time, 2nd edn, London: Routledge.

Nielsen, K. (2005) 'Wittgensteinian Fideism Revisited', in K. Nielsen and D. Z. Phillips (eds), *Wittgenstein Fideism?*, London: SCM Press.

Nietzsche, F. (1986) *Human, All Too Human*, trans. R. J. Hollingdale, Cambridge: Cambridge University Press.

Nussbaum, M. (2001) 'Saving Aristotle's Appearances', in her *The Fragility of Goodness*, Cambridge: Cambridge University Press.

Okrent, M. (1988) *Heidegger's Pragmatism*, Ithaca, NY: Cornell University Press.

—— (2002) 'Equipment, World and Language', *Inquiry* 45: 195–204.

Olafson, F. A. (1987) *Heidegger and the Philosophy of Mind*, New Haven, CT: Yale University Press.

Ott, H. (1994) *Martin Heidegger: A Political Life*, London: Fontana Press.

Owen, G. E. L. (1986) *Logic, Science and Dialectic*, Ithaca, NY: Cornell University Press.

Palmer, A. 'Scepticism and Tragedy: Crossing Shakespeare with Descartes', in D. McManus (ed.), *Wittgenstein and Scepticism*, London: Routledge.

Phillips, D. Z. (1999) *Philosophy's Cool Place*, Ithaca, NY: Cornell University Press.

Philipse, H. (1998) *Heidegger's Philosophy of Being*, Princeton, NJ: Princeton University Press.

Pietersma, H. (1989) 'Truth and the Evident', in J. N. Mohanty and W. R. McKenna (eds), *Husserl's Phenomenology: A Textbook*, Washington, DC: University Press of America.

Pippin, R. (2007) 'Necessary Conditions for the Possibility of What Isn't: Heidegger on Failed Meaning', in S. Crowell and J. Malpas (eds), *Transcendental Heidegger*, Stanford, CA: Stanford University Press.

Plato (1997) *Complete Works*, ed. J. M. Cooper, Indianapolis: Hackett Publishing Co.
Polt, R. (1999) *Heidegger: An Introduction*, London: UCL Press.
Preston, B. (1993) 'Heidegger and Artificial Intelligence', *Philosophy and Phenomenological Research* 53: 43–69.
——(1998) 'Cognition and Tool Use', *Mind and Language* 13: 513–47.
Priest, G. (2002) *Beyond the Limits of Thought*, Oxford: Oxford University Press.
Rentsch, T. (1989) *Das Sein und der Tod*, Munich: Piper.
Richardson, J. (1986) *Existential Epistemology*, Oxford: Clarendon Press.
Rich, A. N. M. (1954) 'The Platonic Ideas as the Thoughts of God', *Mnemosyne* 7: 123–33.
Rouse, J. (1985) 'Science and the Theoretical "Discovery" of the Present-at-Hand', in D. Ihde and H. J. Silverman (eds), *Descriptions*, Albany, NY: State University of New York Press.
——(1987) *Knowledge and Power: Toward a Political Philosophy of Science*, Ithaca, NY: Cornell University Press.
——(1998) 'Heideggerian Philosophy of Science', *Routledge Encyclopaedia of Philosophy*, London: Routledge.
——(2000) 'Coping and its Contrasts', in M. A. Wrathall and J. Malpas (eds), *Heidegger, Coping and Cognitive Science*, Cambridge, MA: MIT Press.
——(2005) 'Heidegger on Science and Naturalism', in G. Gutting (ed.), *Continental Philosophy of Science*, Oxford: Blackwell.
Ryle, G. (1928) 'Review of Heidegger's *Sein und Zeit*', reprinted in his *Critical Essays*, London: Routledge, 2009.
Safranski, R. (1999) *Martin Heidegger: Between Good and Evil*, Cambridge, MA: Harvard University Press.
Sallis, J. (1986) *Delimitations*, Bloomington: Indiana University Press.
Schear, J. (2007) 'Judgment and Ontology in Heidegger's Phenomenology', *The New Yearbook for Phenomenology and Phenomenological Research* 7: 127–58.
Searle, J. (2000) 'The Limits of Phenomenology', in M. A. Wrathall and J. Malpas (eds), *Heidegger, Coping and Cognitive Science*, Cambridge, MA: MIT Press.
Sellars, W. (1956) 'Empiricism and the Philosophy of Mind', in H. Feigl and M. Scriven (eds), *Minnesota Studies in the Philosophy of Science*, vol. 1, Minneapolis: University of Minnesota Press.
Smith, D. W. (2007) *Husserl*, London: Routledge.
Smith, W. H. (2007) 'Why Tugendhat's Critique of Heidegger's Concept of Truth Remains a Critical Problem', *Inquiry* 50: 156–79.
Smith, R. (1995) 'Logic', in J. Barnes (ed.), *Cambridge Companion to Aristotle*, Cambridge: Cambridge University Press.

Sokolowski, R. (1970) *The Formation of Husserl's Concept of Constitution*, The Hague: Martinus Nijhoff.

Stanley, J. and Williamson, T. (2001) 'Knowing How', *The Journal of Philosophy* 98: 411–44.

Stern, D. (2000) 'Practices, Practical Holism, and Background Practices', in M. A. Wrathall and J. Malpas (eds), *Heidegger, Coping and Cognitive Science*, Cambridge, MA: MIT Press.

Strawson, G. (2010) *Mental Reality*, 2nd edn, Cambridge, MA: MIT Press.

Stroud, B. (1991) 'The Background of Thought', in E. Le Pore and R. van Gulick (eds), *John Searle and his Critics*, Oxford: Blackwell.

Sullivan, P. M. (1996) 'The "Truth" in Solipsism, and Wittgenstein's Rejection of the *A Priori*', *European Journal of Philosophy* 4: 195–219.

——(2002) 'On Trying to be Resolute: A Response to Kremer on the *Tractatus*', *European Journal of Philosophy* 10: 43–78.

——(2003) 'Ineffability and Nonsense', *Proceedings of the Aristotelian Society* 77 Supp.: 195–223.

Taminiaux, J. (1991) *Heidegger and the Project of Fundamental Ontology*, trans. M. Gendre, Albany, NY: State University of New York Press.

Tugendhat, E. (1969) 'Heidegger's Idea of Truth', trans. C. Macann, in McCann (ed.), *Critical Heidegger*, London: Routledge, 1996.

——(1970) *Der Wahrheitsbegriff bei Husserl und Heidegger*, 2nd edn, Berlin: de Gruyter.

Turetzky, P. (1998) *Time*, London: Routledge.

Van Buren, J. (1994) *The Young Heidegger*, Indianapolis: Indiana University Press.

Versényi, L. (1965) *Heidegger, Being and Truth*, New Haven, CT: Yale University Press.

Wigner, E. P. (1960) 'The Unreasonable Effectiveness of Mathematics', *Communications in Pure and Applied Mathematics* 13: 1–14.

Williams, B. (1978) *Descartes: The Project of Pure Enquiry*, Harmondsworth: Penguin Books.

Williams, C. J. F. (1976) *What is Truth?* Cambridge: Cambridge University Press.

Witherspoon, E. (2002) 'Logic and the Inexpressible in Frege and Heidegger', *Journal of the History of Philosophy* 40: 89–113.

Wittgenstein, L. (1922) *Tractatus Logico-Philosophicus*, trans. C. K. Ogden, London: Routledge and Kegan Paul.

——(1967) *Philosophical Investigations*, trans. G. E. M. Anscombe, ed. G. E. M. Anscombe and R. Rhees, Oxford: Blackwell.

——(1978) *Remarks on the Foundations of Mathematics*, trans. G. E. M. Anscombe, ed. G. H. von Wright, R. Rhees, and G. E. M. Anscombe, 3rd edn, Oxford: Blackwell.

——(1979) *Notebooks 1914–16*, trans. G. E. M. Anscombe, ed. G. H. von Wright and G. E. M. Anscombe, Oxford: Blackwell.

Wrathall, M. A. (2000) 'Background Practices, Capacities, and Heideggerian Disclosure', in M. A. Wrathall and J. Malpas (eds), *Heidegger, Coping and Cognitive Science*, Cambridge, MA: MIT Press.

——(1999) 'Heidegger and Truth as Correspondence', *International Journal of Philosophical Studies* 7: 69–88.

——(2005) 'Unconcealment', in H. L. Dreyfus and M. A. Wrathall (eds), *A Companion to Heidegger*, Oxford: Blackwell.

——and Malpas, J. (eds) (2000a) *Heidegger, Authenticity and Modernity*, Cambridge, MA: MIT Press.

——and Malpas, J. (eds) (2000b) *Heidegger, Coping and Cognitive Science*, Cambridge, MA: MIT Press.

Wright, C. (2004) 'Wittgensteinian Certainties', in D. McManus (ed.), *Wittgenstein and Scepticism*, London: Routledge.

Index

adaequatio intellectus et rei, see
   correspondence; correspondence theory of truth
ambiguity 161
analytic/continental distinction vii
St. Anselm 38
anxiety 56, 161, 195
appropriation 39, 154, 160–1, 221
St Thomas Aquinas 34, 125, 133, 145, 165
Aristotle 22–3, 28–9, 32, 56, 63, 67, 109, 169, 185, 195, 221–2
assertion 1, 3, 6, 33, 47, 51–2, 55, 58–62, 76, 103, 115, 125–7, 131, 136, 153, 166–7, 177–9, 190, 193, 195, 198–202, 205–6, 208, 210, 215–16, 219, 222, 224
attunement, *see* Befindlichkeit
St. Augustine 18, 105–6, 109, 145
Austin, J. L. 74, 169, 192
authenticity 5–6, 20, 24–6, 39, 62, 120, 138, 153–4, 158–61, 170, 173–4, 180, 194–5, 200, 202, 205–6, 210, 216, 222

background 4, 74–99, 104, 120
Barad, K. 144
Bar-On, D. 117, 181
Beck, A. 54, 105, 153, 161
Befindlichkeit 169, 212
'Being and Time' Project vii, 209–15, 222
Being-in-the-world 1–4, 23, 39, 41–5, 66, 73, 77–8, 104–5, 114, 118–24, 134–5, 140, 165–89, 192, 214
Being-with-others, *see* Mitsein
Bernasconi, R. 193
Bernet, R. 227
biology 93, 148, 159
Blattner, W. D. 3, 11, 15, 37, 53–4, 56–7, 63, 66–73, 103, 135, 139, 170, 183–4, 188, 191, 201, 211, 214
Boghossian, P. 92, 153
Brandom, R. 58, 81–3, 92, 117

Carman, T. 53, 63, 73, 80, 125, 161, 166, 201
Cartesianism 30, 42, 77, 114, 118–19, 179, 186, 226–7

Cartwright, N. 146–7, 151–2, 159
categories 2, 25, 28–41, 51, 78, 112, 170, 183, 200, 202, 205
categorical intuition 114
Cavell, S. 24–6, 168
Cerbone, D. R. 125
ceteris paribus clauses 89–92, 179
Chang, H. 146–7, 151–2, 159
Christiansen, C. B. 53, 85, 92
con-formity 28, 30–1, 34–7, 39–40, 43, 110, 113, 133, 137–8, 140, 142, 149, 153, 155, 160, 162, 171–2, 190–1, 201–2, 214
consciousness 12, 16, 25–6, 36, 41–6, 78, 83, 108, 131, 177, 179, 217, 219, 226–8
constitution 2–4, 11–46, 51, 75, 99, 103, 105–12, 114, 118–19, 136, 151–2, 172, 194, 201, 205, 225
continuity scepticism 117, 180
conventionalism 152
Cooper, D. E. 16, 38–9, 105, 122
correspondence 1, 4–5, 30–2, 36, 41–2, 106, 110, 113, 121–3, 130–3, 136, 138–40, 149, 166–7, 170–1, 174, 179–80, 185–6, 190–1, 208, 210, 220
correspondence theory of truth 4, 107–8, 110, 125–34, 140, 166–7, 179, 183, 208, 210, 214, 217
Craig, E. J. 34
Crowe, B. D. 18
Crowell, S. 28, 38, 48, 105, 173, 213, 227

Dahlstrom, D. O. 16, 46–8, 54, 57, 89, 108–9, 173, 175, 187, 193, 201, 208, 210–11, 213–16, 222–3, 226–7
Dasein 15, 21, 25–6, 36–7, 42, 44–5, 58, 74, 90, 104, 112–14, 116–17, 119–20, 122, 127–9, 138, 153, 166, 168, 171, 174, 177, 181–8, 191, 200–1, 213–14, 224–5
Davidson, D. 117, 151
Davies, P. S. 93
decontextualisation 54, 68, 197, 201
Dependency Claim 128, 181–9, 21
   see also truth

depicturization 81, 84, 178
  see also master thesis
Descartes, R. 22, 25, 40, 43, 87, 113–14, 145, 218, 227
destruction, see historical destruction
devivification 55, 58
dialectical reading, see reactive readings
Diamond, C. 152, 202
direct realism 127, 129, 175–6
disclosure 22–3, 39, 118–21, 129, 152, 157, 160, 166–74, 177, 181, 195, 210, 214
Dreyfus, H. L. 4, 11, 42, 53–4, 56, 59, 67, 74–99, 104, 117, 125, 138, 172, 179, 180, 193, 201
Dreyfus, S. E. 95
Dummett, M. 153

Elden, S. 105
emptiness, in connection with words, descriptions, etc. 5, 138, 154–6, 159–62, 199, 216–21
'empty intending' and 'fulfilment' 4, 18, 105–13, 129–30, 174–6, 180
epoché 14, 226–7

Fell, J. P. 53–6, 69, 196
fetishism, see methodological fetishism; Pythagorean fetishism
finitude 5, 33–4, 65, 124, 166–73
Fodor, J. 24
forgetting, see *Seinsvergessenheit*; *Verstehensvergessenheit*
forgetting of Being, see *Seinsvergessenheit*; *Verstehensvergessenheit*
formal indication 48, 187, 222–3
founding 1, 3–5, 12–13, 51–2, 64, 70, 86–7, 103–4, 130, 133, 135–7, 140–2, 146, 166–7, 190, 193, 202, 208, 214
Frege, G. 11, 57, 58
Friedman, M. 31, 44, 54, 152, 214
'fulfilment', see 'empty intending'
fundamental ontology 1–2, 5, 47, 104–34, 169, 214–15

Gadamer, H.-G. 20
Gardner, S. 33
Gelven, M. 54
Glock, H. J. 182
God 14, 17–20, 34–5, 41, 45, 51, 106, 109, 134, 202, 204–6, 219–20
  see also religious belief

Goldfarb, W. 35
Gorner, P. 53–4, 56, 60, 70, 72
Guignon, C. B. 53–4, 56, 185

Hall, H. 12–13, 227
Haugeland, J. 57, 61, 117, 151–2, 160, 169–70, 173–4, 228
Heal, J. 23–4, 153
Heidegger, later works of 21, 38–9, 47, 57, 105, 112, 118, 129, 135, 153, 158–9, 170, 181, 215, 223–4
Hinblick 105, 111–23, 129, 132–3, 150, 153, 172–5, 193, 196, 212, 224
historical destruction 20, 212
history 20–1, 26, 44, 57, 61, 148, 161, 212, 223
Hoffman, P. 127
horizon 13–14, 26, 64, 107, 115, 134, 170, 211–12, 223
Hume, D. 116
Husserl, E. 2–4, 11–17, 22, 29, 35–6, 38, 41, 66, 77, 105–11, 114, 118, 129–30, 151, 174, 176, 209, 226–8

ideal, the 14, 126, 176–81
idealism vi, 1–5, 12, 28–31, 35–7, 65, 96, 105, 110, 113, 116, 123, 130, 133, 135, 137, 140, 151, 162, 165, 166, 181, 188, 190, 202, 214
idle talk 62, 138, 158, 161, 180, 200, 206, 216, 218, 221
Ihde, D. 144
immodesty, see modest theories of meaning
inauthenticity, see authenticity
indefiniteness, see indeterminacy
indeterminacy, in thought and meaning 25, 118, 138, 160, 186, 200, 216–23
indifference, see ontological indifference
intentionality 2, 14–16, 18, 23, 46, 76–81, 84, 87–8, 91–3, 96–9, 104, 106–8, 110, 123, 127, 133, 151, 153, 165–8, 172, 174–81, 186, 201, 210, 228
internal relations 87, 185–7, 220
intuition 16, 34, 52, 55, 104, 106, 109, 130, 145, 174, 176, 198
Inwood, M. 69, 197, 213

Kant, I. 29, 31–4, 40, 44, 57, 80, 83, 113–14, 124, 133–4, 145, 168, 209, 212–14, 218
Käufer, S. 31, 33, 53, 54–5, 70, 194, 213–14
Kellogg, R. T. 157
Kern, I. 227

Kisiel, T. 19, 26, 28, 38–9, 48, 58, 70, 73, 120, 209, 212–14, 222–3
know-how 77–9, 91, 93, 96, 104, 150, 191
knowledge 5, 11, 16, 19, 21, 22–7, 30, 32, 35, 38, 40, 46, 52, 55, 57, 63–5, 67, 69–70, 72, 77–9, 82–3, 89, 91, 108, 112, 120, 123–4, 132–4, 140, 145, 152, 161, 166–73, 176, 178, 203, 228
  see also science and scientific knowledge; self-knowledge
Kripke, S. A. 92
Külpe, O. 29

ladder metaphor 48, 89, 187, 219
Lafont, C. 3, 47, 54, 129, 132, 135, 152, 170, 181
Last Judgment 19–20, 105, 202, 205–6, 220
later Heidegger, see Heidegger, later works of
'living in' motif 23, 37–8, 111–12, 117, 166–75, 178, 181

manipulating/seeing distinction 144–6
Marbach, E. 227
master thesis 81–8, 98, 178
  see also depicturization
mathematics 22, 55, 60, 64, 156–61, 174, 194, 227
McDowell, J. 39, 76–7, 82–9, 95–8, 117, 170–2, 176–8, 221
McGrath, S. J. 18
McNeill, W. 58, 193
measure 1–2, 4–6, 34, 39, 103–11, 118, 130–6, 139, 141, 165, 171, 174–7, 183, 196, 202, 209, 215–20, 224
measurement, and measuring tools 5, 65–6, 72, 123, 130–1, 136–8, 141–62, 167–77, 180, 183, 191–4
metaphilosophy 6, 11–17, 45–8, 187, 208–25
methodological fetishism 156–61
Mill, J. S. 155
Miller, A. 92
Minar, E. 185, 219
Mitchell, J. 155
Mitsein 23, 42
modest theories of meaning 95–8, 171–2
Moore, A. W. 48, 56, 69, 214
Moran, D. 11, 13–14, 45, 55, 67, 227
Mulhall, S. 54–5, 70, 183, 185, 219
mysticism 6, 48

Nielsen, K. 202
Nietzsche, F. 65, 67
non-subjectivist *a priori* 114, 121, 201
Nussbaum, M. 222

objectivity 63, 114, 124, 128, 148–54, 168, 170, 192
observation 17, 21, 25, 52, 55, 64, 66, 140, 145–6, 148, 150, 153–7, 169, 195, 226
Okrent, M. 6, 48, 105, 117, 132
Olafson, F. 139
ontological indifference 218–21
ontology 11–12, 16, 29, 31, 41, 48, 53, 55, 57, 60, 62, 66, 88, 91, 98, 134, 140, 184, 188, 198, 202, 205, 208, 210, 212–13, 215, 217, 219–21, 223–4
  see also fundamental ontology
original havings 2, 5, 16–27, 119, 121–2, 137, 148, 151, 170, 208–12, 218, 220, 222
Ott, H. 18
Owen, G. E. L. 29, 222

Palmer, A. 221
Parousia, see Last Judgment
perspective 14, 39–41, 73, 98, 121, 148–52, 174, 190, 210–11, 220
phenomenology 5, 11–13, 16–17, 22, 45–47, 69, 79, 83, 86, 98, 105, 197, 200, 214, 216, 218–20, 223–4, 227
Philipse, H. 6, 53–6, 137
Phillips, D. Z. 39, 151, 158
physics 64, 72, 146, 153, 159, 200
Pietersma, H. 13
Plato 23, 34, 38, 110, 222
Polt, R. 153
practice, and the practical 3, 5, 21, 37, 51, 54, 60, 63, 65–80, 86, 90, 95, 104, 117, 120, 125, 133, 135–7, 141–6, 148, 150–3, 156, 167, 169–80, 183–4, 190, 192–3, 202, 213–14, 218, 224
  see also Primacy of Practice Claim; Primacy of Scientific Practice Claim
pragmatism, and pragmatist readings of Heidegger 3, 5, 67, 71–4, 104–5, 150, 156, 191
pre-ontological understanding 105–6, 109, 111, 217–18, 221
presence-at-hand, see *Vorhandenheit*
Preston, B. 54, 79, 92
Priest, G. 48

Primacy of Practice Claim 37, 52, 65, 69–70, 74, 76, 78, 135–7, 201, 214
Primacy of Scientific Practice Claim 63, 65, 135, 141
Prior Projection Claim 63–5, 105, 136–7, 141, 201, 214
projection 36, 64–5, 109–10, 115–17, 136–7, 141–3, 148–50, 157–8, 161–2, 170, 174, 181, 185, 212
  see also Prior Projection Claim
pseudo-problems vi, 23, 29
pure beholding 55, 59, 144–5, 148, 194, 197–8, 202
Pythagorean fetishism 156–8, 194, 217

reactive readings 89, 97, 187–8
readiness-to-hand, see Zuhandenhei
realism 3, 5, 28–9, 34–7, 63, 73, 112, 137–8, 140, 151, 162, 181, 201–2
  see also direct realism
relativism, see idealism
religious belief 2, 17–20, 42, 48, 71–2, 202
  see also God
Rentsch, T. 152
representationalism 76–7, 168
Rich, A. N. M. 34
Richardson, J. 53–4
Rouse, J. 54, 56, 66–8, 70, 72–4, 78, 80, 86, 103, 135, 140–1, 143–5, 151, 183, 185, 191, 200–1, 214
rules 76, 78–99, 179, 220
Ryle, G. 3, 6, 48

Safranski, R. 18
Sallis, J. 68
scepticism 1–2, 5, 14, 24–5, 30, 43, 83, 86, 105, 118, 123–5, 135, 166–9, 217, 226
  see also continuity scepticism
Schear, J. 16, 53, 55, 57, 60, 85
science, and scientific knowledge 4–5, 21, 23, 45–8, 52–3, 55, 57, 59, 62–9, 72–3, 103, 117, 135–8, 140, 144–53, 151, 157–62, 169, 189, 191, 193, 195, 200, 202, 209, 213–18, 224, 226–7
  see also Primacy of Scientific Practice Claim
Searle, J. 11, 85
Seinsvergessenheit 15, 195, 216–17
self 25–7
self-knowledge 5, 25–7, 154, 160–2, 173–4, 205–7, 214, 217, 221, 226
Sellars, W. 33, 117

Sheehan, T. 213
Smith, D. W. 12, 20, 36, 41, 106
Smith, R. 29
Smith, W. H. 125, 170, 173–4
Sokolowski, R. 227
space, and the spatial 14, 113–14, 119–20, 124, 166, 168
Spinosa, C. 201
Stanley, J. 79
State-of-Mind, see Befindlichkeit
Stern, D. 78–80, 95
Stevens, S. S. 155
Strawson, G. 153
Stroud, B. 81–2
subject-correlates 16, 19–24, 29, 42, 45–6, 195, 204–5, 222, 224–5
subject, and subjectivity 1–4, 11–20, 22, 24–7, 33–6, 40–5, 57, 78, 112–18, 123, 131–2, 144, 150, 152, 165–72, 174, 177, 180, 186, 191, 214, 218–19, 226–7
subjectivism, see idealism
substance 28, 53, 60, 168, 202
Sullivan, P. M. 215

Taminiaux, J. 56
thematization, paradox of 47, 201, 208, 211, 215
theology 17–20, 22, 51
Theoretical Attitude 2–5, 17–27, 46–7, 51–2, 54, 58, 60, 62, 64, 68, 103, 193–5, 202–6, 226–7
theory 1, 3–4, 16, 17–23, 43–8, 51–2, 54, 57–8, 61, 63, 64, 66–7, 86, 89, 104, 136, 145–6, 156, 192–3, 195, 204, 206, 209, 210–11, 214, 216, 221, 227
  see also Theoretical Attitude
thrownness 112, 116, 174
time, and the temporal 114, 124, 168, 184, 188, 212–14
traditional theory of truth, see correspondence theory of truth
truth 2–6, 14, 23, 32, 37, 51–2, 105, 107–13, 124–35, 140, 144, 147–52, 158, 166–76, 180–9, 198–9, 208, 210, 214–15, 217, 225
  see also correspondence theory of truth; dependency claim
Tugendhat, E. 109, 124, 128–9, 170, 174
Turetzky, P. 54–5

understanding 1, 3–5, 15–16, 18, 21, 24–9, 32–6, 46, 57–8, 61–5, 70, 77–8, 81–2, 88, 90–1, 93, 97, 105–6, 109–13, 115–17,

121–2, 124, 130, 133, 135–41, 143, 146–7, 149, 167–8, 170, 180–1, 185, 188, 190–3, 195, 197–8, 200, 202, 206–8, 212, 214–18, 221, 224–26
see also pre-ontological understanding; projection; *Verstehensvergessenheit*
untruth 128, 138, 153, 166, 171–3

Van Buren, J. 20, 28, 38, 48, 209, 212–14
Versényi, L. 68
Verstehensvergessenheit 15, 195, 198, 204, 216
'view from sideways on' 39–40, 92, 95–98, 122, 170–1, 180, 191
Vorhandenheit 3, 5, 47, 51–75, 78, 96, 98, 103, 125, 137, 141, 153, 190–208, 211, 214, 216–17, 227
Vorhandenheit in broadest sense 45, 54, 195–207

Wigner, E. P. 156
Williams, B. 152
Williams, C. J. F. 132
Williamson, T. 79
Witherspoon, E. 48
Wittgenstein, L. 39–40, 44–5, 48, 73, 76, 80, 83, 86–7, 89, 110, 131, 138, 143–4, 147–8, 151–3, 156, 167–8, 172, 178–9, 187, 202, 214, 220–4
Woraufhin 111–12, 115–16, 129, 132
worldliness, of *Dasein* 1–2, 5, 25, 42–3, 119, 141, 152–3, 165, 168, 180, 201–2
Wrathall, M. A. 70, 78, 80, 90, 125, 166, 168, 173
Wright, C. 124, 170

Zuhandenheit 3, 5, 52, 54–5, 59, 61, 65–6, 68–75, 78, 96, 98, 103, 119, 137–43, 190–3, 200–1, 204, 214, 224

Printed and bound by CPI Group (UK) Ltd, Croydon, CR0 4YY